JANE MACQUITTY'S POCKET GUIDE TO

AUSTRALIAN & NEW ZEALAND WINES

MITCHELL BEAZLEY

Jane MacQuitty's Pocket Guide to Australian & New Zealand Wines
Edited and designed by Mitchell Beazley International Limited, Artists
House, 14-15 Manette Street, London W1V 5LB.

Copyright © Mitchell Beazley Publishers 1990
Text copyright © Jane MacQuitty 1990
Maps copyright © Mitchell Beazley Publishers 1990

A CIP catalogue record for this book is available from the British Library.

ISBN 0 85533 732 X

The author and publishers will be grateful for any information that
will assist them in keeping future editions up to date. Although all
reasonable care has been taken in the preparation of this book, neither
the publishers nor the author can accept any liability for any
consequences arising from the use thereof or from the information
contained therein.

Editor	Rupert Joy
Art Editor	Gaye Allen
Production	Barbara Hind
Managing Editor	Chris Foulkes
Senior Art Editor	Tim Foster

Typeset by Litho Link, Welshpool, Powys, Wales
Produced by Mandarin Offset
Printed and bound in Malaysia

Contents

Foreword

Until now, all books about Australian wines have been written by Australians. Who better to understand the complexities of our wine industry? The same, of course, applies to the wine industry in New Zealand. They *are* complex industries in spite of a certain degree of international ignorance. For years we have suffered from the inference that all our wines tasted the same, that they had no vintage or regional variations, or that they were full of iron and good for Auntie's itch. And, indeed, Australia's pre-1939 "Empire" wines gave some justification for elements of this thinking.

But, as they say, times change. Australian per capita consumption of table wine is now the highest of the English-speaking countries, and the last 25 years has been a period of dynamic change in the wine, food and hospitality industries. New Zealand, too, has experienced a major turn-around from those quite recent days of pale, thin whites and light, astringent reds. Both countries now produce "international" wines – wines that win world-wide acceptance. The current export boom has seen the appearance of all sorts of Australasian wines in all sorts of countries and on all sorts of lists. We have dozens of different wine regions, hundreds of wineries, thousands of different wines. There they are, judge for yourself.

That's where Jane MacQuitty comes in. Her new book will help you enormously to do so. She has visited both countries often, understands the complexities and nuances of our industries, and is an indefatigable taster and questioner. Her recommendations and criticisms are very worthwhile. So why couldn't an Australian have done the job? Well, we could have, but Mitchell Beazley didn't ask any of us, and in any case I think it's a terrific idea to choose an outsider, for many reasons: perspective, lack of bias, non-chauvinism – all that type of thing. In fact, it's a compliment; Australian wines have "arrived".

I enjoyed the book and I think she has done a first-class job. This is an invaluable guide to Australian and New Zealand wines. I don't agree with everything she says, but it's her book, not mine, and it's great to have an opinion that is neither introspective nor self-indulgent. We might even have to *make* her an Australian.

Len Evans OBE

How to use this book

This book is divided into two main sections: Australian wines and New Zealand wines. Each has an introductory chapter which describes the history, climate, wine-making traditions and wine-styles of the country, followed by chapters on wine-producing areas. Australia is dealt with state by state, while New Zealand's two main islands are tackled separately. Following a summary of each wine region and distinctive wine-styles, the wineries and their wines are examined in detail.

Wineries are listed alphabetically and cross-referenced in bold type throughout the book. At the head of every entry are symbols indicating what kinds of wines are produced, abbreviated as follows:

w	white wine
r	red wine
sw	sweet wine
ft	fortified wine
sp	sparkling wine

In some cases, where certain years have been particularly successful for a producer, recommended vintages appear alongside these wine symbols, for example:

w = 78 88 84	indicates that this winery's best vintage for white wines was 1978, followed by 1988 and then 1984
r = 71 82 86	indicates that this winery's best vintage for red wines was 1971, followed by 1982 and then 1986

All wineries are also given a star rating based on the quality of their wines, ranging from one to four stars as follows:

*	ordinary, but acceptable
**	recommended, above average
***	highly recommended, excellent quality
****	finest

Wineries that produce wines of exceptional quality combined with good value for money feature "star buys", represented by the symbol ♀

Beside each entry is an abbreviation identifying the wine-producing region in which that winery is situated. The following abbreviations are used for the Australian states:

AH	Adelaide Hills (SA)	LN	Launceston (TAS)
AP	Adelaide Plains (SA)	MA	Margaret River (WA)
BV	Barossa Valley (SA)	MB	Mt Barker/Frankland River (WA)
CA	Canberra (NSW)	MC	Macedon (VIC)
CL	Clare (SA)	MD	Mudgee (NSW)
CV	Central Victoria (VIC)	MP	Mornington Peninsula (VIC)
CW	Coonawarra (SA)	MR	Murray River (VIC)
DR	Darling Ranges (WA)	NE	North-East Victoria (VIC)
EG	East Gippsland (VIC)	PA	Padthaway/Keppoch (SA)
GB	Granite Belt (QLD)	PR	Pyrenees (VIC)
GL	Geelong (VIC)	RL	Riverland (SA)
GV	Goulburn Valley (VIC)	RV	Riverina (NSW)
GW	Great Western (VIC)	SO	Southern Vales (SA)
HB	Hobart (TAS)	SV	Swan Valley (WA)
HT	Hilltops (NSW)	SW	South-West Coastal Plain (WA)
HV	Hunter Valley (NSW)	UH	Upper Hunter Valley (NSW)
LC	Langhorne Creek (SA)	YV	Yarra Valley (VIC)

(The symbol § denotes a winery that is not situated within any specific wine-producing region.)

The following abbreviations are used to indicate the wine-producing regions in New Zealand:

AU	Auckland (NI)	ML	Marlborough (SI)
CB	Canterbury (SI)	NL	Nelson (SI)
CO	Central Otago (SI)	NO	Northland (NI)
GI	Gisborne (NI)	WR	Wairarapa (NI)
HW	Hawke's Bay (NI)	WK	Waikato/Bay of Plenty (NI)

AUSTRALIAN WINES

Introduction

Australia makes great wine, and Australians know it. Yet it is only within the last decade of their 200-year history that Australian wines have leapt to the fore. There is a new air of confidence and optimism in the Australian wine industry, fostered by a growing world-wide acclaim for its wines and the vintage experience gained by its wine-makers abroad. Today Australia's flavour-packed wines, made in an unpolluted environment, unhampered by convention, are mounting a surprisingly strong challenge to both the Old World classics of Europe and the New World stars of California.

1788 on ...

Australia's wine history began over two centuries ago with the arrival of the First Fleet. When Captain Arthur Phillip disembarked at Sydney harbour on January 26th 1788, he brought with him vine cuttings from Rio de Janeiro and the Cape. Remarkably, these had survived the long, difficult voyage and were planted out at Farm Cove, close to what are now Sydney's Botanic Gardens. These first vines did not flourish in the sub-tropical conditions, but Phillip and others persevered. More were planted further inland, away from the excessive humidity of the coast, and the vine soon became well established in the new colony. By the 1820s, it had reached the Hunter Valley to the north. The history of Australia's other early plantations in Tasmania, Victoria, Western Australia and South Australia followed a similar pattern: vines arrived with, or soon after, the Westerners.

In true imperial style, the colonists' mother country keenly fostered early wine-making in Australia, envisaging the vast sunny continent as an alternative wine supplier for cold, grey Britain which would oust expensive European wines from British cellars and dining rooms. Somehow this grandiose Victorian vision of Australia as John Bull's vineyard never quite came off. Vast quantities of hefty reds and sweet, sticky fortified wines (fortified partly to withstand the long sea voyage) were shipped to Britain from Australia. But, popular though these Australian wines were with the British, they failed to topple European wines from their pre-eminent position.

Since the 19th century, the fortunes of Australia's wine industry have vacillated. Fortifieds remained dominant until the early 1960s, when table wines – mostly robust reds, often coarse and high in alcohol – began to rival beer as the national drink, encouraged by a new affluence and the example of wine-drinking immigrants. But quality was poor. In the absence of appropriate technology to combat the heat or even the awareness of its necessity, this era was, as Brian Croser of **Petaluma** dubs it, the "Dark Age of Australian wine-making". As red wines grew in popularity, many of Australia's wine-producers were unable to meet the demand, so they stretched what little they had in their cellars, turned white wine into red and fobbed off consumers with Cabernet that was Shiraz or Shiraz that was Grenache, feverishly planting red varieties all the while. The hapless Australian wine drinker responded by buying larger quantities of white wines. Faced with a sudden white wine boom and the simultaneous invention in the 70s of wine casks or "bag-in-box" wines, Australia's grape-growers started a massive replanting programme. The early 80s then saw something of a shift back to reds, as well as a boutique wine boom and a switch from blends to varietal wines.

INDIAN OCEAN

NORTHERN TERRITORY

WESTERN AUSTRALIA

SOUTH

Darwin

Perth

During the mid-80s, Australia experienced a huge glut of both red and white wines, caused by over-production in a sparsely populated country. Kill or cure measures forced some wineries to close down and others to join Government-funded schemes. More recently, the market swung back again and the glut was drunk dry by an appreciative new international clientele whose enthusiasm for Australia's full-flavoured, inexpensive wines coincided neatly with a weak Australian dollar. In one year, 1987-88, exports almost doubled. This boom ground to a halt temporarily when hailstorms devastated vineyards in South Australia, where two-thirds of the country's wines are produced.

At the same time there has been a drop in home consumption and in sales of flagon and cask wines, which still account for just over half of total production. The fall in demand for fortifieds, meanwhile, has continued apace. This apparent overall decline has been offset by an increase both at home and abroad in sales of premium bottled wines, especially fine sparkling wines. Australia is in other words struggling with an under-supply of quality wines. There have been a large number of takeovers in the industry too, big fish swallowing the smaller fry with depressing regularity. In a country of just 16 million, it cannot be healthy for the top 8% of Australia's 550 wine-producers to make 93% of the country's wine, leaving the other 500 or so to carve up just 7% between them. Thankfully, there is now a growing body of informed decision-makers in the industry who are aware of the need to anticipate wine trends rather than reacting to them after the event.

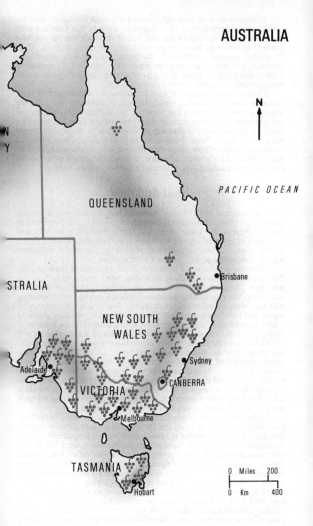

AUSTRALIA

N

PACIFIC OCEAN

QUEENSLAND

STRALIA

Brisbane

NEW SOUTH
WALES

Adelaide

Sydney

CANBERRA

VICTORIA

Melbourne

TASMANIA

Hobart

| 0 | Miles | 200 |
| 0 | Km | 400 |

Tyranny of distance

In the 19th century it took months by boat to reach Australia, half a world away from the birthplaces of its colonial settlers. Once there, the new Australians felt doubly cut off, not just by distance but by season as well – their spring being Europe's winter. Today the Australians rejoice in producing a vintage six months ahead of Europe. This allows them to pip Beaujolais Nouveau to the post and sell their *vin de l'année* before Europe's vines have even flowered. But it would be difficult to overestimate the feeling of isolation among previous generations of Australian wine-producers.

European wine-making skills filtered into Australia slowly with the arrival of different groups of immigrants, such as the Silesians who settled in South Australia's Barossa Valley and later the Italians who made themselves at home in the continent's irrigated regions. Apart from this sporadic settlement, European wine-making input was minimal: few first-class European wines were imported, so Australian wine-makers had no point of comparison, and wine-loving Europeans rarely included Australia in their overseas tours.

Though some Australian wine-producers are still dogged by their isolation from the old wine world, the most troublesome and enduring legacy of the early settlers has been the site of their vineyards. Fear of the unknown, the pressure to produce fruit and the British demand for wine all encouraged the planting of vines close to major settlements such as Sydney, Perth, Melbourne and Adelaide, where many of Australia's vineyards are today. Few of these sites have turned out to be ideal. Some purists even advocate a thorough grubbing-up of the country's vineyards and their relocation in more suitable regions.

Heat and dust

From a European point of view, Australia is a very hot, very dry wine-producing country. Although the search for cooler-climate regions has been underway for some time now, most Australian wine is still produced in irrigated regions such as South Australia's Riverland, one of the hottest, driest wine-making regions in the world. For most regions, the coolest years produce the finest wines.

However, unlike some of their technology-oriented predecessors, the new generation of leading Australian wine-producers act on the principle that great wine begins in the vineyard. Many of them are examining the relationship between yield and quality, experimenting with new sites, clonal selection, trellising, close spacing to control vine vigour and canopy management. The move from the sunbaked plains to cooler hillside sites, some of them benefiting from cool sea breezes, is taking place all over the country from the Barossa Valley to the Perth Hills in Western Australia. The fruit from these new vineyards generally has greater flavour, more balance and better acidity than the flabby, jammy, sun-baked grapes of the hot regions. As more of this finer fruit comes on stream, Australian wines will take another leap forward in quality, as they did in the 70s when new technology revolutionized the industry. In the meantime, wine-producers who cannot wait for their new vines to bear fruit are trucking in grapes from cooler regions such as Tasmania, Western Australia and even New Zealand.

Today vines are planted in every Australian state including, incredibly, the parched Northern Territory. Pinpointing cooler regions with higher levels of rainfall is a major modern preoccupation for every Australian wine-producer. Various methods have been used, but honest wine-makers admit their limitations. In the Barossa Valley, for example, there are significant climatic differences within a radius of only 25 miles (40 km) owing to variations in altitude. California's heat degree days system, which calculates the heat summation during the vine's seven-month growing period, does provide some clues; so too does Australia's own MJT ("Mean January Temperature") rating, which measures the average figure of the warmest month, in Australia's case January. On the basis of these indicators, most Australians agree that the coolest region in the country is Tasmania, followed by Victoria's Yarra Valley, and then South Australia's Adelaide Hills and Coonawarra regions. The Riverland, roughly twice as hot as Bordeaux by this system of measurement, is the hottest.

Irrigation has proved essential to Australia's hot, dry vineyards. However, because of its association with bulk wine regions such as the Riverland it has had, for some, an unfortunate image. Forward-thinking wine-makers realized years ago that excessive vine stress due to drought does not make for quality. Yet surprisingly, even some of the better-informed regions such as Western Australia's Margaret River have only just begun to take action, encouraged by leading viticulturist Dr Richard Smart. In this and other such wine regions, wine-makers are installing drip-irrigation that will enhance their fruit quality and ensure higher grape yields. Another problem is phylloxera. Australia is not a phylloxera-free country and, like Europe, felt its scourge in the late 19th century. Today, Victoria's vineyards, especially those in the north-east, still suffer from phylloxera as do those in the south of New South Wales, yet few grape-growers bother to graft onto American rootstocks more resistant to the destructive aphid.

Technology rules

Australian wine technology is awesome. Now a distinguishing feature of wine-making in this country, it started as a backlash against the poor-quality wines of the 1960s. Faced with leathery, tannic, alcoholic reds often reeking of hydrogen sulphide (bad eggs) and flabby, oxidized whites, Australian wine-makers brought in every gadget available in modern wine weaponry to combat the heat. At the same time, they built up an arsenal of their own, with inventions such as the labour-saving Potter fermenter. This superior new technology, used chiefly in the production of white wines, actually began in the early 50s when **Orlando** imported the first pressure fermenter and was taken up in the 60s by one or two other enlightened firms such as **Leo Buring**. But it was not until the 70s that this wine technology evolved to the point where it began to reach the industry as a whole. Anyone visiting even a small Australian winery today can expect to see expensive high-tech stainless steel, Vaslin and Willmes presses, and a well-equipped laboratory. Meanwhile, on the huge vineyards such as the **Wynns** Coonawarra plots, mechanical pruning helps to keep down costs.

Briefly, Australian wine technology revolves around protecting and preserving the quality of the fruit and keeping it in a cool, anaerobic atmosphere at all times. Mechanical harvesting at night combats the cruel midday sun and is one way of bringing in cool grapes. Smaller boutique wineries achieve the same results by storing their fruit overnight in a cool room and fermenting early the next day. Once the grapes have been pressed (in the case of white wine), must-chilling, cold-settling, filtering and even centrifuging the juice all help to create a pristine product. Red and white wines are routinely innoculated with a chosen yeast strain followed by a cool fermentation and oak ageing; barrel fermentation in cool rooms sometimes also plays a part in the wine-making process.

This "squeaky clean" school of wine-making is not universally admired in Australia. There are many who claim, with some reason, that innoculated yeasts lend too many uniform exotic fruit salad or passion fruit aromas to white wine, and a few traditionalists such as Murray Tyrrell of **Tyrrell's** still insist on using the natural yeasts present on grape skins and ferment their red wines in open fermenters. There will always be different approaches to wine-making, but one factor which has helped to change the industry out of all recognition over the last 20 years has been the willingness to experiment. This owes much to the Australian system of wine shows with well-organized competitions judged by knowledgeable, tough, yet fair panels.

It is difficult to assess the influence of the old school on the new generation of trained wine-makers, though many are now deserting Australia's leading wine schools, Roseworthy and Riverina, for French institutions such as Bordeaux and Dijon or venturing further afield to Davis and Fresno in America. What is clear is that, having fought hard against the heat to rank among the world's finest wine technologists, the Australians are now stepping back from their technically pure corner and evaluating their grapes and juice not by machine but by using their own taste-buds. Australians now have the confidence to experiment with some of the more traditional French ideas, such as allowing pre-fermentation skin contact for Chardonnay and other white varieties and giving this grape extra time on its flavour-enhancing lees or sludgy sediment. The Pinot Noir grape is also now treated in a more Burgundian manner using warm fermentation. The next generation of Australian wine-makers will be neither technocrats nor traditionalists, but take the best from both schools.

Grape varieties

Although the vine arrived in 1788, Australia is still a very young wine-producing country: its modern wine era did not begin until the 1960s. In not much more than two decades the Australians have mastered the new technology needed to conquer their climate. What they have yet to conquer is their vineyards. It took Europeans centuries to work out where each grape variety grows best and which varieties blend most harmoniously with each other. Given the Australian drive to experiment and excell it is likely to take them a fraction of this time. Most Australians now realize that if the 60s, 70s and 80s formed the era of the wine-maker then the next two decades belong to the viticulturist.

Just as Australia's first vineyards were planted with scant regard for factors such as terrain and climate, so early grape-growers were undiscriminating about which varieties they planted where. To begin with a wide range of different vines were planted, working no doubt on a hit-and-miss principle. Many of these vines were selected from France and Spain by the Antipodean wine pioneer James Busby and brought back to Australia in 1832. It soon became clear that all-purpose (though not necessarily top-quality) grapes such as Shiraz, Grenache and Mataro, which could be made into both table and fortified wines, were the safest choice for reds. Australia's early white selection consisted mainly of sherry, fortified and brandy grapes such as Muscat, Palomino, Pedro Ximenez, and Doradillo. These varieties dominated Australian vineyards until the table wine boom of the 60s.

Today high-quality table wine grapes are gradually beginning to feature as a significant proportion of the 500,000 tonnes of grapes produced yearly from Australia's 133,000 acres (54,000 ha) under vine. Shiraz (known to Europeans as Syrah) may still be the most widely planted red variety by far, but Cabernet Sauvignon has ousted Grenache from second place and is treading on its tail. The white varietal list is more complicated. Because of Australia's important dried fruit industry, the all-purpose Sultana grape (better known as Thompson's Seedless in California), which can be turned into wine, table grapes or dried grapes, is easily the most widely planted variety. Next in line is Muscat Gordo Blanco, another all-purpose grape, also known as Muscat Alexandria or "Fruity 'Lexia". These are followed by Rhine Riesling, Semillon and the increasingly fashionable Chardonnay.

The complex task of matching vine to region, site, soil and micro-climate is still largely in its infancy. But a handful of marriages between grape and region have proved distinctly successful. Rhine Riesling has been coupled effectively with Clare in South Australia and Mount Barker in Western Australia. The forgiving Chardonnay vine has settled down well almost everywhere, but is especially happy in Coonawarra, the Margaret River, the Adelaide Hills and even the Hunter. Australians vinify this grape in two distinct styles: either, as James Halliday of **Coldstream Hills** puts it, "a rich, fat, full-bodied peaches-and-cream Dolly Parton style" or an elegant, leaner, more restrained version. Cabernet Sauvignon has thrived in Coonawarra for many years and is flourishing in the Margaret River, where Shiraz also does well. Shiraz and Semillon have both produced memorable Hunter wines, while pernickety Pinot Noir has made itself at home in the Margaret River and may soon be thriving in Victoria's Yarra Valley. North-East Victoria remains the perfect region for fortified wines such as Muscat Blanc (or Muscat à Petits Grains), better known in Australia as Frontignac. Luscious fortifieds are also made here from the Tokay grape, known to Europeans as Muscadelle.

Wine-styles

It is sometimes difficult for newcomers to accept the tremendous thwack of flavour Australian wines deliver. Unlike European vines, grapes here ripen under sunny, rain-free skies which endow them with more fruit, more flavour, more alcohol and less acidity. More does not always mean better, but where wine-makers have striven for balance Australian wines can provide exciting taste trips unrivalled in the world.

Since Australia is still evaluating which vines should go where it is not surprising that few great, truly indigenous wine-styles have developed. Leading Australian wine authorities include North-East Victoria's lovely fortified Muscat and Tokay in this category, as well as fine Hunter Valley Semillon, whose smoky, toasty flavours challenge the world's top Chardonnays. It would be impossible to leave out the distinctive tarry delights of glorious Australian Shiraz like **Penfolds'** Grange Hermitage. But many wine-styles, alas, continue to ape their European forbears. It is disconcerting, for example, to see Australian wine labels bearing the titles "Claret", "White Burgundy" or "Chablis", especially when one considers that the grapes used to make these wines frequently vary from the European original.

Pseudo-European wine labels and what they mean

- "Chablis" on an Australian label indicates a fresh, clean, crisp dry white table wine, which could be made from a number of grapes, though rarely Chardonnay.
- "Dry White Burgundy" means a medium to full-bodied white, often with a touch of oak, which should not show any sweetness. Like "Chablis", it could be made from a variety of grapes other than Chardonnay.
- "Moselle" translates into sweet white table wine with a distinctly flowery bouquet, not usually made from the Rhine Riesling grape.
- "Hock" is generally a dry aromatic wine, again rarely made from Rhine Riesling.
- "Claret" signifies a firm, full-bodied dry red, based usually on Shiraz though Cabernet Sauvignon is beginning to feature in the blend.
- "Burgundy", also mostly a Shiraz-based red, should have a soft, round, velvety palate without the astringency of "Claret".

Fortunately these pseudo-European labels are beginning to disappear, their demise encouraged by a wine show system that seldom recognizes such titles now, adopting instead the international language of "full-bodied, firm-finish dry reds" and "dry white table wines – full-bodied". Another confusing aspect of the Australian wine label are bin numbers. Originally they must have indicated that the wine came from a particular bin which had in turn been bottled from a specific vat. Today they are not much more than a glorified marketing device.

It is worth remembering that, though an Australian bottle may be labelled Cabernet Sauvignon, it can still by law have as much as 20% of another grape such as Shiraz in the blend without this grape appearing on the label; this accounts for those Australian Cabernets with distinctive, rich, earthy, chocolatey Shiraz overtones. Blends that are made from less than 80% of one single variety must announce their other component parts on the label in descending order of proportion: this is why one encounters Australian wines labelled, for example, Cabernet Sauvignon-Shiraz-Malbec. Similarly, any Australian wine quoting a region of origin on the label must be at least 80% made from that region's wines, and if a vintage year is quoted at least 95% of the wine within has to be of that year's vintage.

What won't be confusing to Australian wine buyers is any legal *appellation* jargon: there isn't any. Some individual regions such as Mudgee in New South Wales have their own local *appellation* stamp based on a sensory evaluation of the wine, but there is no move by the Government to create a quality control system for the country as a whole. However, it has recently insisted on a compulsory Universal Recording System (URS) to be kept by every winery in order to keep track of grapes, wine and must; this is essential given the Australian propensity for moving grapes from one end of the country to the other.

New South Wales

New South Wales produces a quarter of all the grapes grown in Australia. Given that this is Australia's oldest wine-producing state it is perhaps surprising that the figure is not higher. The Hunter Valley, planted with vines in the 1820s, was the country's first successful wine-making region and remained the grape-growing stronghold of New South Wales throughout the 19th and early 20th centuries. As pioneering settlers carried the vine to other parts of the continent, grapes were also planted in the Upper Hunter and Hilltops regions, and in Mudgee where Australia's second-oldest producing winery, founded in 1858, can be visited today at **Craigmoor**.

With the completion of the Burrinjuck Dam in 1912, **McWilliam's** planted the first irrigated vines in New South Wales' hot Riverina region. Three-quarters of the state's output now comes from here – far more than the production of its leading quality wine region, the Hunter Valley. For all that the Hunter has an impressively high profile both within the country and abroad, though cynics like to claim that this region is responsible for 90% of the state's wine reviews, but only 10% of its wines. In fact, the state as a whole is too hot to grow high-quality grapes. Even in the famous Hunter, irrigation is essential to produce decent yields. This is why the majority of New South Wales' vineyards are situated in the cooler eastern areas of the state which benefit from coastal breezes.

Wine-producing regions

CANBERRA (CA)

Owing to land restrictions within the Australian Capital Territory, almost all vineyards in the Canberra area are actually situated in NSW, just outside the ACT proper. Most are clustered around Lake George, some on slopes as high as 2,800 feet (860 m) where the cooler climate produces fine fruit. Canberra's wineries are all small family-owned concerns that survive on day-trippers from the capital. Frosts and summer droughts are a problem.

HILLTOPS (HT)

The Hilltops wine-making region is concentrated on the Young, Boorowa and Harden triangle of towns south-west of Sydney. Both table and wine grapes were produced on these slopes in the 19th century but viticulture slowly died out and was not revitalized until the early 1970s. There are now about 100 acres (40 ha) of vines in the region, and much of their production is bought by outside wineries, especially in Canberra. Hilltops has moderate rainfall and good soil; cool nights account for its longer ripening period.

HUNTER VALLEY (HV)

The Hunter Valley (or Lower Hunter), situated close to Cessnock some three hours north of Sydney, is Australia's oldest wine-making region. The first plantings were established here on the fertile Hunter River flats in the 1820s, but the vineyard boom took place during the second half of the century. In spite of its long association with the vine, the region is far from ideal for viticulture. While not as scorching as the Riverland (SA), the Swan (WA) or even NSW's own Riverina, its climate is much too hot for the vine. High levels of summer rainfall and rain at harvest time, combined with the heat, allow mildew to run riot. However, a number of factors do help to alleviate these sub-tropical features: afternoon cloud cover reduces the heat; the Hunter's rich red volcanic soil produces some remarkable white wines; and modern sprays keep rot under control. The proximity of Sydney encouraged new producers to start up here in the 1960s and tourists will continue to ensure the buoyancy of cellar-door sales.

Distinctive regional wine-styles

HUNTER VALLEY SEMILLON
Traditionally sold as Hunter Valley Riesling, Hunter Semillon starts life a shy and somewhat dull, verdant wine. Yet, given five years' bottle age, it transforms into an amazingly complex explosion of toasty-oaky flavours overlaid with rich, honeyed, lime-like tastes. This quality is not achieved by ageing in new oak casks, though first-time tasters would swear it was. Nowhere else in the world does the Semillon grape develop in this fashion. Modern Hunter Valley Semillons are increasingly vinified to be drunk young and show rich, buttery qualities early on. Whether these wines will take on the same toast and lime character with age is another matter.

HUNTER VALLEY SHIRAZ
Blood, guts and thunder Hunter Shiraz is about as close to old-fashioned Australian red wine as the modern drinker will get. Dark in colour, with an enormous, burnt, beefy, alcoholic palate reeking of tar, creosote and farmyard scents, the wine takes on a leathery quality with age that locals have dubbed "sweaty saddles". This is not a style for the faint-hearted, but it should be experienced. Modern vinification techniques are replacing traditional flavours with richer, fruitier reds that display some of the peppery Syrah (Shiraz) attributes of the Rhône.

MUDGEE (MD)
Situated on NSW's central-west tablelands about 160 miles (260 km) north-west of Sydney and an hour's drive west of the Upper Hunter, "the nest in the hills", as the aborigines call Mudgee, tends to be ignored by overseas wine visitors. Once described as "Mudgee mud" the region's wines have improved over the years, partly as a result of its *appellation* scheme under which wines are judged blind by the region's producers. Mudgee's vineyards start on the river flats and follow gentle slopes almost to the top of the Great Dividing Range, whose hills protect it on either side. This altitude, averaging about 1,550 feet (500 m), creates a longer ripening period and grape-growers here harvest about a month later than the Hunter. Beneficial summer rain helps to relieve vine stress from the heat, but unlike the Hunter there is no rain at vintage time; floods and frosts are an occasional problem. The region's rich red loam soils contain both limestone and ironstone. Good Chardonnay is produced, but Mudgee's best wines are reds such as Cabernet Sauvignon and Shiraz.

RIVERINA (RV)
The hot, arid Riverina region, also known as Griffith-Leeton or the Murrumbidgee Irrigation Area, lies due west of Sydney, half-way to Adelaide. Like Australia's other large irrigated wine region, SA's Riverland, the Riverina processes vast quantities of grapes – producing 20% of the country's total output. Over a quarter of the plantings are Semillon, followed by Trebbiano, Shiraz, Gordo and lesser quantities of Colombard. Before the advent of irrigation in 1912, nothing much grew along the Murrumbidgee River. The wine industry took off with the arrival in the 1920s of Italians immigrants who made fortified wines. However, the switch from fortifieds to table wines did not come until the late 50s and early 60s when **McWilliam's** followed SA's lead by introducing new techniques such as cold fermentation; today mechanical harvesting and pruning keep costs down. **De Bortoli's** success with Semillon/Sauternes, and to a lesser extent with Chardonnay, has revealed glimpses of the region's potential. But the Riverina, with its 12,400 acres (5,000 ha) of high-yielding vines, will always be a bulk producer, home to cask wines, flagons and cheap (mostly *spumante*-style) sparklers; the word Riverina is rarely seen on wine labels.

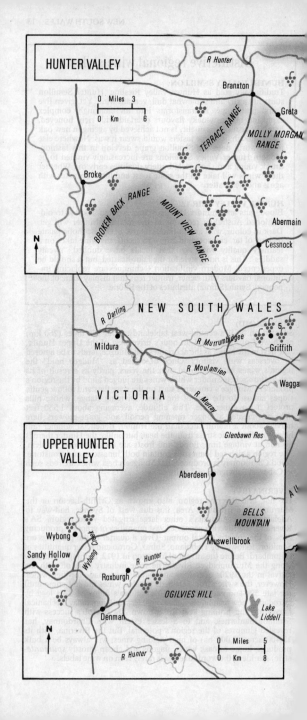

NEW SOUTH WALES

Wine Regions

1 CANBERRA
2 HILLTOPS
3 HUNTER VALLEY
4 MUDGEE
5 RIVERINA
6 UPPER HUNTER VALLEY

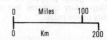

| | Miles | 100 |
| Km | | 200 |

UPPER HUNTER VALLEY (UH)
Vines were first grown in the Upper Hunter Valley during the 19th century, but until the arrival of **Rosemount** in the 1970s the region was always regarded as poor relation to the Lower Hunter. **Penfolds** bought land in the 60s, building a large, well-equipped winery just north of Sandy Hollow at Wybong. It was not a success: the relatively low rainfall here caught the non-irrigated vines unprepared. However, other wineries moving into the region in the late 60s, which planted drip-irrigated vines in the rich volcanic river flat soils, were rewarded with impressive yields. The Upper Hunter, unlike the Hunter itself, has always principally been a white wine producer, as illustrated by Rosemount's success with Chardonnay and Semillon. But its lush, fruity whites are vinified as ready-to-drink wines and lack the cellaring potential of, say, Hunter Valley Semillon. This is a perfectly legitimate commercial approach, but don't expect Upper Hunter wines to improve with age: they won't, they will just fall apart.

OTHER WINERIES (§)
NSW has a greater number of solitary wineries lying outside the recognized wine-making regions than any other state in Australia. Most of these are scattered around the south-east corner of the state to the south of the Hunter Valley and Mudgee, fanning out in a wide semi-circle west of Sydney. **Cassegrain** and **Gilgai** up in the north are the most isolated wineries. The smaller concerns exist chiefly by offering cellar-door sales to the tourists as they drive past.

New South Wales wineries

AFFLECK VINEYARD   CA
244 Gundaroo Road, Bungendore, NSW 2621

w, r, ft *
Ian Hendry produces just 150 cases a year from his 5 acres (2 ha) of vines close to Lake George. Most of these are premium table wines but he also produces Muscat and port.

ALLANDALE   HV
Lovedale Road, Pokolbin via Maitland, NSW 2321

w, r, sw, sp *
Bill Sneddon is the new wine-maker/general manager of this 15-acre (6-ha) estate planted equally to Pinot Noir, Semillon and Chardonnay. Allandale, founded in 1978, buys in most of its grapes from local growers to produce about 10,000 cases a year, Chardonnay being its most popular wine. 1988 was the first sparkling wine vintage.

ALLANMERE   HV
Lovedale Road, Allandale, NSW 2321

w, r *
This small family-owned winery, founded in 1985, makes red wines from 12 acres (5 ha) of Cab Sauvignon and Shiraz. Whites, including Chardonnay, Semillon and a mainly Chardonnay-based Trinity blend, are made from bought-in Hunter grapes.

AMBERTON   MD
Henry Lawson Drive, Mudgee, NSW 2850

w, r *
Amberton is one of three Mudgee wineries in the **Wyndham Estate** group and shared its Italian-born wine-maker, Carlo Corino, with the other two until his recent decision to leave the group. About 5,000 cases are made here from 80 acres (32 ha) of vines. Most of this is Semillon but Chardonnay, Sauv Blanc and Cab Sauvignon are also made. Amberton's young vineyards will provide finer wine when they mature. The current 87 Sauv Blanc is fresh, grassy but dull; so are the 86 Cabernet, whose pleasant blackcurrany scent leads onto a raw palate, and the gutsy, peppery 86 Shiraz. The 84 Cabernet had some finer truffley-cedary qualities, but suffered like the 86 vintage from raw acidity on the palate.

ARROWFIELD UH
Jerry's Plains, NSW 2330

w, r, ft, sp *←→

This 260-acre (105-ha) estate, run by wine-maker/chief executive Simon Gilbert, produces a long list of table, fortified and sparkling wines from a wide range of vines. Arrowfield has had its share of problems but according to Australian judges wine quality here has much improved; its Reserve wines, especially the Semillon, are well regarded. Some tip this winery to become **Rosemount Estate's** most serious competitor in the Upper Hunter.

AUDREY WILKINSON HV
De Beyers Road, Pokolbin, NSW 2321

w, r *

Although **Murray Robson** now leases part of this vineyard, a limited number of traditional Hunter wines are still made here.

AUGUSTINE MD
Airport Road, Mudgee, NSW 2850

w, r, ft *

Barry Platt makes wines for the local syndicate which founded Augustine in 1980. These are sold via a mailing list or at the cellar door.

BARWANG VINEYARDS HT
Barwang Road, Young, NSW 2594

w, r, ft *

Barwang, owned by the Robertson family, produces table and fortified wines from 25 acres (10 ha) planted to a variety of grapes including Semillon and Muscat.

BELBOURIE HV
Branxton Road, Rothbury, NSW 2321

w, r, sp *

Owned by the Roberts family, Belbourie's 15 acres (6 ha) of vines supply about half its grapes; the remainder is bought in locally. Wine-maker Bob Davies makes Belah (Semillon), Bungan (a red blend), Quartz (*méthode champenoise* fizz) and other "low-tech, traditional, big, ageing wines".

BENFIELD ESTATE CA
Fairy Hole Road, Yass, NSW 2582

w, r, ft *

The Fetherstons own this 27-acre (11-ha) estate planted to mixed vines. Until 1985 plantings come on stream, table and fortified wines will continue to be made partly from bought-in grapes.

BOTOBOLAR MD
Botobolar Lane, Mudgee, NSW 2850

w, r, ft *

With its 66 acres (26 ha) of vines and annual 6,000-case production, Gil and Vincie Wahlquist's easterly Mudgee outpost is larger than most in the region. Wines range from Crouchen and St Gilbert Dry Red (a Cabernet/Shiraz blend) to Marsanne, Chardonnay and Cab Sauvignon. All vines are organically grown.

BRAMHALL MD
Cassilis Road, Mudgee, NSW 2850

w, r, ft *

Ian and Kathy Lindeman make table and fortified wines from 37 acres (15 ha) of Mudgee Traminer, Cab Sauvignon and Shiraz.

BRIAR RIDGE VINEYARD HV
Mount View Road, Mount View, NSW 2325

w, r *←→

Formerly the Robson Vineyard, this wooden winery situated in a pretty corner of the Hunter Valley has passed through a turbulent period since **Murray Robson** left to set up a new firm. His assistant wine-maker,

Kees van de Scheur, has now started the Briar Ridge Vineyard on the same premises; his first vintage was 1988. Van de Scheur's stylish salmon-pink labels are as different as can be from the old regime's, but he still aims to maintain a "small specialist boutique winery". Briar Ridge's own 19 acres (8 ha) of vines, supplemented by one of its new owners' vineyards, produce about 7,000 cases a year. Chardonnay is the big line, followed by Hermitage, Semillon and a Merlot/Cabernet blend. The 88 Briar Ridge Early Harvest Semillon with its fresh, grassy passion fruit mouthful is pleasant, and the 88 Tradition Semillon not dissimilar. The light, fresh, melon and pineapple-like 88 Chardonnay was better, but the grassy, plummy, acidic 88 Merlot/Cabernet nothing special.

BROKENWOOD   HV
McDonalds Road, Pokolbin, NSW 2321

                                  w=86 87 84, r=86 87 85   *→***

This exciting "spare time" winery was founded in 1970 by partners Tony Albert, John Beeston and James Halliday. They made the first few vintages from 1973 onwards by working every weekend and taking holidays at vintage time. New partners joined, new vines were planted – there are now 40 acres (16 ha) – and wine-maker Iain Riggs arrived in 1982. Under his supervision Brokenwood has gone from strength to strength. Annual production is now up to 15,000 cases. Extra fruit is bought in from the Hunter and Coonawarra (SA); by 1991 Brokenwood will be bringing in fruit from the Yarra (VIC) too.

Brokenwood's bestseller is its Semillon: the 88 with its fresh, light, waxy, lemony fruit makes a great aperitif. The delicate, mango and pineapple-like 88 Chardonnay was less successful. Shiraz is another strength here: the 86 Graveyard Hermitage boasted rich, robust, earthy, truffley flavours, while the fine, flavoursome 87 had some spicy black pepper scents reminiscent of the northern Rhône. Cabernets are less impressive, though the 87 Graveyard version has a lovely wine with a light, smoky cassis scent and big, chocolatey flavours on the palate. Brokenwood has even produced a creditable 87 Pinot Noir. Its juicy, fruity taste of strawberries and redcurrants is a bit light and jammy, but this is an impressive start with a tricky grape. Don't worry, incidentally, about the "Graveyard" label – though originally planned as a cemetery, the vineyard here was never used as one.

BURNBRAE   MD
Hargraves Road, Mudgee, NSW 2850

                                                          w, r, ft   *

Robert Mace's lifelong interest in wine began with a vineyard in Hampshire, England. He and his wife Pamela bought this somewhat run-down estate in the early 80s and are still reorganizing their 36-acre (15-ha) vineyard and winery. At present they make about 3,000 cases, of which a Cab Sauvignon/Malbec blend and a Grenache Rosé are the bestsellers. New wines include a Nouveau style and Blush Rosé.

CALAIS ESTATES   HV
Palmers Lane, Pokolbin, NSW 2321

                                                          w, r, ft   *

Now owned by the Petersons, this winery remains independent of the main **Petersons** operation. Calais' 60 acres (24 ha) of vines such as Semillon and Hermitage are turned into table and fortified wine.

CALOOLA   MD
Henry Lawson Drive, Mudgee, NSW 2850

                                                          w, r, ft   *

This small estate, run by the wine-making Cross family, specializes in fortified wines such as Muscats and also makes a few table wines.

CAMDEN ESTATE   §
Lot 32, Macarthur Road, Camden, NSW 2570

                                                          w, r   *

Roseworthy-trained wine-maker Norman Hanckel produces 10,000 cases of varietal wines – mostly Chardonnay and a Traminer blend – from 42 acres (17 ha) of vines.

CARTOBE   HT
Young Road, Boorowa, NSW 2586

w, r   *

Cartobe, about an hour's drive north of Canberra, is one of the oldest Hilltops wineries. Wine-maker Geoff Carter has 8 acres (3 ha) of mainly Rh Riesling close to the winery, which supplies half his fruit; the rest, including Chardonnay, is bought in. Annual production is 2,500 cases, of which Boorowa Chardonnay is the bestseller. Tastings are held in the late 19th-century winery. Cartobe hopes to buy a new vineyard and double production over the next two years.

CASELLA'S   RV
Farm 1471, Yenda, NSW 2681

w, r, sp *

John Casella owns this small family operation in the north-east of the region, selling bulk wines and bottled *spumante* at the cellar door.

CASSEGRAIN   §
Fernbank Road, Port Macquarie, NSW 2444

w, r   *→

Situated in the Hastings Valley near the coast, this family-owned winery is run by John Cassegrain who trained at **Tyrrell's** in the Hunter. When opened in 1985 it revived a Hastings wine-making tradition broken in 1919. There are 40 acres (16 ha) of grapes surrounding the winery and part of its fruit comes in from the Hunter. Output is likely to increase dramatically soon with Claude Cassegrain's new 380-acre (155-ha) plantations. Production stands at 45,000 cases, but within three years Cassegrain hopes to reach the 250,000-case mark. The big sellers are Chardonnay, Gewurztraminer and Cab Sauvignon, produced using a combination of "tradition and technology". The 85 Semillon was a pleasant, soft, citric, but unexciting mouthful.

CHATEAU FRANCOIS   HV
Broke Road, Pokolbin, NSW 2320

w, r   *

Donald Francois, a wine-loving American with a doctorate in fish research, is owner/wine-maker at this 6-acre (2.5 ha) estate founded in 1969. He produces just 1,200 cases a year of Semillon, Chardonnay and a Shiraz/Pinot Noir blend which he rates as his best wine.

CHATEAU PATO   HV
Thompson's Road, Pokolbin, NSW 2321

w, r   *

Small quantities of one white (Gewurztraminer) and one red (Hermitage) are made here and sold via a mailing list.

CLONAKILLA WINES   CA
Crisps Lane, Gundaroo Road, Murrumbateman, NSW 2582

w, r   *

Dr John Kirk and his family own Clonakilla. The vineyard here was planted in 1971 and the first commercial vintage was produced in 1976. Production is only 300 cases, half made from the 3 acres (1 ha) of vines adjoining the winery and half from local bought-in grapes.

COGNO BROTHERS   §
Cobbity Road, Cobbity, NSW 2570

w, r, ft, sp *

Giovanni and Joe Cogno produce Italian-influenced table, fortified and sparkling wines here from 25 acres (10 ha) of vines.

THE COLLEGE   HT
Boorooma Street, North Wagga Wagga, NSW 2650

w, r   *

The Riverina-Murray Institute of Higher Education – better known as "Wagga" – has, along with Roseworthy in SA, become an important stepping-stone to Australian wine-making. The wine course here was set up by Brian Croser and Dr Tony Jordan. Output is variable.

COOPERS ETTAMOGAH WINES   §
Lot 4, Burma Road, Tabletop, NSW 2641

w, r, ft, sp   *

Lindsay Cooper is owner/wine-maker at this 13-acre (5-ha) winery in
the touristy Ettamogah Pub Complex close to the Victorian border.
Coopers produces 2,000 cases of a wide range of wine-styles including
port, Muscat, *spumante* and straight varietals such as Cab Sauvignon.
One-third of Coopers' fruit is bought in.

COWRA WINES   §
Cowra, NSW 2794

w, r   *

This 100-acre (40-ha) estate, one of the largest in the Cowra area, lies
inland from Sydney. Chardonnay, Traminer, Rh Riesling and Pinot
Noir grapes are grown and mostly sold to other wineries. A limited
range of table wines are made for Cowra by **Arrowfield**.

CRAIGMOOR   MD
Craigmoor Road, Mudgee, NSW 2850

w, r, ft   *

Founded in 1858 by Adam Roth, a German settler, Craigmoor is the
oldest surviving Mudgee winery and the second-oldest in Australia after
Olive Farm Wines (WA); it was also the first in the country to plant
Chardonnay. In the late 1960s the Roth family sold out and it eventually
became part of **Wyndham Estate's** Mudgee interests. Craigmoor has
140 acres (55 ha) of Chardonnay, Shiraz, Cab Sauvignon, Semillon and
Trebbiano, from which it makes just 20,000 cases of wines; remaining
grapes are used by Wyndham. Semillon/Trebbiano is the big seller,
followed by Cab Sauvignon, Chardonnay, a Chablis blend and Shiraz.
New plantings will include 80 acres (32 ha) of vineyards on original
Craigmoor property. The 88 Semillon/Chardonnay was an agreeable,
but unexciting, zesty, pineappley fruit salad of a mouthful. The 88
Chardonnay offered soft melon and vanilla flavours, the 86 Shiraz a
farmyard scent and a big, beefy, brambley palate.

CRUICKSHANK CALLATOOTA ESTATE   UH
Wybong Road, Wybong, NSW 2333

r   *

This winery was founded in 1973 by John Cruickshank, whose son
Andrew is now wine-maker. With just 22 acres (9 ha) of mainly Cab
Sauvignon vines and an annual 3,000-case production, Cruickshank
Callatoota Estate is by no means the biggest player in the Upper Hunter.
At present, it makes Cabernet and Cabernet Rosé wines; Cab Franc
plantings will come on stream in 1990.

D'AQUINO   §
129-133 Bathurst Road, Orange, NSW 2800

w, r, ft, sp   *

Rex and Leo d'Aquino make a wide range of Italian-style table, fortified
and sparkling wines here.

DAWSON ESTATE   HV
Londons Road, Nulkaba, NSW 2325

w   *

The Dawson family's 20 acres (8 ha) of vines surrounding the premises
are planted mostly to Chardonnay, with a little Traminer. About 5,000
cases of white wine a year are produced at this winery, under the
Allandale and Dawson labels.

DE BORTOLI   RV
De Bortoli Road, Bilbul, NSW 2680

w, r, sw=82 84, ft, sp   *—*×**

Vittorio de Bortoli founded this firm in 1928. His son Deen is now
Managing Director, his Roseworthy-trained grandson Darren wine-
maker and his granddaughter Leanne in charge of sales. De Bortoli'
Italian traditions are typical of the Riverina, as are its dead-flat, dead
straight 250 acres (100 ha) of irrigated vineyards. What separates it

wines from other local produce is their quality. The luscious, sweet late harvest botrytis-affected Sauternes (Semillon-based) made here are a match for Bordeaux originals. The 82 Semillon Sauternes – remarkably the family's first attempt at this style – has deservedly been covered with gold medals and trophies. When the de Bortolis struck gold in the following year with a lighter 83 botrytis Semillon Sauternes and yet again in 84 with another full-bodied offering, Australia's cynics stopped dismissing their success as a fluke.

The winery's own Riverina vineyards supply just 10% of its fruit, the rest coming from local growers. A vast range of wines is made. At the upper end are sweet botrytis offerings including the sensational four-star silky, flowery 82 Botrytis Semillon, the glorious, rich, *crème brulée*-like 84 and the sappier, more raisiny 82 Botrytis Pedro, which is cheaper. One step down are premium varietals such as the light, clean, pineappley 87 Chardonnay and the big, rich, lemony-sherbetty 87 Semillon, both thoroughly acceptable. The family is pleased with the light, sweet, juicy fruit 86 Merlot and the drinkable, herbaceous, cassis-like 85 Cab Sauvignon. Marginally better is the 86 Pinot Noir with its plum and rose fruit. Port, Muscat, sherry, the Jean-Pierre *méthode champenoise* fizz, wine casks, flagons, Italian-influenced sparklers and German-influenced table wines complete the range.

DENMAN ESTATE UH
Denman Road, Muswellbrook, NSW 2333

w, r, ft ★

Bought by **Rothbury** in 1988, Denman now contributes most of its grapes to the Rothbury wines. A small range of "fighting varietals" such as Cab Sauvignon and Chardonnay are still available at the cellar door.

DOONKUNA ESTATE CA
Barton Highway, Murrumbateman, NSW 2582

w, r ★→

Sir Brian Murray, Doonkuna's wine-maker, once hired Dr Tony Jordan to assist him here. With some 12 acres (5 ha) of mixed vines, this is a large operation by Canberra standards and its wines are already being hailed as the best in the region.

DRAYTON'S BELLEVUE HV
Oakey Creek Road, Pokolbin, NSW 2321

w, r, ft, sp ★

The Drayton family grows Shiraz and Cab Sauvignon here, making a wide range of table, fortified, flavoured and sparkling wines. The 86 Shiraz is a typical big, beefy, burnt, "sweaty saddles" Hunter Shiraz.

ERUDGERE VINEYARDS MD
Hill End Road, Erudgere, Mudgee, NSW 2850

w, r ★

This small winery, which sells most of its grapes to other concerns, occasionally uses outside wine-makers.

EVANS FAMILY HV
Palmers Lane, Pokolbin, NSW 2321

w, r ★★→★★★

Wine supremo Len Evans is the man behind this label. The hillsides surrounding his beautiful house in the Hunter are planted to 20 acres (4 ha) of mostly Chardonnay, with Pinot Noir and a little Gamay. These yield about 2,000 cases of first-class wines most years, vinified at Evans' **Rothbury** winery. The delicate pineappley fruit and light, oaky taste of the 87 Chardonnay, his latest vintage, need time but will eventually no doubt be as delicious as the rich, buttery, flowery 86 and the fine, rich, soft, toasty 84. Evans' first Pinot Noir is eagerly awaited.

FRANCO'S WINES RV
Irrigation Way, Griffith, NSW 2680

w, r, sw, ft ★

Salvatore Franco makes table and fortified wines in various styles here and sells them at the cellar door.

FRASER VINEYARD   HV
Wilderness Road, Rothbury, NSW 2320

w, r *

This new winery run by Peter and Beverley Fraser produces small
quantities mostly of whites such as Semillon, and a Shiraz.

GILGAI   §
Tingha Road, Gilgai, NSW 2360

w, r, ft *

The Whish family owns 15 acres (6 ha) of a wide variety of vines close to
Inverell. These are turned into table and fortified wines, including the
Gilgai Red and White table wine brands.

GLENFINLASS   §
Elysian Farm, Parkes Road, Wellington, NSW 2820

w, r *

Brian and Nyasa Holmes' 5 acres (2 ha) of Shiraz, Cab Sauvignon and
Sauv Blanc vines are made into small quantities of table wines.

GOLDEN GRAPE ESTATE   HV
Oakey Creek Road, Pokolbin, NSW 2321

w, r, ft, sp *

Owned by the large German Pieroth group, Golden Grape's 105 acres
(43 ha) of vines are turned into a German-influenced range of table,
fortified and sparkling wines. There is also a wine museum and gift shop.

GREVILLEA ESTATE   §
Buckajo Road, Bega, NSW 2550

w, r *

Grevillea's 16 acres (6 ha) are owned by the Collins family. Sisters Beth
and Nicky are wine-maker and vineyard manager respectively. A wide
range of table wines are produced, as well as a kiwi fruit wine.

HELM'S WINES   CA
Butts Road, Murrumbateman, NSW 2582

w, r *

Founded in 1974, this winery is situated about half an hour from
Canberra. Ken Helm and his family, whose ancestors came from the
Rhineland in 1854 to grow grapes, own only 5 acres (2 ha) of vines with
another 25 acres (10 ha) under contract. About 1,500 cases of various
table wines were produced in 1988, but the Helms expect production to
double in a few years and are making plans to release a *méthode
champenoise* sparkler soon.

HERCYNIA   HT
Prunevale, NSW 2587

w, r *

Lawrence Doldissen's small family-operated winery has 12 acres (5 ha)
of Kingsvale vines, including Pinot Noir and Chardonnay.

HILL OF GOLD   MD
Henry Lawson Drive, Mudgee, NSW 2850

w, r, ft *

The 30 acres (12 ha) of vines here, planted to Pinot Noir and Cab
Sauvignon, are turned into table and fortified wines.

HOLLYDENE ESTATE   UH
Merriwa Road, Hollydene, via Denman, NSW 2333

w, r, ft *→→**

Hollydene's 225 acres (90 ha) of vines, managed by the ebullient Brian
McGuigan, are now part of the **Wyndham Estate** winery group and its
commercial wines, which are meant to be drunk young, are not
dissimilar to Wyndham's. The soft, leafy-buttery scent and taste of the
87 Semillon/Chardonnay is good, while the 87 Chardonnay boasts a
good, clean, fruity, lemon-lime palate. The 86 Cab Sauvignon has a
fresh, zesty, blackcurrant pastille-like taste and the 86 Shiraz has stacks
of loganberry-like fruit: probably not for purists.

HORDERNS WYBONG ESTATE UH
Yarraman Road, Wybong, NSW 2333

w, r ★

Horderns, one of the Upper Hunter's most northerly wineries, was founded in 1963 and is run by Dr Robert Smith and his wife Theo. The 90 acres (36 ha) of vines here are vinified by Roseworthy-trained Vicky-Louise Bartier-Roberts in a winery made from blocks of the old Bengalla prison. Some 3,000 cases of table wines are produced, about 5% of their fruit coming from Cowra and Mudgee. Horderns rates its 89 Shiraz and Chardonnay highest.

HORSESHOE VINEYARD UH
Horseshoe Road, Horseshoe Valley, NSW 2328

w, r ★

This small vineyard produces limited quantities of a Chardonnay, a Semillon and a Shiraz Nouveau; 1987 was the first vintage.

HUNGERFORD HILL HV
Broke Road, Pokolbin, NSW 2321

w, r, ft, sp ★→★★

Hungerford Hill was founded in 1967 and now has a motel, restaurant, art gallery, craft shop and convention centre all on the same site. While clearly designed as a tourist attraction, this "wine village" has been quite skilfully (if not entirely tastefully) executed. The winery, which produces about 100,000 cases a year, owns nearly 100 acres (40 ha) in the Hunter and another 170 acres (70 ha) or so in Coonawarra (SA); grapes are also bought in. Wine-maker Adrian Sheridan, formerly with **Arrowfield**, makes a varied range of wines including red Nouveau, sparkling red Burgundy, ports, Muscats and sparklers; Dry White, Dry Red and Pokolbin Chardonnay account for most of the output. The rich, ripe flavours of the 86 Show Reserve Pokolbin Chardonnay are fair without being fine. The 81 Show Reserve Coonawarra Cab Sauvignon with its big, rich, green pepper and blackcurrant flavours is better. Down-market from these are the Hungerford Hill Collection wines: the 86 Coonawarra Rh Riesling had some fine, fresh, lime juice flavours while the 86 Cabernet/Merlot/Malbec had a light, sappy, grassy palate. Hungerford Hill still has plenty of room for improvement.

HUNTER ESTATE HV
Deasey's Road, Pokolbin, NSW 2321

w, r, ft ★

Yet another member of the **Wyndham Estate** empire, this winery is also run by Jon Reynolds. Besides vinifying its own 280 acres (115 ha) of fruit, it buys in grapes from Mudgee and the Hunter, producing large quantities of table, fortified and flavoured wines.

HUNTINGTON ESTATE MD
Cassilis Road, Mudgee, NSW 2850

r=84 83 79, w=79 82 ★→★★★

Huntington Estate is by far the finest wine-producer in Mudgee. Its elegant, cedary Cabernets and its fine, flavoursome Chardonnays effortlessly reveal the region's aptitude for first-class wines. Bob and Wendy Roberts, Huntington's owners, came here in the late 1960s with the encouragement of Len Evans, purchasing two blocks of land on which they planted vines and built a winery in 1968. Their love of music recently led them to build a concert hall as well. The 100 acres (40 ha) surrounding the winery are planted mainly to Shiraz and Cab Sauvignon, with large plantings of Semillon and Chardonnay, and a little Merlot and Pinot Noir. Bob Roberts, who is self-taught, believes that Mudgee has an "over-supply of everything: in flavour, tannin and colour, it's hard to make a bad wine". The quality of other Mudgee vines does not support this theory, but he has clearly learnt how to get the best from the region. There is no high-tech white wine equipment – and indeed the elegant, flavoursome, melon and pineapple-like 88 Chardonnay does not need any; nor does the fresh, apricot-like 88 Medium Dry Semillon. Reds here receive long, cool fermentation and ageing in large American ovals.

Huntington produces around 24,000 cases a year of which Cab Sauvignon has the largest share: the 88 Cabernet is a big, rich, oaky, cassis-like mouthful. Other wines include a jammy "Beaujolais-style" 88 Barton Rouge and a Dry Rosé that goes down well chilled with curry. With age, Huntington's reds move into a different class. The ripe, choclatey, cassis and capsicum-like 84 Cab Sauvignon is good, and the 84 Cabernet/Merlot blend with its elegant, truffley, cedary style is finer still. 1984 was obviously a good Mudgee year, for even the 84 Shiraz/Cabernet had an extra dollop of elegant, peppery, chocolatey Shiraz fruit. Huntington's finest wine is the 83 Cab Sauvignon with its elegant spice-box layers of fruit and flavour. Wines here are all very reasonably priced – especially bulk dry reds such as the 86 Bin HB Shiraz/Cabernet with its spicy, chocolatey, oaky flavours.
♀   Star buy: All Huntington Estate wines, esp Bin HB

JASPER VALLEY WINES   §
Crozier's Road, Berry, NSW 2535

w, r, ft, sp   ★

John and Ann Jorgenson produce a full range of table, fortified, flavoured and sparkling wines from 14 acres (6 ha) of vines.

JEIR CREEK WINES   CA
Gooda Creek Road, Murrumbateman, NSW 2582

w, r   ★

Small quantities of bought-in table wines are sold at this half-finished winery in the Canberra region.

KYEEMA WINES   CA
Belconnen, ACT 2616

w, r   ★

Andrew McEwin makes small quantities of red and white table wines at Kyeema from bought-in grapes.

LAKE GEORGE   CA
Federal Highway, Collector, NSW 2581

w, r   ★

Dr Edgar Riek's 8 acres (3 ha) of vines produce only 500 cases, mostly of Chardonnay and Pinot Noir. These are sold locally as "a retirement pleasure more than a commercial venture".

LAKE'S FOLLY   HV
Broke Road, Pokolbin, NSW 2321

w, r   ★→★★

Max Lake, another ex-medical man, is one of the Hunter's characters. Not everyone agrees with his idiosyncratic and occasionally bizarre views on wine but no one could deny his unique contributions to the Hunter. Lake became the first of a new wave of Australian boutique wine-makers when he planted Cab Sauvignon here in 1963. This vine had not been grown in the Hunter for 20 years: Lake had the foresight to realize its potential and press ahead in spite of local opposition. His distinctive white A-frame winery was erected in 1964 and the first vintage "foot-stamped" there in 1966; Lake's soft, cigar box-like 66 is still holding up now. Not content with Cabernets such as the grassy herbaceous 83 (which Lake rates as "outstanding") or the equally herbaceous, chunky 86, he planted Chardonnay in 1969, releasing the first vintage in 1974. The 81 Chardonnay was an intense, oaky, vanilla-like wine; the musky, flowery, lemony 86 is also worthwhile. Stephen, Max's son, has now taken over the wine-making at this 35-acre (14-ha) estate. Scarcely 6,000 cases of Cab Sauvignon and Chardonnay are made, and these sell out rapidly.

LARK HILL   CA
Gundaroo Road, Bungendore, NSW 2621

w, r   ★

Just south of Lake George in the high country is the Carpenters' Lark Hill winery. At 2,800 feet (860 m), with winter snowfalls, they believe i is one of the highest wineries in Australia. Sue Carpenter makes almost

2,000 cases a year, mostly of Chardonnay, Rh Riesling and a Cabernet/ Merlot blend, from 10 acres (4 ha) of vines. Production is set to increase soon when a further 5 acres (2 ha) come on stream. Lark Hill's 87 Chardonnay had a passion fruit scent and a light, lemony, somewhat acidic palate.

LESNIK FAMILY HV
Branxton Road, Pokolbin, NSW 2321

w, r, sw, ft, sp ∗

Josef Lesnik and his family, Australians of Austrian descent, own 52 acres (21 ha) of vines on the site of Joseph Holmes' 1840s vineyard. The Lesniks formerly sold all their grapes but since 1983 Josef has been making a 6,500-case range of table wines besides Muscats, ports and a *méthode champenoise* fizz.

LILLYPILLY RV
Lillypilly Road, Leeton, NSW 2705

w, r, sw, ft ∗

Lillypilly, situated at Leeton in the southern Riverina region, was founded in 1982. Wine-maker Robert Fiumara produces 8,500 cases a year from 40 acres (16 ha) of vines, Cab Sauvignon and Shiraz accounting for almost half. Lillypilly's wide range includes Muscats, ports, a sweet, well-thought-of botrytis-affected Spatlese Lexia and table wines such as Chardonnay and Fumé Blanc. A Traminer and Semillon blend is sold under the name "Tremillon".

LINDEMANS HV
McDonalds Road, Pokolbin, NSW 2321

w, r, sw, ft, sp ∗→∗∗∗

Dr Henry John Lindeman, an enlightened Victorian Englishman keen to try his hand in the "Lucky Country", arrived in Australia in 1840 and planted vines three years later close to the Paterson River at Cawarra (aboriginal for "by running waters"). In spite of a fire which burned down the winery in 1851, Cawarra flourished and in 1860 he opened an office and bottling hall in Sydney. More vineyards were purchased and after Lindeman's death in 1882 the company continued to thrive under his sons. Today Lindemans (itself owned by Philip Morris) owns **Leo Buring** and **Rouge Homme** in SA, and is one of the most important wine firms in the country. Its principal winery is at Karadoc in the Murray River (VIC), but its origins are in the Hunter and some of its finest wines are still made here at the sprawling Hunter River Winery, presided over by genial Dutchman Gerry Sissingh.

Apart from its 2,500 acres (1,000 ha) of Hunter vines which provide a third of its grapes, Lindemans has sizeable acreages at Padthaway and Coonawarra (SA), and at Karadoc. The company first became involved in Coonawarra in 1967 and planted further vines there in 1972; plantings at nearby Padthaway began in 1969. Lindemans therefore has access to fine mature vines in two quality regions, vinifying its Coonawarra fruit at the Rouge Homme winery. The Karadoc winery is responsible for its cask wines, which represent two-thirds of the company's sales. Besides being Lindemans' fortified wine GHQ, this winery also makes its Matthew Lang range whose dull, citric White Burgundy and spicy, jammy Claret will not set the wine world alight.

Like most Australian cask wines, Lindemans' 4-litre Cellar Pack range is not very exciting. The Gordo-based Cellar Pack Riesling is a simple, fresh, grapey mouthful and the Shiraz/Grenache-based Cellar Pack Claret is a light, jammy, inky wine. Together with the 2-litre Mirrabook casks, these are Lindemans' humblest wines. The next two levels up are the beverage wines, such as Ben Ean Moselle, and the Premier Selection "mid range", which includes wines such as the pleasant, earthy 88 Premier Selection Chardonnay and the soft, burnt, liquorice-like 86 Shiraz/Cabernet. A special range of award-winning regional and varietal wines is produced by Lindemans for export markets. These wines – such as the ripe, musky, pineappley 88 Bin 65 South-East Australian Chardonnay and the zesty, fresh, passion fruit-like 88 Bin 95 Sauv Blanc – are blended to be consistent year after year and not to show vintage variations.

The next step up in quality are the Hunter River wines, such as the pleasant, peachy-citric 88 Bin 7255 Semillon. There is a 30-year tradition here of keeping back top wines from the best vintages and releasing them at their peak. Latest releases include a 70 Bin 3855 Semillon, whose fresh, toasty, citric style is a classic example of aged Hunter Valley Semillon. The smoky, earthy, almost bloody 70 Shiraz Bin 4110, another classic release, has also aged well. A more traditional Hunter style is the 86 Steven Hermitage Bin 7210, whose intense, chunky palate of black and red fruits is backed up by a leathery, sappy note. Further up the scale are the single vineyard wines. These include the splendid, strong, elegant, herbaceous-gooseberry 87 Padthaway Vineyard Sauvignon, which Lindemans describes as "Australia's answer to New Zealand's **Cloudy Bay**". The Coonawarra single vineyard reds are on this level too. The 85 St George Cab Sauvignon is a fine rich, velvety, blackcurranty, eucalyptus-like mouthful and the equally velvety 85 Limestone Ridge Shiraz-Cabernet with its chocolatey, brambley flavours is not far behind. The firm, robust, truffley 86 Coonawarra Pyrus, a Bordeaux-inspired equal blend of Cab Sauvignon, Cab Franc, Malbec and Merlot, needs time. Fortifieds such as the delicate, raisiny, tea-leaf-like Old Liqueur Muscat should not be overlooked.

LITTLE'S   HV
Lot 3, Palmers Lane, Pokolbin, NSW 2321

w, r, ft   *

Founded in 1983, Little's is run by wine-maker Ian Little and viticulturist Tuula Little, who have about 35 acres (14 ha) of vines. They are particularly proud of their Chardonnay and vintage port.

McMANUS   RV
Farm 1347, Yenda, NSW 2681

w, r, sw   *

The McManus family's 25 acres (10 ha) of Shiraz, Semillon and other grapes are turned into table wines including White Burgundy.

McWILLIAM'S   HV
Mount Pleasant, Marrowbone Road, Pokolbin, NSW 2321

w = 86 87, r = 83 86 87, ft, sp   *→**

McWilliam's biggest wineries are at Yenda, Hanwood and Beelbangera in the Riverina, but its best wines are made in the Hunter which is why it is covered here. Samuel McWilliam founded the firm in 1877 and, remarkably, 19 of his descendants still work for McWilliam's today, making it "the biggest private family wine company in Australia". Samuel planted vines at Corowa, but his son John James spotted the Riverina's potential and harvested his first grapes at Hanwood in 1916. Discovering that irrigated vines could provide vast quantities of grapes at low costs, McWilliam's expanded into Yenda in 1923, Beelbangera in 1943 and finally Robinvale (VIC) in 1961; this last winery now provides most of its sherries and ports. The Mount Pleasant winery in the Hunter originally belonged to Maurice O'Shea, a partner of McWilliam's in the 1930s who was eventually bought out. O'Shea's famous Hunter reds are still revered and his tradition of naming wines after royalty – for example Elizabeth Riesling and Philip Hermitage – continues today.

New technology has started to shape up the Mount Pleasant wines which have often lacked fruit and freshness, as a result of spending too long in old unsavoury casks. Each McWilliam's winery is distinguished by a row of tall, slim, stainless steel fermenters and drainers, invented by Glen McWilliam, which ensure that a long, slow, clean separation of white wine juice from its solids takes place. McWilliam's does not publish its production figures, but it is among the top five in the country. Its 700 acres (280 ha) of vines supply just 5% of its fruit, the Mount Pleasant vineyards producing about half of its Hunter grapes.

McWilliam's produces a vast range including small sachets of wine, inexpensive sparklers such as Markview, wine casks, coolers, flagons, bulk wines, fortifieds and brandies, as well as the Hanwood and Mount Pleasant varietal range. Inheritance, McWilliam's popular red and white pair, consist of a chunky, fruity 87 Shiraz/Cabernet and a grassy, appley 87 Semillon. The Hanwood varietal range includes the soft, citric 88 Semillon/Chardonnay, the earthy 85 Shiraz and the jammy, peppery 85 Cab Sauvignon. The straight 85 Mount Pleasant Shiraz was a not unpleasant, chunky, burnt, coffee bean-like wine. McWilliam's bestsellers are its Semillon-based 82 Mount Pleasant Elizabeth Riesling and Cream Sherry, but the firm rates Mount Pleasant 83 OP and OH Hermitage as its best wines, along with its Show Series Muscats. Overall it is an ordinary range of wines, lit by occasional flashes of brilliance such as the greeny-gold 78 Maria Riesling with its intense, sweet, flowery, lime-like palate, but improvements are on the way. Visitors to Hanwood (open Mon-Sat, 9am-5.30pm) can admire the giant barrel-shaped tasting hall and Hanwood Bottle, which houses a museum.

MADEW WINES   CA
Furlong Road, Queanbeyan, NSW 2620

w, r *

The Madew family makes small amounts of table wines here, which are sold at the cellar door.

MANSFIELD WINES   MD
Eurunderee Lane, Mudgee, NSW 2850

w, r, sp *

This small family-owned Mudgee winery, run by Peter Mansfield, produces table and sparkling wines.

MARSH ESTATE   HV
Deasey's Road, Pokolbin, NSW 2321

w, r, ft *

Peter Marsh, wine-maker at this small family-owned estate, produces table and fortified wines from varieties such as Hermitage and Semillon.

MILLSTONE VINEYARD   HV
Talga Road, Allandale, NSW 2321

w, r, ft *

The 20 acres (8 ha) of vines here, planted to varieties such as Ruby Cabernet, Pinot Noir and Shiraz, are made into a range of table, fortified and sparkling wines by the Ross family.

MIRAMAR   MD
Henry Lawson Drive, Mudgee, NSW 2850

w, r, ft *

Miramar's Ian MacRae makes 12,500 cases of various wines including Semillon, Riesling, Chardonnay, Cab Sauvignon and vintage port from 60 acres (24 ha) of vines.

MIRANDA   RV
57 Jondaryan Avenue, Griffith, NSW 2680

w, r, sw, ft, sp *

Frank Miranda and his sons Jim, Luigi and Sam produce large quantities of *spumante* under the Golden Gate label and a wide variety of other wines. Their premium table wine range is St James.

MOLLY MORGAN   HV
Talga Road, Allandale, Pokolbin, NSW 2321

w *

Small amounts of Wood-Matured Semillon are produced at this Hunter winery and sold at the cellar door.

MONTROSE   MD
Henry Lawson Drive, Mudgee, NSW 2850

w, r, ft *→

Founded in 1974, this is the flagship winery of **Wyndham Estate's** Mudgee group. Most Montrose wines are made from its own 280 acres (115 ha) of grapes but much of its Chardonnay fruit is bought in locally to produce 20,000 cases a year of this wine. Shiraz, Cab Sauvignon and Semillon are the other major wines here, previous products such as sparkling and carbonic maceration wines having given way to Wyndham's "big company philosophy" of putting table wines first. Montrose has 100 acres (40 ha) of new plantings, is beginning to switch from hand-picking to mechanical harvesting and is now building a winery extension. The fresh, apricot-like 88 Semillon with its soft, barley sugar palate is a pleasant enough aperitif style. However, the dumb-nosed 88 Chardonnay and the wood-fermented 84, which developed into rich, elegant, pineappley fruit, both need time. The best reds are the 86 Cab Sauvignon/Merlot with its plummy scent and somewhat coarse palate and the richer, cassis-like 85 Special Reserve Cab Sauvignon.

MOUNT VINCENT MEAD   MD
Common Road, Mudgee, NSW 2850

w, r   *

Jane Nevell is owner/wine-maker at this 3-acre (1-ha) estate founded in 1972. As the name suggests, most of her output is mead but she does produce about 1,000 cases of Cab Sauvignon and a blended white.

MOUNTILFORD   MD
Mount Vincent Road, Ilford, NSW 2850

w, r   *

Don and Helen Cumming make about 650 cases of wines, including Chardonnay, a blended Vineyard Red and Vineyard Riesling, from 15 acres (6 ha) of vines just south of Mudgee.

MUDGEE WINES   MD
Henry Lawson Drive, Mudgee, NSW 2850

w, r, ft   *

Jennifer Meek, chief executive/wine-maker at this 18-acre (7-ha) winery, grows a variety of vines including Crouchen, Trebbiano and finer offerings such as Chardonnay and Cab Sauvignon.

MURRAY ROBSON WINES   HV
De Beyers Road, Pokolbin, NSW 2321

w, r   *→→**

Indefatigable Murray Robson, who left **Briar Ridge** to start a new winery in mid-career, is an example to all who think that life ends at 40. Since starting this venture in 1988, he has taken on new partners and now leases 125 acres (50 ha) of vines from **Audrey Wilkinson**, buying in about one-fifth of his needs locally. His 10,000 cases of Shiraz, Chardonnay, Cabernet, Semillon and Sauv Blanc are vinified at **Richmond Grove** as there is no winery here. Robson has continued his old practices of sending out an informative quarterly newsletter to loyal customers and signing the label on every bottle. Such attention to detail is the key to his success and this venture is likely to prosper. His first vintage was in 1988. The light, elegant, apricot-citric 88 Early Harvest Semillon, the 88 Semillon Traditional and the fresh, light, pineappley 88 Chardonnay all pleased Australian judges.

THE MURRUMBATEMAN WINERY   CA
Barton Highway, Murrumbateman, NSW 2582

w, r, ft   *

Geoff and Trish Middleton run a restaurant here and make table and fortified wines from 9 acres (3.5 ha) of vines.

NIOKA RIDGE   HT
Barwang Road, Young, NSW 2594

w, r   *→

Nioka, founded in 1979, has 12 acres (5 ha) of vines in the high country between Young and Harden. Wine-maker Philip Price produces Rh Riesling, Chardonnay and Cabernet/Malbec wines among others here.

OAKVALE   HV
Broke Road, Pokolbin, NSW 2321

w, r   *

Former Sydney lawyer Barry Shields is owner/wine-maker at this revamped establishment founded originally in 1893. Barry and his wife Jan, who purchased Oakvale in 1985, now have 30 acres (12 ha) of vines close to the winery and another 20 acres (8 ha) planted in 1989, but 90% of their fruit is bought locally to make up a 4,000-case output. All fruit is hand-picked at daybreak; the reds are fermented traditionally in open concrete fermenters and hand-plunged.

PETERSONS HV
Mount View Road, Mount View, NSW 2325
w, r *→**
Ian Peterson, his wife Shirley and son Colin run this winery with wine-making help from Gary Reed. Although grapes were planted here in 1971, wine was not produced until 1981. With an annual production of 6,000 cases, made from 40 acres (16 ha) of Chardonnay, Semillon, Shiraz, Pinot Noir and Cab Sauvignon, this is a small operation; indeed, the Petersons regularly win the Small Wine-makers' gong at the Sydney show. Try the fresh, zesty, lemon and lime-like 86 Semillon, the robust, velvety 86 Cab Sauvignon or the restrained, peppery 85 Shiraz. The Petersons rate the soft, flowery-citric 86 Chardonnay as their finest wine.

PIETER VAN GENT MD
Black Springs Road, Mudgee, NSW 2850
w, r, ft *
Pieter and Sheila van Gent make 4,000 cases of wine from 30 acres (12 ha) of vines. Wine-maker Pieter is the fourth generation of his family to work in the industry. All his wines except Muscat are home-grown. Chardonnay, Frontignan, Shiraz and "Angelic White" (a Gordo-based dessert wine) are the most popular but Pipeclay Port is the bestseller.

PLATT'S MD
Mudgee Road, Gulgong, NSW 2852
w, r *
The Platts founded this winery in 1982 and now have 25 acres (10 ha) at Gulgong, leasing a larger acreage at Mudgee itself. Barry Platt produces 4,000 cases of wines such as Semillon and Cab Sauvignon.

RALEIGH §
Walter Street, Raleigh, NSW 2454
w, r *
At Raleigh, close to scenic Coffs Harbour, John Gorton produces a small range of wines which he sells at the cellar door.

RICHMOND ESTATE WINES §
Gadd's Road, North Richmond, NSW 2754
r *
Tom Allen produces table wines from almost 17 acres (7 ha) of Malbec, Shiraz and Cabernet vines here.

RICHMOND GROVE UH
Rylstone Road, via Muswellbrook, NSW 2333
w, r *
Richmond Grove's wide range of table wines, like those of other Hunter and Mudgee wineries in the extensive **Wyndham Estate** group, are made and marketed by Wyndham.

RIVERINA RV
Hillston Road, Griffith, NSW 2680
w, r, ft, sp *
Antonio and Angelina Sergi have nearly 17 acres (7 ha) of Riverland Cab Sauvignon and Shiraz vines. These are mostly made into bulk table and fortified wines, but small quantities of bottled wines are also released under the Riverina and Ballingal Estates labels.

ROSEMOUNT ESTATE UH
Rosemount Road, Denman, NSW 2328
w=87 84 80, r=86 80, ft, sp *→***
Rosemount is one of Australia's great modern success stories. From its humble start in 1970 when the present Chairman Bob Oatley and his son Sandy made small batches of wine, Rosemount has leapt to the forefront of the industry, its Show Reserve Chardonnay in particular

helping to trigger the Australian wine boom in Britain. The Oatleys had already built a coffee and cocoa empire before they moved into wine, buying 3,600 acres (1,450 ha) of land in an attractive corner of the Upper Hunter north-west of Denman. Vines had in fact been grown here in the mid-19th century, although the Oatleys did not realize this when they planted the vineyard in 1969. The Oatleys soon took over **Penfolds'** old Wybong property and now own the vast, well-tended Roxburgh vineyard with its red volcanic loam, as well as Yarrawa and Waroona. All told, Rosemount has 1,000 acres (400 ha) under vine in the Upper Hunter and Coonawarra (SA), most of it mechanically harvested. This supplies about 80% of its fruit. The rest, destined for the inexpensive Diamond label wines, is bought in from Mudgee and from McLaren Vale (SA). With new plantings at most of its vineyards, Rosemount hopes to be almost self-sufficient in three years' time.

Rosemount has been devoted to the production of popular 100% varietals since it launched its first reds in 1974. There are four ranges: the basic Diamond label generic wine-styles; the varietal range; the Show Reserve level; and the single vineyard wines such as Roxburgh and the new Giants Creek label. Purists claim that wine-maker Philip Shaw deliberately ages his wines for immediate appeal, so that they do not mature in bottle. This may be true, but his approach has done much to popularize Australian wines at affordable prices. The agreeable Semillon-based 88 Diamond Reserve White (topped up with Sauv Blanc) is a soft, fruity, citric wine and the Diamond Reserve Red (mainly Cab Sauvignon/Shiraz-based) is blessed with some zesty, raspberry-like carbonic maceration fruit. At the next varietal level Rosemount's Sauv Blanc wines are not as full-flavoured as its Semillons – the rich, buttery Wood-Matured 87 and the rich, herbaceous, nutty 87 Show Reserve. Rosemount's straight 88 Rh Riesling is worth buying too for its fresh, lively, lime-like flavours.

The firm's reputation stems mostly from its Chardonnays. These start with the fresh, oaky, buttery, vanilla-like 88, working up to the fuller, richer, more perfumed Show Reserve 88 and the intense, oaky-toasty 87 Roxburgh. Finer still (although Rosemount rates it beneath the Roxburgh) is the new Giant's Creek 87 Chardonnay, whose spicy, restrained, cinnamon and vanilla style is worth seeking out. Rosemount's reds are getting better by the minute. The new star is the 86 Show Reserve Coonawarra Merlot whose rich, fleshy, plummy palate is a delight. The 85 Show Reserve Coonawarra Cabernet with its luscious, blackcurrant, mint and eucalyptus-like palate is better still. Rosemount's 86 Show Reserve Shiraz is not dissimilar in style and even the straight 87 Cabernet with its soft, ripe, easy-drinking cassis fruit is worthwhile; the leafy, vegetal Show Reserve Pinot Noir is getting there. Look out for Rosemount's delicious Show Reserve Noble Semillon with its sweet palate of butterscotch and peaches.

♀ Star buy: Rosemount Show Reserve wines

ROSSETTO'S WINES   **RV**
Farm 576, Rossetto Road, Beelbangera, NSW 2680

                                                          w, r, ft, sp *

The Rossetto family, originally from Treviso in Italy, has been making wine in the Riverina since 1930. In those days, the Rossettos processed 25,000 litres of wine a year. Some 60 years later they are still in charge here, but produce a more modest 6 million litres. Their 25 acres (10 ha) of Shiraz and Semillon vines supply only a fraction of the fruit they need to make over 40,000 cases; the rest is bought in locally. Wines include Mount Bingar and Beelgara table wines, ports, Muscats and liqueurs such as Mother Machree Shamrock Cream.

THE ROTHBURY ESTATE   **HV**
Broke Road, Pokolbin, NSW 2321

                                          r=87 86, w=86 84, sw *→*★★★★

Len Evans, who founded Rothbury with a group of wine-loving investors in 1969, has had more influence on the modern development of Australian wines than any other figure. Wine-writer, restaurateur, television personality, Chairman of **Petaluma** (SA) and Chairman of Judges at the Sydney, Adelaide and Canberra wine shows – this man *is*

Mr Australian Wine. Born in Wales, Evans has spent most of his adult life in Australia as a "New South Welshman". But it is his European perspective that has made him so valuable to his adopted land: he has run two French châteaux, Château Padouen in Barsac and Château Rahoul in Graves, and dabbled for a while in California's Napa Valley.

The aim of Rothbury's founders was to promote Hunter wines using the finest modern techniques. Persistent financial problems stemmed not from the quality of its wines, which has never been in doubt, but from the difficulty of predicting market trends. For the first time since its foundation, Rothbury has sailed out of financially troubled waters into a prosperous calm. Previously most wines were sold to "Friends of Rothbury", a group which met for grand dinners in the vast, 50-foot (15-m) high cask hall here. Today Rothbury's 150,000 cases have a wider audience. There are now six separate vineyards at Rothbury, Herlstone, Brokenback, Homestead Hill, Cowra and Denman. The original low-yielding Rothbury home plot planted in 1968 produces wines with the most pronounced Hunter character. In 1988, Rothbury bought the Denman Estate vineyard and well-equipped winery in the Upper Hunter. In accordance with Rothbury's restructuring plans, devised in 1984, the soaring white winery at Broke Road will be enlarged to include a new cool barrel-ageing area and other extensions. All Rothbury fruit will be vinified here by wine-maker David Lowe.

The switch of emphasis from reds to whites was Rothbury's salvation and Chardonnay has had much to do with this renaissance; the Reserve in particular has won world-wide praise. White wines here, such as the fresh, light, lemony 88 Hunter Valley Semillon and the delicate, oaky-pineappley 88 Chardonnay, are vinified for immediate appeal. Older vintages of Semillon from the mid-70s boast wonderful toasty-smoky, lime-like characters. Rothbury's Chardonnay Reserve with its gold bullrush label is fermented and aged in new barrels. The 88 had a rich, well-made cinnamon oak style but needed time to fill out; the 87, which won Australia glory in the Qantas Cup competition against America, had a buttercup-gold colour and delicious rich, buttery, elegant, cinnamon taste. The Hunter may not be ideal for Pinot Noir, but Rothbury's best offerings suggest otherwise. Try the agreeable liquorice and leaf-mould-like 88 Pinot Noir, the classic Burgundian 83 Directors Reserve Pinot with its rich, plummy, vegetal flavours, or the lighter, elegant, rose-scented 85. Rothbury's Shiraz has lightened over the years, as shown by the spicy, black pepper 87; the 86 is more robust and displays leathery-peppery Hunter scents. Watch out for the intense, marmalade and raisin 84 Botrytis Semillon and the inexpensive Len Evans 88 Semillon/Chardonnay.

♀ Star buy: Rothbury Semillon & Chardonnay

RUBERTO'S WINERY
Moama Street, South Hay, NSW 2711

RV

w, r, sw, ft, sp   ∗

The Roberts family makes Italian-influenced table, fortified and sparkling wines at this winery in the Riverina.

SAN BERNADINO
Leeton Road, Griffith, NSW 2680

RV

w, r, ft, sp   ∗

This 300-acre (120-ha) Italian winery is owned by Stan Aliprandi. Wine-maker Walter Suntesso produces an extraordinarily wide range including *spumante* sold under the Castella label, wine casks, ports, sherries, Muscats and non-alcoholic products. Table wines are sold under the Rushton Bend, Woodride and San Bernadino labels.

THE SAND HILLS VINEYARD
Sandhills Road, Forbes, NSW 2871

§

w, r   ∗

Swiss-born Lucien Bourcier planted the first vines here and built the winery in the early 1920s. John Saleh, the present owner, has 20 acres (8 ha) of vines from which he makes 150 cases, mostly of carbonic maceration red. Plans to replant the vineyard and modernize the winery should improve quality.

SAXONVALE   HV
Fordwich Estate, via Broke, NSW 2330

w, r, ft   *

Purchased by **Wyndham Estate** in 1985, Saxonvale has two extensive
vineyards at Fordwich and Spring Mountain, each covering over 150
acres (60 ha) of vines. Saxonvale's wine-maker, Alasdair Sutherland,
whose Semillons and Chardonnays are widely admired, produces both
table and fortified wines.

SCENIC HILL   RV
Beelbangera, Griffith, NSW 2680

w, r   *

Table wines are made here but most of this winery's output is sold in
bulk to other concerns.

SHINGLE HOUSE   CA
209 Gundaroo Road, Bungendore, NSW 2621

w, r   *

Max Blake has 5 acres (2 ha) planted to Mataro, Chardonnay and other
vines, from which table wines are made.

THE SILOS WINERY   §
810 Princes Highway, Jaspers Brush, NSW 2535

w, r, ft   *

Wine-maker Alan Bamfield and his sister Marie manage this family-
owned winery and restaurant situated two hours south of Sydney. Their
12 acres (5 ha) of vines, with another 3 acres (1 ha) just planted, supply
three-quarters of their grapes. Founded in 1985, Silos is still in its early
stages but a full list of table wines are on offer, including Wiley's Creek
Claret, Dry White and tawny port. The Bamfields rate the Shiraz and
Sauv Blanc as their finest wines.

SIMON WHITLAM   HV
Wollombi Brook Vineyard, Broke Road, Broke, NSW 2330

w, r   **→****

Simon Whitlam was founded in 1982 by wine merchant Andrew Simon
and banker Nicholas Whitlam. Together with David Clarke, another
banker, they run this firm and its 20 acres (8 ha) of Chardonnay,
Semillon, Cab Sauvignon and Pinot Noir. Wines are made at **Arrowfield**.
The first wine was released in 1983 and from the beginning quality was
superb. The 85 Cab Sauvignon has been admired by Australian and
British judges. The magnificent 87 Chardonnay is a rich, exciting,
refined wine whose spicy cinnamon scent leads to an even more
appealing, complex pineappley palate.

SIMONS WINES   CA
274 Badgery Road, Burra Creek, NSW 2620

w, r   *

Small quantities of white and red table wines are made at this Canberra
winery by Lloyd Simons.

SOBELS   HV
McDonalds Road, Pokolbin, NSW 2321

w, r, ft   *

Kevin and Margaret Sobels turn 45 acres (18 ha) of Shiraz, Cab
Sauvignon and Semillon vines into table and fortified wines at this
Hunter Valley winery.

STEIN'S WINES   MD
Pipeclay Lane, Mudgee, NSW 2850

w, r, ft   *

Wine-maker Robert Stein and family, whose wine-producing forebears
came to Australia from the Rheingau in 1837, started Stein's in 1976.
Their 10 acres (4 ha) of vines have recently been supplemented by
5 acres (2 ha) more. Some 2,500 cases a year are made here, including a
Semillon/Riesling medium white, a dry Shiraz red and a Chardonnay,
as well as ports and Muscats.

SUTHERLAND WINES HV
Deasey's Road, Pokolbin, NSW 2321

w, r, sp ✳→

Neil and Caroline Sutherland, owners of this winery since 1979, have 55 acres (22 ha) of vines from which they make 7,000 cases of wines using "cold fermentation techniques to preserve flavour and character". Semillon and Chardonnay are the big sellers, and a Chenin Blanc-based *méthode champenoise* Cremant their newest wine. The 87 Semillon has a pleasant lime and lemon style, and the 87 Chardonnay offers ordinary oaky flavours.

TALLARA MD
Cassilis Road, Mudgee, NSW 2850

w ✳

Owned by Richard and Jenny Turner, Tallara sells most of its grapes to local producers. Its one wine, a Chardonnay, is made by **Platt's**.

TAMBURLAINE HV
McDonalds Road, Pokolbin, NSW 2321

w, r, sw ✳→

Tamburlaine was founded in 1966 but its owner/wine-makers Mark Davidson and Greg Silkman have been here only since 1986. They make about 6,000 cases of table wines from 40 acres (16 ha) of vines, including a light, aromatic Blanc de Noir. The 88 Chardonnay was a pleasing soft, ripe, pineappley offering, the 86 Syrah an ordinary spicy-leathery wine. Dry Semillon is the bestseller.

TERRACE VALE HV
Deasey's Road, Pokolbin, NSW 2321

w, r ✳

Terrace Vale's 18 partners own 90 acres (36 ha) of Hunter vines between them. These are turned into 8,000 cases of table wines by Frenchman Alain le Prince. Semillon, Shiraz and Chardonnay, which le Prince considers Terrace Vale's best wine, are the big sellers.

THISTLE HILL MD
McDonalds Road, Mudgee, NSW 2850

w, r, ft ✳

David and Lesley Robertson own 27 acres (11 ha) of Mudgee vines just west of Mudgee. Their organically-minded, "minimal intervention" winery produces just 2,000 cases a year, mostly from home fruit.

TILBA VALLEY §
Glen Eden Vineyard, Tilba, NSW 2546

w, r ✳

Tilba Valley's 22 acres (9 ha) of coastal vineyards, some 200 miles (320 km) south-east of Sydney, are owned by Barry and Val Field. They make 2,500 cases of table wines such as Semillon and Chardonnay.

TIZZANA §
Tizzana Road, Ebenezer, NSW 2756

w, r ✳

This small winery just north of Windsor produces tiny quantities of a Cabernet/Shiraz blend.

TOORAK RV
Farm 279, Toorak Road, Leeton, NSW 2705

w, r, ft, sp ✳

Frank Bruno makes a wide range of wines from his 74 acres (30 ha) of vines planted to Gordo, Shiraz, Semillon and Cab Sauvignon.

TULLOCH HV
Glen Elgin Estate, De Beyers Road, Pokolbin, NSW 2321

w, r, ft, sp ✳→✳✳

After several changes of ownership, Tulloch is now part of the **Penfolds** group but still managed by Jay Tulloch, grandson of the founder. Tulloch has developed considerably since 1893, when shopkeeper John

Tulloch accepted vineyard land as payment for a bad debt and started to make wine. Today, with annual production at 40,000 cases, the firm's aim is to produce the "best wines in the distinctive styles of the Hunter Valley". Tulloch's 65 acres (26 ha) of Hermitage, Semillon and Chardonnay provide about two-fifths of its grapes; the rest is bought in locally. Other wines in the Tulloch range include White Burgundy, Chablis, a new Verdelho, port, and a popular *méthode champenoise* sparkler. Whites here are better than reds, the Select Vintage range being Tulloch's finest. Try the delicious, fresh, toasty, pineapple and cinnamon spice of the 87 Chardonnay or the aromatic, perfumed, fruit salad-like 88 Verdelho. Also in the Select Vintage range is the sappy, spicy, chunky 85 Hermitage. The basic Hunter River Tulloch selection is good, rather than great, but the 88 Hunter River White with its fresh, zesty fruit is a worthwhile buy.

TYRRELL'S   HV
Broke Road, Pokolbin, NSW 2320

w=86 83 79, r=85 87, ft, sp   *→****

The Hunter Valley would not be the same without Murray Tyrrell, so-called "mouth of the Hunter", who runs Tyrrell's with his son Bruce, now General Manager of the firm. The first Tyrrell to settle here was Edward Tyrrell, nephew of the Anglican Bishop of Newcastle, who in 1858 applied for a 320-acre (130-ha) plot in the shade of the Broken Back Ridge and planted vines there. His original ironbark shack is still standing today in front of the winery. Subsequent generations of Tyrrells made wine here, selling it in bulk until Murray Tyrrell took charge in the early 1960s. Murray began bottling wines under the Tyrrell's label and was soon doing well in wine shows. He also planted the first Chardonnay grapes in the Hunter, amazing the wine world with the quality of his Vat 47 Chardonnay in 1971 and 1977. Tyrrell's also had an early success with its Pinot Noirs, the 76 coming top in the 1979 Gault Millau Wine Olympiad.

Tyrrell's has some 380 acres (155 ha) of vines in the Hunter and Upper Hunter, which supply about a third of the fruit needed to make its 360,000 cases. The rest, destined mainly for cheaper wines, is mostly bought in locally. Tyrrell's adopts a traditional approach to wine-making, using natural yeasts and large open stone fermenters for red wines besides its stainless steel and complicated cooling system. The winery's rabbit warren of old earth-floor cellars is filled to the ceiling with a jumble of old and new oak casks.

The bestseller by far is Tyrrell's tannic, black fruits-like Long Flat Red, a Shiraz-based wine topped up with Cab Sauvignon and Malbec, which sells 105,000 cases a year – but the spicy, flowery 88 Long Flat White, a Semillon blend with 5% Traminer, is better. The 86 HVD Semillon is worthwhile for its rich, toasty scent and lime juice palate: classic Hunter Semillon. Tyrrell's rates its Vat 47 Chardonnay as its finest wine: the buttercup-gold 87 with its fragrant, toasty, vanilla quality is a fine offering; the 86 developed into a big, rich, vegetal, almost aged Chablis style, and the delicious smoky, cinnamon-like 84 was more like a Côte d'Or Burgundy. Tyrrell's 85 Pinot Noir with its garnet colour, rich damson-like palate and vegemite scent is a splendid wine and the nearest Tyrrell's has got in recent years to the Burgundy original, but the leathery, tobacco and leaf-mould-like 81 is drying out now. Tyrrell's 83 Shiraz with its enormous, rich, intense flavours of creosote and sweaty saddles is classic Hunter Hermitage. This wine was offered as a "future" to customers, who paid some of the price in advance while it matured in cellar for four years. Tyrrell's also makes first-class *méthode champenoise* wines.

VERONA   UH
Aberdeen Street, Muswellbrook, NSW 2333

w, r, ft, sp   *

The Yore family makes table, fortified and sparkling wines from 55 acres (22 ha) of vines at Muswellbrook and a few more at Pokolbin. Most of their fruit is sold to other wineries. The Yores also have a new high-altitude development in the Barrington Tops area situated to the north of the Hunter Valley.

VICARY'S §
Northern Road, Luddenham, NSW 2750

w, r, ft, sp *

Ross Carbery makes a wide range of table, fortified and flavoured wines from 20 acres (8 ha) of vines at Luddenham.

WEST END WINES RV
1283 Brayne Road, Griffith, NSW 2680

w, r, ft *

William and Lena Calabria's 15 acres (6 ha) of Riverina land supply about half their fruit; the rest is bought in locally. Their annual 2,000-case production includes Italian specialities such as Lambrusco and Australian favourites such as Goldminer's Port.

WESTERING VINEYARD CA
Federal Highway, Collector, NSW 2581

w, r *

Geoffrey Preston Hood and family have owned 7 acres (3 ha) of vines near Lake George since 1973. Just over 400 cases are made, mostly of Cab Sauvignon and Chardonnay; surplus grapes are sold.

WOODROW WINES §
Woodrow, Junee, NSW 2663

w *

Brian and Cathy Edwards turn their 3 acres (1 ha) of Junee vines into just 200 cases a year of Dry and Medium Dry White, made from various grapes, and a Sauv Blanc. They also hope to produce Cabernet and port before long.

WYNDHAM ESTATE HV
Government Road, Dalwood, via Branxton, NSW 2321

w, r, ft, sp *→***

Wyndham Estate, the Hunter's biggest producer by far, is run by larger-than-life Brian McGuigan, his almost as ebullient brother Neil and wine-maker Jon Reynolds. The McGuigans' father, who was wine-maker at **Penfolds'** Dalwood Estate, bought the winery when Penfolds pulled out of the Hunter. Since then Brian and his wife Fay, in charge of exports, have built a massive empire on his father's foundations. Wyndham Estate, now a public company in which Brian has a third share, owns **Hollydene**, **Saxonvale**, **Richmond Grove** and the **Hunter Estate** in the Hunter Valley as well as **Montrose**, **Craigmoor** and **Amberton** in Mudgee.

The McGuigans deliberately vinify all their wines for "softness, fruit and appeal" – an easy-drinking approach which, though it may not please purists, has made their wines very popular with the public. So don't bother to hang onto to any Wyndham Estate wines: they will not grow old gracefully and are all, without exception, far better drunk young. The 86 Bin 888 Cabernet/Merlot with its deep purple-black colour and soft, velvety, herbaceous, green pepper style is Wyndham's best offering and the soft, ripe, velvety cassis and eucalyptus-like fruit of the 84 Bin 444 Cab Sauvignon is almost as appealing. The gutsy, beefy 81 Bin 555 Hermitage is probably too aggressive for most Wyndham customers. There are two styles of Chardonnay made: the soft, toasty, oaky, nutty 85 Oak Cask Chardonnay and the perfumed 84 Bin 222 Chardonnay. Look out for the 81 Auslese Rh Riesling whose peachy *crème brulée* style is worthwhile.

YASS VALLEY WINES CA
Crisps Lane, Murrumbateman, NSW 2582

w, r *

The Griffiths family owns 6 acres (2.5 ha) of vines from which they make a variety of table wines sold at the cellar door.

Victoria

The vine arrived in Victoria when it was already well established in New South Wales, Tasmania and Western Australia. The first cuttings came from Tasmania but it appears that these were not successful. It was not until nine vines were planted in the late 1830s at what is now **Yeringberg** in the Yarra that Victoria's wine history truly began. During the 1840s, vineyards were also started in and around the city of Melbourne, and at Geelong. Gold was the spur and phylloxera the downfall of the early Victorian wine-makers. Many prospectors who arrived with the gold rush stayed on and planted vines only to have their hopes dashed by the arrival of phylloxera. Although this vine scourge failed to wipe out all of the state's vineyards, it ruined most plantations in Geelong, the Goulburn Valley and Central Victoria.

Victoria's vineyards did not spring back into life until the 1960s and 70s. Today Victoria has more wine-producing regions than any other Australian state. Almost every conceivable wine-style is produced: from whites and reds to sparkling wines, from youthful red Nouveau wines to intensely sweet fortified Muscats. The irrigated vineyards of the hot, arid Murray River region still produce the lion's share of Victoria's wines, but the preponderance of bulk wines is offset by the recent arrival of small, quality-minded wineries in regions such as the cool Yarra Valley, where Cabernet Sauvignon and Pinot Noir wines have reached new standards.

Wine-producing regions

CENTRAL VICTORIA (CV)
Also known as Bendigo-Ballarat, this wine-making region came into being after the discovery of gold here in 1851. New-found wealth and the demand for wine led to the foundation of about 100 wineries around Bendigo with over 500 acres (200 ha) of vines. But phylloxera, as it had already done in Geelong, brought the region's wine-making activities to a close in 1893 when the Government insisted that all the vines were to be grubbed up. It was Stuart Anderson's foundation of **Balgownie** in 1969 that put Central Victoria back on the wine map. Given the size of this sprawling region there are significant local variations in soil and climate. However, red wines have clearly been more successful than whites.

EAST GIPPSLAND (EG)
This small remote wine region lies clustered around a series of lakes to the south of Bairnsdale, some 217 miles (350 km) directly east of Melbourne. There were vineyards here in the 19th century, but not many, and today only a few thousand cases of wines are made from East Gippsland grapes. To meet visitors' demands most producers supplement their own grapes with bought-in fruit. Close to both lakes and the sea, the region's climate is humid and maritime-influenced, sea fogs, mists and cool breezes bringing a long growing season.

GEELONG (GL)
Drive west along the coast across Melbourne's West Gate Bridge for an hour or so and Geelong's vineyards will come into view. The first vines were planted here in the 1840s by Swiss immigrants. By the 1860s it was the most important quality grape-growing area in the state and by the 1870s there were 100 vineyards here. Sadly, phylloxera struck and the Government over-reacted by ordering all vines to be systematically destroyed. The Seftons of **Idyll Vineyard** were the first to breathe life back into the wine industry in 1966. Geelong's climate is cooler than most due to cool sea breezes whistling in off the Bay and the Bass Strait beyond. Within the region's 150 acres (60 ha) of vines there are various micro-climates and soils, including black volcanic soil.

GOULBURN VALLEY (GV)

About 60 miles (100 km) due north of Melbourne are the rich river flats of the Goulburn Valley. The region's warm climate, fertile soils and plentiful water supplies made it an ideal site for early Australian vignerons. The first vines were planted at **Chateau Tahbilk** in 1860 and thrived until the arrival of phylloxera in the 1890s. Strangely, given the valley's fertility, it was not until the Osicka family arrived in 1955 that another vineyard was established here. The final seal of approval on the Goulburn Valley's viticultural merits came when **Mitchelton's** extensive plantings were established in the late 60s and early 70s. The region has now expanded to take in the areas north and south of Tabilk, still its heart. Its most unusual grape variety is the Rhône's Marsanne, warmly embraced by both Chateau Tahbilk and Mitchelton. Over half of the world's plantings of Marsanne are now grown here.

GREAT WESTERN (GW)

North-west of Melbourne on the southern edge of the Great Dividing Range is the Great Western region, principal site of Australia's 19th-century gold rush. The region's first wines made in the 1860s must mostly have catered to the needs of miners, but when they left the vineyards continued to thrive. Most vineyards here today are scattered around Avoca and Stawell. **Seppelt**, the region's great wine-maker, continues to make fine sparkling and table wines in a handsome winery whose vast cellars were dug by ex-miners. The altitude and climatic influence of the Dividing Range encourage high rainfall, cloud cover and cool evenings, all of which help to make this the state's third-coolest region after the Yarra and Geelong.

MACEDON (MC)

Also situated north-west of Melbourne, within the triangle made by Kyneton, Romsey and Sunbury, this small hilly region is centred on the town of Macedon. The first wineries were established in the 1860s as a result of land concessions and Sunbury once boasted eight flourishing vineyards, only two of which remain. Macedon's wineries start just half an hour outside Melbourne and even the most far-flung are only about an hour's distance, yet the region has numerous different soils and micro-climates, wind being its greatest drawback. Given their proximity to the city and the famous Hanging Rock, Macedon's wineries are hoping that day-trippers will increase sales.

MORNINGTON PENINSULA (MP)

One hour's drive south-east of Melbourne on a boot-shaped peninsula jutting out into the Bass Strait, this maritime-influenced, frost-free region was developed in the 1970s. It is warmer than the Yarra Valley and suffers from harsh, salty winds and a humid climate in which vine diseases thrive. Nevertheless, the Mornington Peninsula's articulate growers feel that their region could well become another Yarra. At present, with only around 260 acres (105 ha) under vine and 17 wineries, this appears a fanciful notion. But there have been some promising Chardonnay and Cabernet Sauvignon wines, as well as a spectacular Shiraz. Many more wineries are on the way.

MURRAY RIVER (MR)

The Murray River is Victoria's answer to NSW's Riverina and SA's Riverland regions, although production here is much smaller. Its irrigation plan was designed in the late 19th century by the Californian Chaffey brothers, who created a similar scheme in the Riverland. Fed by the mighty Murray River, the region is planted to high-cropping, low-quality vines (Gordo and Sultana among others), most of which end up in cask wines produced by the giant juicing factories. Salinity is a problem, albeit a lessening one. The region covers an extensive area, taking in both the vineyards between Mildura and Robinvale, home of Australia's once-booming dried grape industry, and the more southerly vineyards centred on Swan Hill. The big players here, such as **McWilliam's** Robinvale development and **Lindemans'** Karadoc, are better known for their NSW wines and are therefore covered in that section; VIC's own **Mildara** does have a base here though.

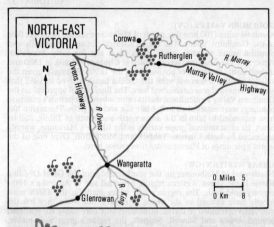

NORTH-EAST VICTORIA

Corowa
Rutherglen
R Murray
Murray Valley Highway
Ovens Highway
R Ovens
Wangaratta
R King
Glenrowan

N

0 Miles 5
0 Km 8

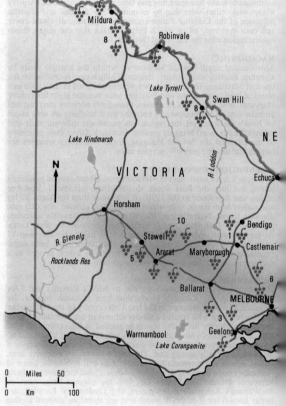

N E

Mildura
8
Robinvale
Lake Tyrrell
Swan Hill
8
Lake Hindmarsh
VICTORIA
R Loddon
Echuca
N
Horsham
Bendigo
Castlemair
R Glenelg
Stawell
10
Maryborough
1
Rocklands Res
5
Ararat
Ballarat
6
MELBOURNE
Warrnambool
Lake Corangamite
Geelong
3

0 Miles 50
0 Km 100

VICTORIA

INDIAN OCE

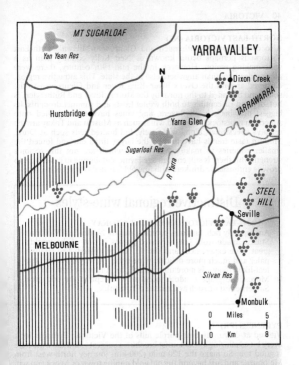

YARRA VALLEY

MT SUGARLOAF

Yan Yean Res

N

Hurstbridge

Dixon Creek

TARRAWARRA

Yarra Glen

Sugarloaf Res

R Yarra

STEEL HILL

Seville

MELBOURNE

Silvan Res

Monbulk

0 Miles 5

0 Km 8

UTH WALES

hepparton

Wangaratta 9

Albury

R Murray

our

Lake Eildon

A U S T R A L I A N   A L P S

R Snowy

Yarra

Bairnsdale

2

Sale

Wine Regions

1 CENTRAL VICTORIA
2 EAST GIPPSLAND
3 GEELONG
4 GOULBURN VALLEY
5 GREAT WESTERN

6 MACEDON
7 MORNINGTON PENINSULA
8 MURRAY RIVER
9 NORTH-EAST VICTORIA
10 PYRENEES
11 YARRA VALLEY

NORTH-EAST VICTORIA (NE)
Also called Corowa-Rutherglen and Glenrowan-Milawa, North-East
Victoria is perhaps better known as Ned Kelly country than as a
wine-making region. However, in the mid-19th century, there were
more vines here than anywhere else in the state. This attractive region,
clustered around the Ovens River, King River and Glenrowan to the
south and bounded to the north by the Murray River and Rutherglen, is
hot, dry and susceptible to both winter frosts and summer droughts. Its
biggest drawback is phylloxera, and vines have to be grafted onto
American rootstocks. Fortified wines such as Muscat and Tokay are the
region's specialities, along with beefy, full-bodied reds such as Durif.
Modern taste trends have pushed the larger firms out and forced the
smaller wineries to make white wines, which are not this region's
strength. But there is still enough aged wine slumbering in casks here to
provide enthusiastic drinkers with fine old fortifieds for years to come.

Distinctive regional wine-styles

NORTH-EAST VICTORIAN MUSCAT & TOKAY
An intensely rich, luscious, complex, raisiny North-East Victorian
Muscat made from late-harvested grapes is one of the world's
great wine experiences and should not be missed. The region's
paler and much more delicate wine-style – tawny-coloured, tea-
leaf-like Tokay – is more unusual still, for it is made from the rare
Muscadelle grape (seldom found now except in the odd great
Sauternes estate such as Château d'Yquem).

PYRENEES (PR)
Viewed at dawn, the blue-purple hills of the Victorian Pyrenees look
every bit as alluring as the tourist brochures suggest – and the wine here
is good too. So make the 120-mile (200-km) journey north-west from
Melbourne and just beyond the old gold mining town of Avoca you will
come across a series of small hills studded with vineyards. The Pyrenees
is another compact VIC wine region planted with vines in the mid-19th
century which did not revive until the 1960s – in this case, when
Chateau Remy arrived. The hills, with their cool climate and gravel
over clay soils, create a thin rain belt well-suited to viticulture.

YARRA VALLEY (YV)
Just 20 miles (35 km) east of Melbourne lie the wide, open fields of the
Yarra Valley, dotted here and there with windbreaks of spruce and
conifer. After Tasmania, this is Australia's second-coolest region and its
grape-growing prowess has never been in doubt. The valley's wine
industry was started by Swiss immigrants in the mid-19th century – de
Castella at **Yering** and de Pury at **Yeringberg**. In its heyday from 1860-
90, the Yarra gained a great reputation for its wines, but lack of
customers led to its demise by the 1920s. During the late 1960s and
early 70s vines were gradually planted again and, with the arrival of
large firms such as **Domaine Chandon** and **Coldstream Hills**, there
was a dramatic increase in vineyards. The total now stands at 800 acres
(325 ha) of vines, half of them new plantings. Viticultural problems here
appear to be few. The quality of Yarra red wines, especially Pinot Noir
and Cabernet, has been very encouraging and occasionally outstanding.

Victorian wineries

ALL SAINTS VINEYARD   NE
All Saints Road, Wahgunyah, VIC 3687

                                                    w, r, sw, ft, sp *
The Sutherland Smith family owns All Saints' 350 acres (140 ha). A
mixture of table and traditional fortified grapes, such as Brown Muscat,
Palamino and Tokay, are grown here; sparkling wine is also produced.

AVALON   NE
Whitfield Road, Wangaratta, VIC 3670

w, r *

Doug Groom produces small quantities of table wines at this North-East Victorian winery, made from King Valley grapes.

BAILEYS   NE
Taminick Gap Road, Glenrowan, VIC 3675

w, r, sw, ft *→*****

Dour-looking Varley Bailey, whose photograph graces most Baileys labels, was an Englishman who emigrated from Manchester in the mid-19th century. He planted vines here in 1866, making his first wines in 1870. Bailey clearly understood the relationship between vine and soil for he planted them out precisely on a small bank of red granite soil at the foot of the Warby Ranges. Today the Baileys vineyard covers some 110 acres (45 ha) of this soil, which wine-maker Stephen Goodwin (also from Manchester) regards as a prime quality factor for the estate. With an annual production of 30,000 cases, Baileys has to buy in a third of its fruit locally and from SA and NSW at present, but Goodwin aims to double the acreage of vines here soon.

Baileys does not have vast stocks of old material, preferring like **Morris** to work on a solera system, blending old and new wines. Its wines are in the same league as those of Morris, if not a shade ahead. The big, beefy red table wines do not have universal appeal, but the Muscats certainly do – as anyone who has tasted the 84 Muscat with its fine, fragrant rose scent and luscious palate will tell you. Equally impressive is the Baileys HJT Muscat with its full brown colour and yellow rim indicating age, backed up by a rich, nutty, caramelized flavour. More widely available, and almost as good, is Baileys Founder Muscat with its paler colour, distinctive rose bouquet and soft, rich palate.
♀ Star buy: Baileys Founder Muscat

BALGOWNIE ESTATE   CV
Hermitage Road, Maiden Gully, VIC 3551

w = 78 82 84, r = 76 80 85 *→***

Stuart Anderson, founder of Balgownie, describes himself nowadays merely as "consultant director/wine-maker" for his brainchild has been bought by the giant **Mildara** group. There are two ranges of Balgownie wines: the superior Estate range made from grapes grown here at Maiden Gully and the Premier Cuvee range, which is made from various Mildara wines blended at Balgownie. Anderson regards this second commercial selection as a vehicle for marketing its wines – similar to Mouton Rothschild's Mouton Cadet brand.

Formerly a pharmacist in Bendigo, Anderson became convinced of the region's wine-growing potential and planted about 25 acres (10 ha) of vines in 1969. Building on his pharmaceutical knowledge he went in search of practical experience at **Lake's Folly** and Château Cissac. This rapidly paid off for, since 1973, Balgownie's immaculate traditional cellar has produced a number of first-class wines, using methods that Anderson feels are distinctly French but with "modern temperature control and monitoring". There are now 35 acres (14 ha) of vines here planted mainly to Cab Sauvignon and Chardonnay, with lesser amounts of Shiraz and Pinot Noir. These vines produce some 6,000 cases of Balgownie Estate wines and contribute a percentage of the fruit needed to make the 9,000-case Premier Cuvee range.

Balgownie's biggest Premier Cuvee seller is the strong, herbaceous, cabbagey 87 Petit Blanc, a mix of Hunter Semillon and Coonawarra Sauv Blanc that will not suit every palate. Other wines in the range include the rich, brassy 87 Chardonnay and the pleasant, fragrant, chocolatey 86 Cabernet/Hermitage. Of the Estate wines, Balgownie's 87 Estate Chardonnay has beefy, vanilla-like flavours; the inky 87 Hermitage and tannic, coffee bean 86 Cab Sauvignon are nothing special either. However, the 87 Cabernet with its elegant, robust fruit is better, and so is the spicy, fruity, perfumed 87 Pinot Noir. Past Balgownie glories included a fine, rich, buttery-pineappley 82 Chardonnay as well as a superlative 80 Pinot Noir, a three-star wine blessed with glorious, plummy Burgundian flavours.

BALLANCLEA   GL
The Barrabool Hills, VIC 3221

W *

Fred Meeker has 5 acres (2 ha) of Sauv Blanc here, from which he
intends to make a Bordeaux-inspired dry white wine.

BALNARRING VINEYARD   MP
Dromana Road, Balnarring, VIC 3926

w, r *—→

Bruce and Stan Paul's 12-acre (5-ha) winery has been releasing wines
for five years. **Elgee Park** made the first wines, but **Tarrawarra** has
taken over. Balnarring wines, especially the reds, are well thought of.

BANNOCKBURN VINEYARDS   GL
Midland Highway, Bannockburn, VIC 3331

w, r *—→**

With Roseworthy training and experience of three vintages at Domaine
Dujac in Burgundy, Gary Farr is well equipped to look after the 45 acres
(18 ha) of vines here. Bannockburn, founded by Stuart Hooper in 1974,
now produces 8,000 cases a year, mainly of Chardonnay, Pinot Noir
and Cab Sauvignon. The winery "is commited to making great wine
from Pinot Noir" using traditional methods such as close-spacing vines
and fermenting grapes in open fermenters. The 83 Chardonnay made a
lively mouthful, as did the pleasant, juicy berry-fruit of the 82 Pinot
Noir. The 86 Chardonnay had some fine musky, pineappley, cinnamon
flavours, but the hefty, burnt, liquorice and creosote-like flavours of the
82 Cabernet were overdone.

BELVEDERE CELLARS   GV
399 High Street, Nagambie, VIC 3608

w, r *

Belvedere Cellars used to sell all its grapes but now makes small
quantities of red and white wines.

BEST'S WINES   GW
Western Highway, Great Western, VIC 3377

w, r, ft, sp *—→

Best's dates from 1886 and now has 125 acres (50 ha) of vines, half of
them at Lake Boga on the Murray River and the remainder at Concongella. Trevor Mast, who owns **Mount Chalambar** and works at **Mount
Langhi Ghiran**, used to be the wine-maker but has handed over to Viv
Thomson, the fourth generation of her family to work here. Best's
produces an 8,000-case range of Concongella table, sparkling and
fortified wines sold under the Great Western label. Wines made from
Murray River and bought-in fruit are sold under the St Andrews label.

BIANCHET   YV
Lot 3, Victoria Road, Lilydale, VIC 3140

w, r *

Lou Bianchet and family planted vines here in 1976. 1980 was his first
commercial vintage and he has now expanded the vineyard to nearly 12
acres (5 ha). A short list of table wines are produced, a Verduzzo white
and a Merlot red emphasizing his Italian origins.

BLANCHE BARKLY WINES   CV
Rheola Road, Kingower, VIC 3517

r *

David Reimers is chief executive at this tiny winery which produces Cab
Sauvignon and Shiraz, selling most of it at the cellar door.

BLUE PYRENEES ESTATE   See **Chateau Remy**.

BOROKA VINEYARDS   GW
Pomonal Road, Hall's Gap, VIC 3381

w, r, ft *

Bernard and Cordelia Breen produce table and fortified wines here
from 20 acres (8 ha), planted to a mix of red and white varieties.

BROWN BROTHERS   NE
Glenrowan-Myrtleford Road, Milawa, VIC 3678

w=82 86 88, r=82 86 88, sw, ft   *→**

Brown Brothers has remained entirely family-owned for a century.
Today 74-year-old John Charles Brown and his four sons all live and
work happily together at Milawa. The business is big enough for each to
have his own sphere of interest: John Graham Brown, the eldest, is
wine-maker; Peter, the second-eldest, viticulturist; Ross, the next,
marketing man; and Roger, the youngest, overseer of vine propagation
and harvesting. It was their Scottish great-great-grandfather, John
Francis Brown, who founded the firm in 1889. Brown Brothers has
since gone from strength to strength. It now has 390 acres (160 ha) of
vines, from which it produces a long list of single varietal table wines
and a small selection of fortifieds. The two largest vineyards are at
Milawa and Mystic Park in northern Central Victoria, with smaller
plantings at Hurdle Creek just south of Milawa and at Whitlands in the
foothills beyond the King Valley. The Browns buy in about 50% of their
grape needs from local contract growers in the King Valley and from the
northern part of the state.

   The Browns consider themselves Australia's "varietal wine special-
ists" – which is true – and aim "to produce deeply-flavoured varietal
wines rather than generic styles or copies" – which is more debatable.
Certainly Brown Brothers was one of the first in the country to make
stylish single varietal table wines using modern methods such as night-
harvesting, must-chilling, pre-fermentation filtering and cold fermentation. But a few years back their white wines had a disturbingly uniform
style. This is lessening with each vintage and the Browns are obviously
aware of the problem for they have now built a "kindergarten" winery
near their vast processing plant at Milawa, where small batches of first-
class grapes will be carefully treated. Zinfandel and Nebbiolo will be
some of its first releases.

   One of the Browns' most popular white wines is the scented,
aromatic 87 Dry Muscat Blanc, whose aniseed, sherbet and barley sugar
taste is in the same style as the 88 Semillon with its spicy, vanilla and
citric taste. The soft, buttery, lemon-clove-like 86 Family Reserve
Chardonnay is also worthwhile, but the grassy-appley 87 Sauv Blanc is
an ordinary wine. The Browns were the first wine-makers in Australia
to produce a late harvest botrytis-affected Riesling in the early 1960s
and the first to make a wine from the Tarrango grape a decade later.
Their newest wines include a Pinot Noir Chardonnay Brut sparkling
wine and a fruity, creosote-like 85 King Valley Cab Franc/Merlot blend.
Brown Brothers' finest red, however, is its single-vineyard Koombahla
Cab Sauvignon, whose 85 vintage boasts a delicious, rich, velvety,
peppermint and eucalyptus-like palate.
Υ   Star buy: Brown Brothers Koombahla Cab Sauvignon

BULLERS CALLIOPE   NE
Three Chain Road, Murray Valley Highway, Rutherglen, VIC 3685

w, r, sw, ft   *

The Bullers and their three sons, who have overseas wine-making
experience, produce a range of Muscat, Tokay, Frontignac, port and
hearty red table wines. Their Murray Valley development at Beverford
produces spirits for Rutherglen fortifieds and table wines.

CAMPBELLS   NE
Murray Valley Highway, Rutherglen, VIC 3685

w, r, ft   *→

Scotsman John Campbell planted the vineyard here in 1870 and
completed the cellar in 1885. Successive generations of Campbells
added to both. Today fourth-generation Colin Campbell, the Roseworthy-
trained wine-maker, and his viticulturist brother Malcolm continue
family traditions, producing 30,000 cases a year from 120 acres (50 ha)
of vines, dominated by Shiraz and Brown Muscat. Their bestseller is
Dry Graves, a blended white. The Campbell brothers also produce good
quantities of Bobbie Burns Shiraz, a strong, typical Rutherglen wine,
and a long list of fortifieds including the light, flowery-raisiny Liqueur
Muscat and vintage port.

CAPOGRECO WINES   MR
Riverside Avenue, Mildura, VIC 3500

w, r, ft, sp *

This winery's 50 acres (20 ha) of Sultana, Palomino, Muscatel, Mataro,
Cab Sauvignon, Shiraz and Rh Riesling vines are owned and managed
by Bruno Capogreco and family. They produce a wide range of Italian-
style table, fortified, sparkling and flavoured wines.

CATHCART RIDGE ESTATE   GW
Byron Road, Cathcart, VIC 3377

w, r *→

Cathcart Ridge's Dr Bertuch has 32 acres (13 ha) of vineyards planted
to Cab Sauvignon, Shiraz, Chardonnay and Rh Riesling, from which he
makes a well-thought-of table wine range with Trevor Mast's help.

CHAMBERS ROSEWOOD   NE
Off Corowa Road, Rutherglen, VIC 3685

w, r, sw, ft *→→***

Englishman William Chambers from Norfolk planted a vineyard here in
1860 and started to make wine some three years later. Today his great-
great-grandson Bill Chambers, an experienced wine judge, makes wine
from 110 acres (45 ha) of vines. Annual production exceeds the 7,000
cases sold but a lot of wine is aged in wood for some years at the winery.
This casual, if not chaotic, small family winery believes firmly in tradition.
A long list of table wines are produced, including sweet wines such as
Sauternes and Moselle: try the soft, lime-like Riesling or reds such as
the rich, ripe, full Blue Imperial Alicante Bouchet. The Chambers
family's finest offerings are the Old Liqueur Muscats and Tokays, whose
base wine dates from 1928. The Old Liqueur Tokay with its green edge
and intense rancio flavours is a four-star offering, and the glorious,
silky, perfumed Liqueur Muscat is not far behind.

CHATEAU DORE   CV
Mandurang Road, Mandurang, VIC 3551

w, r *

Chateau Dore was founded in 1866 when Jean Theodore de Ravin
planted the first vines at Sheepwash Creek in Mandurang. By the 1870s
he was producing wine, much of it no doubt enjoyed by Bendigo's gold
diggers – hence perhaps the name of the winery. By 1895 he had the
largest vineyards in the region, but Chateau Dore's prosperity was
brought to an abrupt end by the arrival of phylloxera, not because its
vines were attacked but because they fell within the state's compulsory
grubbing-up radius. De Ravin continued to make wine from neighbours'
grapes in the solid sandstone cellars that he had built in 1893 and which
can still be seen today. When disaster struck again in the shape of an
excise officer who denatured 13,000 gallons of Chateau Dore's wine
because it contained a banned wine preservative, de Ravin had enough
and devoted the rest of his life to mining. Happily his great-grandsons,
Ivan and Jan Grose, re-established Chateau Dore in 1975. There are
now 10 acres (4 ha) of vines here, planted equally to Shiraz, Cabernet,
Rh Riesling and Chardonnay, and new Chardonnay plantings are on
the way. About 1,500 cases are made annually by traditional methods.
The Groses regard the Hermitage as their best wine. This historic
survivor is open Tue-Sun, 10am-6pm.

CHATEAU LE AMON   CV
Calder Highway, Bendigo, VIC 3550

w, r *

Philip Leamon has 10 acres (4 ha) of Big Hill vines, planted to Rh
Riesling, Semillon, Shiraz and Cab Sauvignon.

CHATEAU REMY   PR
Vinoca Road, Avoca, VIC 3467

w, r, sp *→**

Founded in 1960 by Rémy Martin, Chateau Remy has had its problems.
The original idea was to make brandy – which is why the vineyard still
has sizeable Ugni Blanc plantings, gradually grafted over to finer

varieties. By the time the vineyard was producing, the bottom had dropped out of the Australian brandy market so, executing a dramatic u-turn, Chateau Remy transformed itself principally into a sparkling wine house. Vincent Gere, the new wine-maker, has 250 acres (100 ha), including 150 acres (60 ha) of sparkling wine grapes surrounding the winery. The remainder is divided between 67 acres (27 ha) of white varieties at the Australis and 33 acres (13 ha) of red varieties at Blue Pyrenees; Clare Valley fruit is also bought in for the Clos Saint Charles label. Three-quarters of Chateau Remy's 40,000-case production consists of sparklers, such as the well-made Cuvee Speciale Brut, rosé and vintage fizz. The remaining quarter offers table wines such as the convincing, cherry-like "Beaujolais" Kindilan Nouveau and the big, mainly Cabernet-based 84 Blue Pyrenees Estates with its unusual, robust, eucalyptus and sandalwood palate.

CHATEAU TAHBILK   GV
Tabilk, VIC 3607

w=80 82, r=81, sw   *→**

Chateau Tahbilk, founded in 1860, is VIC's oldest family-owned winery. The winery is part of the huge Tahbilk grazing estate on the east bank of the Goulburn River, run by the Purbrick family. Several generations of Purbricks have run Chateau Tahbilk since the family arrived here in 1925. Young, Roseworthy-trained Alister Purbrick is the current chief executive/wine-maker. Tahbilk's magnificent underground cellars topped with a distinctive wooden tiered tower date from 1860, and the "new cellar" adjacent from 1875. Wandering through the capacious cellars, where original grape presses and oak fermenters have been preserved, it is easy to imagine what late 19th-century Australian wine-making must have been like – back-breakingly hard work. The tiered tower had a practical purpose: grapes were transported from the vineyard in tubs, tipped into a hopper at ground level and then pulled up to the crusher on the first floor; the second floor stored oats for the horses; and the third was a look-out level. Tahbilk changed its name to Chateau Tahbilk in 1879, but no one knows where the "h" in the name came from. When phylloxera hit Tahbilk in 1890, two-thirds of its vines were destroyed, but the estate survived because some of its vines were planted on sandy soils naturally resistant to the aphid.

There are now 300 acres (120 ha) of vines here. Marsanne is the biggest planting, followed by Cab Sauvignon, Chardonnay, Shiraz and Rh Riesling. The reds, made using traditional Bordeaux methods, have "cellaring potential of 10 to 40 years" according to Alister Purbrick. He regards the Cabernet as his finest wine, but the Marsanne (of which **Mitchelton** acquired cuttings) is his biggest seller. The Tahbilk wine style is distinctive. All of the red wines boast a big, rich, fruity taste underpinned by lots of oak and tannin to give them the ageing quality that the Purbricks rate so highly. The 81 Cabernet with its rich intense mulberry-like fruit was a classic Chateau Tahbilk wine. The Marsanne is interesting, but it is hard to get too enthusiastic about its big, citric, peachy flavours. Chardonnay and Sauv Blanc are recent additions. Visitors to the state (who are welcome here Mon-Sat, 9am-5pm and Sun 12-5pm) should make a point of seeing this historic property.

CHATEAU YARRINYA   YV
Pinnacle Lane, Dixon's Creek, VIC 3775

w, r, ft   *

Yarrinya's extraordinary crenellated grey-brick building does perhaps deserve to be called a "château". Now belonging to **De Bortoli** of NSW, its vineyards were planted in 1971 and today there are 32 acres (13 ha) of vines here. Besides premium table wines, such as Chardonnay, Pinot Noir and Cabernet, Chateau Yarrinya also produces vintage port.

CHERRITTA WINES   CV
Henty Highway, Branxholme, VIC 3302

w, r, ft   *

Cherritta's table and fortified wines are made by owner John Sobey. There are 25 acres (10 ha) of vines here including Rh Riesling, Shiraz, Cab Sauvignon and Chardonnay.

CLYDE PARK GL
Midland Highway, Bannockburn, VIC 3331

w, r ∗

Clyde Park, founded in 1981, is owned by wine-maker Gary Farr and his wife Robyn. Gary runs it in his spare time from **Bannockburn** but, with only 8 acres (3 ha) of vines and no more than 2,000 cases produced, this is not a big operation. Small quantities of Chardonnay, Cab Sauvignon and Pinot Noir are made and bottled at Bannockburn.

COLDSTREAM HILLS YV
Lot 6, Maddens Lane, Coldstream, VIC 3770

w, r = 88 87 ∗→∗∗∗

James Halliday, Australia's leading wine-writer, first tried his hand at the real thing in the 1970s at **Brokenwood** in the Hunter (NSW), but his involvement there came to an end when his law firm moved from Sydney to Melbourne. In 1985, after first buying parcels of Pinot Noir from the Yarra and vinifying them at **Elgee Park**, Halliday bought this property and planted close-spaced hillside vineyards here. Coldstream's 86 and 87 vintages were made from bought-in Yarra grapes and vinified at **Yarra Ridge**, a winery run by one of Halliday's legal partners. When an adjoining property came up for sale, he and his PR-trained wife Suzanne bought it, turning Coldstream Hills into a public company (in which **Thomas Hardy** of SA has a 20% share). The stylish, well-equipped winery was completed in time for the 1988 vintage, and there are now 37 acres (15 ha) of vines here. The bulk of these are divided equally between Pinot Noir and Chardonnay, the remainder mostly between Cab Sauvignon, Cab Franc and Merlot. This supplies about a third of the Hallidays' fruit; the rest is bought in locally.

A second James Halliday label for the export market will offer wines from other regions, such as the 88 Coonawarra Cabernet. All told, the Hallidays intend to produce 10,000 cases – rising, hopefully, to 30,000 cases by 1992. Making a classic Pinot Noir in Australia using traditional Burgundian methods is clearly a challenge for Halliday. His 87 Lilydale Pinot Noir with its gamey, vegetal scent and soft, rich, velvety palate of plums and roses, shows that he has succeeded; so does his light, zesty, damson, plum and liquorice-like 88 Four Vineyards wine. His fresh, flowery, pineappley 87 Lilydale Chardonnay and elegant 88 Four Vineyards Chardonnay with its firm, cinnamon-like bite are equally good. Better still is the ripe cassis and capsicum-like 87 Lilydale Cab Sauvignon with Merlot and Cab Franc in the mix.

♈ Star buy: Coldstream Hills 87 Lilydale Pinot Noir

CRAIGLEE MC
Sunbury Road, Sunbury, VIC 3429

w, r ∗

Craiglee is another historic Macedon winery founded, like **Goonawarra**, in the late 19th century (1865) and replanted over a century later (1978). At its four-storey bluestone winery, Pat Carmody makes a variety of table wines including Shiraz, Cabernet and Chardonnay.

CRAWFORD RIVER WINES CV
Crawford, via Condah, VIC 3303

w, r, sw ∗

Started in 1977, Crawford is run by "owner, wine-maker and dogsbody" John Thomson. The Thomsons now have 17 acres (7 ha) of vines and produce 1,500 cases; Rh Riesling and Cab Sauvignon are their big lines.

DALWHINNIE PR
Taltarni Road, Moonambel, VIC 3478

w, r ∗

Architect Ewan Jones and his wine-making son David named this winery after Dalwhinnie in Scotland. Founded in 1973, Dalwhinnie now has 26 acres (11 ha) of vines at 1,150 feet (350 m), next door to **Taltarni**. The first wines were released in 1980 and today just 4,000 cases are made each year. Jones' principal wine is the pleasant, fresh, eucalyptus-like 85 Cabernet. Other offerings include the lively, spicy-oaky 88 Chardonnay and the surprisingly light, flowery 85 Shiraz.

DELATITE   CV
Stoney's Road, Mansfield, VIC 3722

w=82 87, r=86 87 *→***

Set in some of the state's wildest and most beautiful "sub-alpine" country in the foothills of the Great Dividing Range, Delatite is very much a family-run concern. Robert and Vivienne Ritchie are the owners, Roseworthy-trained daughter Rosalind the wine-maker and brother David the marketing man. Delatite (meaning "devil's river" in aboriginal) is named after a nearby stream that meanders down from the mountains blowing its banks during the winter floods. In the early days after its foundation in 1982, the Ritchies received considerable help from **Brown Brothers**, Oenotec and Dr Tony Jordan. Outside wine-making expertise of this calibre ensured that the wines were good from the start. The Ritchies first planted vines on the steep north-facing slopes of rocky ironstone in 1968, gradually adding new varieties. Today they have 60 acres (24 ha) of vines which supply about two-thirds of their needs; the rest of their fruit, used only for the three second label wines, is bought in from other cooler-climate areas.

Annual production stands at around 14,000 cases, made in the functional winery designed by Oenotec. Delatite produces a wide range of table wines, with more whites than reds. Rh Riesling is its most celebrated offering, and deservedly so, for the 87 was a delicious three-star zesty, lime-juice mouthful and the spicy, elegant, lychee-like 87 Gewurztraminer was almost as good. Delatite's latest red wines are its best as shown by the minty-stalky 86 Cabernet/Merlot and the soft, simple 86 Malbec; even the mint and eucalyptus-like 86 Pinot Noir is a step in the right direction. Delatite expects to release its first Sauv Blanc in 1990 and a Pinot Noir-based sparkler the following year.
℣ Star buy: Delatite 87 Rh Riesling

DIAMOND VALLEY VINEYARDS   YV
Kinglake Road, St Andrews, VIC 3761

w, r *→

Named after the local creek which it overlooks, Diamond Valley was founded by David and Cathy Lance in 1976. David, a chemist by training, was one of **St Hubert's** founding fathers and broke away to set up his own winery, planting 8 acres (3 ha) of vines on sloping hillsides here. The vineyard supplies fruit for Chardonnay, Pinot Noir, Rh Riesling and a Cabernet-based blend, but half of Diamond Valley's fruit is bought in locally. These outside grapes go into the Blue Label range, the biggest share of the winery's 4,000 cases, which includes the new Germanic white blend, White Diamond. Diamond Valley's owners rate the Pinot Noir as their finest wine.

DOMAINE CHANDON   YV
Maddens Lane, Coldstream, VIC 3770

sp *→

After many years of trial wines and vineyard analysis, sister companies Moët et Chandon of Champagne and Domaine Chandon of California chose this property, just down the road from **Coldstream Hills**, as the site of their Australian operation. As Managing Director they acquired Dr Tony Jordan, joint founder of the Oenotec wine consultancy, whose wine-making skills and knowledge are hard to beat. Founded in 1985, Domaine Chandon has 50 acres (20 ha) of vines, two-thirds planted to Chardonnay and one-third to Pinot Noir, with a dash of Pinot Meunier. This will supply half of the winery's grapes, the other half coming in from regions as far-flung as TAS and Coonawarra (SA). So far Jordan has released only one wine, a crisp, lemony 86 Cuvee Chardonnay; his second sparkler, a Pinot Noir/Chardonnay-based wine, will be out late in 1989. A lavish winery and visitors' centre is due to open soon.

DONOVIEW VINEYARD   GW
Pomonal Road, VIC 3380

w, r *

Peter Donovan is in charge here, but wine-making is left to Chris Peters. Some 20 acres (8 ha) of red and white table wine varieties are grown, including the unlovely Crouchen. Donoview's Shiraz is well regarded.

DROMANA ESTATE   MP
Harrisons Road, Dromana, VIC 3936

w, r   *⟶

Gary Crittenden looks after the 10 acres (4 ha) of grapes grown in sandy
grey loam here, also buying in SA fruit to make Dromana's admired
Schinus Molle, or peppercorn tree, label. He produces 1,500 cases here
and acts as consultant elsewhere. The 84 Dromana Estate Cabernet is
an intense, verdant, tutti-frutti mouthful, the pricier 88 Schinus Molle
Chardonnay a pleasant ripe, pineappley wine.

ELGEE PARK   MP
Wallace's Road, Merricks North, VIC 3926

w, r   *⟶

Founded by Sidney Baillieu Myer, Elgee has the oldest vineyard and
largest winery in the region. The 10 acres (4 ha) of vines, split equally
between whites and reds, are planted to Cab Sauvignon, Cab Franc,
Merlot and Chardonnay. Wine-maker Tod Dexter produces wine for
several other local concerns as well. The 84 Cabernet and Chardonnay
both boasted bright, clean fruit.

FAIRFIELD VINEYARD   NE
Murray Valley Highway, Brown's Plain via Rutherglen, VIC 3685

w, r, sw, ft   *

Wine-maker Stephen Morris produces table and fortified wines from 25
acres (10 ha) of vines such as Shiraz and Muscat.

FERGUSSON'S WINERY   YV
Wills Road, Yarra Glen, VIC 3775

w, r   *

With 18 acres (7 ha) of vines and a restaurant to run, Peter and Louise
Fergusson employ Kerrie Haydon as wine-maker. Some 5,000 cases are
produced, mostly of Shiraz and Cab Sauvignon but also of Riesling and
Chardonnay, 50% made from their own fruit.

FITZPATRICK ESTATE   MR
Campbell Avenue, Irymple, VIC 3498

w, r, ft, sp   *

The Fitzpatrick family and wine-maker Neville Hudson manage 87
acres (35 ha) of vines, turning them into a long 20,000-case list of table,
fortified, flavoured and sparkling wines. Once known as Bonnonee
Wines, this estate grows bulk wine grapes such as Gordo, Sultana,
Crouchen and Ruby Cabernet alongside more noble vines, selling large
quantities of juice to other producers. Popular wine-styles such as
Moselle are sold under the Bonnonee label, with the Mildura Vineyards
label covering other products such as Passion Wine; Victoria Gardens
Estate is another Fitzpatrick label.

FLOWERDALE   CV
Yea Road, Flowerdale, VIC 3717

w, r   *

Ros Ritchie from **Delatite** is the contract wine-maker at this small
6-acre (2.5-ha) estate in Central Victoria, planted to Chardonnay,
Chenin Blanc, Traminer and Pinot Noir.

FLYNN & WILLIAMS   MC
Flynn's Lane, Kyneton, VIC 3444

r   *

This small winery run by John Flynn and Laurie Williams produces Cab
Sauvignon and Shiraz, most of it sold at the cellar door.

GARDEN GULLY   GW
Western Highway, Great Western, VIC 3377

w, r   *

Garden Gully is a new label for the fine fruit produced from two old
Great Western vineyards called Salinger and Chalambar, once owned
by **Seppelt** but now deemed insufficiently productive. The new owning
group has not yet released wines.

GAYFER'S CHILTERN NE
Hume Highway, Chiltern, VIC 3683

w, r, sw, ft *

At Gayfer's Chiltern, on the site of an old mine, the Gayfer family produces table and fortified wines.

GEHRIG BROTHERS NE
Murray Valley Highway, Barnawartha, VIC 3688

w, r, sw, ft *

Brian Gehrig is wine-maker at this 50-acre (20 ha) estate, established in 1858. Table and fortified wines are made here from vines such as Cabernet and Trebbiano.

GIACONDA CV
McClay Road, Beechworth, VIC 3747

w, r *→

Rick Kinzbrunner, Giaconda's well-travelled wine-maker, produces a short list of quality table wines that have pleased Australian judges. The 88 Chardonnay was a pleasant fresh, sherbetty-buttery wine.

GLENMOUR ESTATE GV
Johnsons Lane, Northwood, VIC 3660

w, r *

Small quantities of red and white table wines are made for Glenmour by wine-maker Alister Purbrick of **Chateau Tahbilk**.

GOLVINDA EG
Lindenow South Road, Lindenow, VIC 3865

w, r *

Robert Guy produces a range of table wines at this East Gippsland winery, most of them sold at the cellar door.

GOONAWARRA MC
Sunbury Road, Sunbury, VIC 3429

w, r *

Goonawarra may not sound the most elegant of names to European ears, but its meaning in the local aboriginal dialect – "resting place of the black swan" – is certainly that. The estate was founded in 1863 by James Goodall Francis, an early Victorian Premier, who built the bluestone winery and its extensive terraced vineyards, but these fell out of use in the 1900s. The Barniers replanted Goonawarra in 1983 and released their first wines in 1987. Goonawarra and **Craiglee** are now the only 1860s wineries remaining in Macedon. Made from 12 acres (5 ha) of various vines (mostly Chardonnay and Cab Franc), Goonawarra wine is a "low-tech, hand-made product".

HALCYON DAZE YV
Lot 15, Uplands Road, Lilydale, VIC 3140

w, r *

Richard and Cheryl Rackley, with 9 acres (3.5 ha) of Yarra soil to their name and another 25 acres (10 ha) planned, make under 1,000 cases of Cabernet, Riesling and Chardonnay.

HANGING ROCK WINERY MC
Jim Road, Newham, VIC 3442

w, r *→

Named after the mysterious and dramatic Hanging Rock nearby, this winery was established in 1983 and produced its first vintage in 1987. Wine-maker/manager John Ellis hopes its location will tempt tourists making the 40-mile (70-km) journey north-west from Melbourne to visit the winery. Ellis has 15 acres (6 ha) of high-altitude vines; an additional 60 acres (24 ha) of fruit is bought in from all over VIC. The close-spaced Macedon vines are mainly intended for a future Pinot Noir/Chardonnay sparkler, while the others are selected to produce "specific regional wine-styles" such as Victorian Semillon, Faraday Chardonnay, and King Valley Pinot Noir and Riesling. Grapes grown in suburban Melbourne are turned into Melbourne Rosé.

HARCOURT.VALLEY VINEYARD   CV
Calder Highway, Harcourt, VIC 3453

w, r   *

Founded in 1980 as a partnership of two families, the Honeymans and the Livingstones, this 12-acre (5-ha) establishment now sells almost 4,000 cases a year, mostly of Cab Sauvignon, Shiraz and a Cab Sauvignon/Merlot blend. Wine-maker Philip Honeyman produces, among others, a special Shiraz wine made from century-old vines. New releases include Pinot Noir and Chardonnay.

HAYWARD'S OF WHITEHEADS CREEK   GV
Hall Mayne, Seymour, VIC 3660

w, r   *

This small wine-making concern in the Goulburn Valley is run by the Hayward family.

THE HEATHCOTE WINERY   CV
183-185 High Street, Heathcote, VIC 3523

w, r   *

Doris and Kenneth Tudhope own this winery and their daughter Elain is wine-maker. With 40 acres (16 ha) planted and more due, Heathcote is bigger than most family concerns. Some 5,000 cases are produced, with Chardonnay the big seller followed by Pinot Noir and Traminer.

HENKE   GV
Henkes Lane, Yarck, VIC 3719

r   *

Herb Henke planted the vines here in 1969. With just 10 acres (4 ha) of vines planted equally to Shiraz and Cabernet, his daughter and son-in-law Tim and Caroline Miller now produce only 250 cases of each.

HICKINBOTHAM WINE-MAKERS   CV
2 Ferguson Street, Williamstown, VIC 3016

w, r   *—→

The Hickinbothams must be one of Australia's most talented wine-making families. Grandfather Alan Robb Hickinbotham was an early Roseworthy teacher and his son Ian helped to establish **Wynns'** good name in Coonawarra (SA), also initiating Australia's bag-in-box wine package. The third generation has performed as impressively as the first two: Stephen, trained in Bordeaux, invented a unique Australian version of *macération carbonique* before dying in an air crash; Burgundy-trained Andrew works in the Mornington Peninsula; and Jenny is a trained viticulturist. This winery, founded in 1981, has just 7 acres (3 ha) of vines and buys in grapes from elsewhere in VIC to produce 5,000 cases of high-quality table wines. By 1992 it hopes to complete the establishment of a vineyard in the Mornington Peninsula.

HJT VINEYARDS   NE
Keenan Road, Glenrowan, VIC 3675

w, r, sw   *—→

HJT is owned by Catherine and Henry James Tinson, previously wine-maker at **Baileys**. They have just 5 acres (2 ha) of vines planted to well-thought-of premium varietals, from which 1,000 cases are made.

HONEYMAN   MC
Old Post Office Road, Metcalfe, VIC 3448

r   *

This new winery is not strictly in Macedon, but the Honeymans feel more at home here than anywhere else. So far it has produced only small quantities of red wines such as a Cabernet/Merlot blend.

HUNTLEIGH VINEYARD   CV
Tunnecliff's Lane, Heathcote, VIC 3523

w, r   *

Leigh Hunt founded this 13-acre (5-ha) winery in 1975. With over half of this acreage planted to Cab Sauvignon, and a little Shiraz and Traminer also made, he produces just 300 cases a year.

IDYLL VINEYARD
Ballan Road, Moorabool, VIC 3221

GL

w, r *→

Daryl and Nini Sefton, Idyll's enthusiastic co-owners, developed this concern from 1966 onwards. Daryl's great-grandfather was one of Geelong's pioneering Swiss wine-makers, and the Seftons feel that they too have done their bit for the rebirth of the Geelong wine industry. Idyll has 50 acres (20 ha) under vine, concentrating on Cab Sauvignon, Shiraz and Gewurztraminer. These are turned into a straight dry, spicy Gewurztraminer, Shiraz rosés called Idyll Blush and Idyll Glow, a hefty Cab Sauvignon/Shiraz blend and a lighter summer red called Bone Idyll. Nini's colourful oil paintings provide Idyll with its labels.

INNISFAIL VINEYARDS
Cross Street, Batesford, VIC 3221

GL

w, r *

Ron and Sharon Griffiths founded Innisfail in 1980. From their 10 acres (4 ha) of Geelong grapes they make just 500 cases of mixed table wines, led by Chardonnay which they have sold since 1988.

JASPER HILL VINEYARD
Drummonds Lane, Heathcote, VIC 3523

CV

w, r *

Ron and Elva Laughton make 2-3,000 cases of wine from 45 acres (18 ha) of vines, most of it sold under the Georgia's Paddock Shiraz label. Sadly a bushfire prior to the 87 vintage ravaged the vineyard and a "Friends" Shiraz made from the fruit of vigneron friends has now taken its place. The 87 Friends Shiraz is a hefty wine and the burnt, chunky, creosote-like 87 Shiraz/Cab Franc is bigger still.

JOHN GEHRIG WINES
Oxley via Wangaratta, VIC 3678

NE

w, r, ft, sp *

John and Elizabeth Gehrig own 12 acres (5 ha) of vines on the banks of the King River, producing table, fortified and sparkling wines.

JOLIMONT
Murray Valley Highway, Rutherglen, VIC 3685

NE

w, r, ft, sp *

Table, fortified and sparkling wines are made in Jolimont's handsome century-old cellars by Howard Anderson. There are also a restaurant and conference facilities on site.

JONES WINERY
Jones Road, Rutherglen, VIC 3685

NE

w, r, ft *

Les Jones and family manage 30 acres (12 ha) and a winery dating from the 1860s, which came into their family in 1927. Just over 1,000 cases of table wines and vintage port are made.

KARINA VINEYARD
Harrisons Road, Dromana, VIC 3936

MP

w, r *

Ian and Graeme Pinney founded Karina in 1984. Their 1988 crop yielded just 320 cases of wine – mostly Rh Riesling and a little Sauv Blanc – with labels designed by their daughter Caroline. A similar output is expected from their first crop of Cab Sauvignon and Merlot.

KELLYBROOK
Fulford Road, Wonga Park, VIC 3115

YV

w, r *

Founded in 1960 by Darren and Farley Kelly, Kellybrook now has 20 acres (8 ha) of vines. Originally better known as cider-makers, the Kellys now produce a long list of products including a new *méthode hampenoise* fizz, apple brandy, cider and "champagne cider", alongside the more usual Yarra offerings of Chardonnay and Cab Sauvignon. They also run their own restaurant.

KINDILAN NOUVEAU   See **Chateau Remy**.

KINGSLEY   CV
50 Bancroft Street, Portland, VIC 3305

                                                              W   *
So far this Central Victorian winery has released only one wine, a Rh
Riesling, which was made for it by **Seppelt**.

KNIGHT'S WINES   MC
Baynton via Kyneton, VIC 3444

                                                            w, r   *→
Founded in 1978, this winery's 22 acres (9 ha) of vines are managed by
chief executive Gordon Knight and wine-maker Llewellyn Knight.
Production is divided equally between Shiraz, Cabernet, Riesling and
Chardonnay, with a little Semillon. The Knights' two brands, Granite
Hills and Arthur's Creek, cover a full range of table wines, the most
famous being their fine, black pepper spice-like Shiraz.

LANCEFIELD ESTATE   MC
Woodend Road, Lancefield, VIC 3435

                                                            w, r   *
Another winery close to Hanging Rock, Lancefield is run by Andrew
and Anne Pattison, whose table wine range includes Gewurztraminer,
Chardonnay, Merlot and Pinot Noir.

LANDRAGIN   CV
102 Fisken Road, Mount Helen, VIC 3350

                                                             sp   *→
Dominique and Anna Landragin have retained their French style after
many years in Australia. Born into a French Champagne family,
Dominique was previously wine-maker at **Yellowglen** and it is likely
that he will make a similar style of fresh, strong sparkling wine here.

LILLYDALE VINEYARDS   YV
Davross Court, Seville, VIC 3139

                                                            w, r   *→
Alex White and Martin Grinbergs, formerly at **St Huberts**, split off to
plant Lillydale's 25 acres (10 ha) in 1976. Today Lillydale produces
10,000 cases of well-regarded wines a year, making it the second-largest
producer in the valley after St Huberts. Seven different wines are made
– principally whites such as Chardonnay and Rh Riesling, but with
small quantities of Pinot Noir and Cab Sauvignon also released.

LONG GULLY ESTATE   YV
Long Gully Road, Healesville, VIC 3777

                                                            w, r   *
Reiner Klapp and his wife bought Long Gully as a weekend retreat.
Now they have 38 acres (15 ha) of vines, from which wine-maker Peter
Florence produces 8,000 cases of wines. 1989 saw the first releases,
Riesling and Chardonnay taking the largest share.

LONGLEAT WINERY   GV
Old Weir Road, Murchison, VIC 3610

                                                            w, r   *
Longleat is owned by Peter and Jenny Schulz, who have 45 acres (18
ha) of vines here and a further 20 acres (8 ha) of contract vines in the
King Valley. Peter and his son Mark make 4,000 cases of wine with the
help of **Chateau Tahbilk's** Alister Purbrick. Shiraz and Cab Sauvignon
are the two big sellers, accounting for half their output. A further 15
acres (6 ha) of Merlot and Cabernet are planned.

McALISTER VINEYARDS   EC
Golden Beach Road, Longford, VIC 3851

                                                              r
Only one wine is made here by Peter Edwards from his 12 acres (5 ha)
of vines – the McAlister, a Cab Sauvignon-based red with a little Merlot,
Cab Franc and Petit Verdot blended in.

McIVOR CREEK WINES
Costerfield Road, Heathcote, VIC 3523

CV

w, r, sw, ft　*

Peter and Robyn Turley own 15 acres (6 ha) of vines surrounding their winery, which supply 20% of the grapes for their annual 5,000-case production. The rest is bought in, Central Victoria supplying their dry table wine fruit and Riverina (NSW) their fortified and sweet table wine grapes. Drip-irrigation should increase production here soon.

MAIN RIDGE ESTATE
William Road, Red Hill, VIC 3937

MP

w, r　*→

The 7 acres (3 ha) at Main Ridge, founded in 1975, are owned by Nat White and family. They produce 800 cases of Pinot Noir, Chardonnay and Cab Sauvignon. Main Ridge was the first commercial winery/vineyard on the Mornington Peninsula and the Whites intend to keep it small, concentrating on quality. Their vegetable, liquorice-like 83 Pinot Noir is a step in the right direction, as is the herbaceous 84 Cabernet.

MAIR'S COALVILLE
Coalville Vineyard, Moe South Road, Moe, VIC 3825

EG

r　*

Tiny quantities of Cab Sauvignon, blended with Merlot, are made here in the north of the East Gippsland region.

MARKWOOD ESTATE
Morris Lane, Markwood, VIC 3678

NE

w, r, ft　*

Rick Morris is wine-maker at this 12-acre (5-ha) estate. Cab Sauvignon, Palomino and other varieties are made into small quantities of table and fortified wines, sold at the cellar door.

MERRICKS ESTATE
Thompsons Lane, Merricks, VIC 3916

MP

w, r　*→→**

The Kefford family, as their labels proudly state, are the owners of this 7-acre (3-ha) property planted in 1978 "after much experimentation". They grow Chardonnay, Cab Sauvignon and Shiraz vines, producing just 650 cases a year. Wine-making help is provided by **Dromana's** Gary Crittenden and Alex White from **Diamond Valley** in the Yarra. The 83 Cabernet has big, intense mint and eucalyptus-like fruit. Merricks' 84 Shiraz, with its elegant, spicy, tea-rose perfume and rich, juicy fruit palate, is a three-star wine.

MILDARA
Wentworth Road, Merbein, VIC 3505

MR

w, r, sw, ft　*→→**

Mildara, one of Australia's new stock exchange-listed wine giants, has been hot on the acquisition trail during the last few years. It now owns **Yellowglen** and **Balgownie** in VIC, **Krondorf** in SA and **Morton Estate** in New Zealand. Mildara has by far the largest winery (capable of crushing 15,000 tonnes of grapes) and bottling plant in the group. It was the Chaffey brothers, designers of this region's irrigation scheme, who founded Mildara when they planted vines in 1888 at Mildura, not far from Merbein. The adapted town's name eventually became the name of the firm. Mildara's early years were as troubled as those of the region, but new management in the 1930s brought the company round. Under Ron Haselgrove, whose son Richard is the present Chairman, the company started producing quality sherries and brandies, and in 1955 purchased some 30 acres (12 ha) in Coonawarra (SA); it now owns 630 acres (255 ha) there. Mildara's famous yellow label red wines of the 50s, 60s and early 70s owed much of their reputation to the portions of Coonawarra Shiraz and Cabernet in the mix.

With an annual production of 550,000 cases, including all the group's table wines, fortifieds and brandies, Mildara buys in 80% of its grapes from contract growers. The most basic of its several ranges is the Flower Series range made from irrigated Murray River fruit. The spritzy, passion fruit-like 88 Fumé Blanc and the soft, grassy-peppery Cabernet/ Merlot are not very exciting, but they are pleasant enough. One notch up are wines such as the Coonawarra Rh Riesling, the strong, murky Coonawarra 86 Hermitage and the much finer Coonawarra 86 Cab Sauvignon with its generous herbaceous and cassis palate. Mildara also produces Jamiesons Run, a white and red Coonawarra pair blended for "drinkability". The white is a fresh, fruit salad-like blend of Sauv Blanc, Chardonnay and Semillon, and the red a mainly Shiraz-based wine rounded off with Merlot, Cab Sauvignon, Malbec and Cab Franc. Both wines have done extremely well in Australia since 1987. Alexander's, Mildara's flagship Bordeaux-inspired Coonawarra red, is a three-star wine. The 86 (mainly Cab Sauvignon with a dollop of Cab Franc, Merlot and Malbec) was a purple-black, rich, spicy, refined, scented wine, backed up by a delicious, silky, cassis and oak palate.

Apart from table wines, Mildara still makes sherries, ports such as the popular Benjamin and Cavendish Ports and brandies such as the Extra Reserve Pot Still Brandy. Its overseas labels include the discount Mark Swann, Roo's Leap and Koala Ridge ranges which are sold in America and joint-venture wines which are sold in Japan under the Mercian Mildara label.

MITCHELTON   GV
Mitchellstown, Nagambie, VIC 3608

w=86 81 88, r=86 84 87, sw, sp   *→**

Driving out from Mitchellstown it is impossible to miss this winery, topped with its witch's hat observation tower. Mitchelton is named after Major Thomas Mitchell, the first European to cross the Goulburn River in 1836, who set up camp on the site now occupied by the vast, multi-million dollar show-piece winery. This whole complex, complete with restaurants, conference centre, swimming pool, souvenir shops, aviary and wildlife sanctuary, has a distinctly Californian feel to it. Now owned by the Valmorbida family, Mitchelton may not get quite the hordes of visitors that it would like but its wines, made by Don Lewis, have been getting better year by year.

There are 500 acres (200 ha) of land at Mitchelton, by no means all of them under vine. Apart from the home plot, the winery has 20 acres (8 ha) of vines at Fernlea in the cool Strathbogie Ranges and buys in about a third of its needs from other producers in these areas. About 10,000 cases of wines are made. The new Thomas Mitchell range, whose labels depict the man himself crossing the Goulburn, is the cheapest. More up-market are the Mitchelton wines, topped by the Print Label series, and finally the Classic Releases. The wine that invites more column inches than any other (although Mitchelton is also well known for its fine Rh Rieslings) is the Cab Mac, first produced in 1986. As its name suggests this wine is made by carbonic maceration, but using a distinctly Australian interpretation of the Beaujolais process developed by the late Stephen **Hickinbotham**. The end result, based mainly on Shiraz but with Cab Sauvignon and Grenache in the mix, is a respectable light, jammy, raspberry and cherry-like mouthful.

The basic Thomas Mitchell range is good value for money, its best offerings being the fresh, flowery, musky 88 Rh Riesling and the pleasant oaky-pineappley 88 Chardonnay. In the superior Mitchelton range the wines to choose are the 86 Cab Sauvignon, with its ripe berry-fruit, and the elegant, ripe wood-matured 87 Chardonnay. Mitchelton is keen on its well-made, perfumed, waxy, glacé-fruit-like Marsanne. But neither this nor the rich, jammy, blackcurrant pastille-like flavours of the 85 Cab Sauvignon/Merlot Print Series and the jammy, cassis-fruit of the 82 Cab Sauvignon Classic Release are worth paying the extra money for. Mitchelton's strength lies at the lower levels.

♀ Star buy: Thomas Mitchell range, esp 88 Rh Riesling

MONBULK   YV
Macclesfield Road, Monbulk, VIC 3797

w, r   *

The Jaborniks produce kiwi fruit wines as well as the usual kind at this 8-acre (3 ha) property. Their first vintage was in 1986, when they released Chardonnay, Rh Riesling, Shiraz and Cab Franc wines.

MONICHINO WINES   GV
Berry's Road, Katunga, VIC 3640

w, r, ft, sp   *

Carlo Monichino and family have 60 acres (25 ha) of vines, including Orange Muscat and Frontignac. From this acreage they make a wide range of table, flavoured, fortified and sparkling wines.

MONTARA   GW
Chalambar Road, Ararat, VIC 3377

w, r, ft   *

Montara's 42 acres (17 ha), planted to Chasselas, Ondenc and finer varieties, are turned into a wide range of table and fortified wines.

MOOROODUC ESTATE   MP
Derrill Road, Moorooduc, Mornington Peninsula, VIC 3936

w, r   *

Dr McIntyre owns Moorooduc's 6 acres (2.5 ha) of Chardonnay, Pinot Noir, Cab Sauvignon, Merlot and Cab Franc vines, making wines with the help of wine-maker Nat White and viticulturist Gary Crittenden.

MORRIS   NE
Mia Mia Vineyard, Murray Valley Highway, VIC 3685

w, r, ft, sp   *→→****

Mick Morris is the great-grandson of George Morris who planted this region's first vines at Fairfield in 1859. The vineyard here was established by Charles Morris, Mick's grandfather, in 1890. Today it covers 200 acres (80 ha) of Brown Muscat, Durif, Muscadelle, Shiraz and Cab Sauvignon. The Morris style has remained traditional under its new owners, **Orlando** of SA, with earth floors, open concrete fermenters and hydraulic basket presses still in evidence. Mick ages most of his excellent Muscats in old wood. This allows about 4% evaporation per year, gradually concentrating the flavour of the Muscat and old wood. The sweet, intoxicating scent of great old Muscats evaporating in this cellar is a great experience. Reds such as the hefty, gutsy 81 Durif or the intense, big 83 Shiraz are worth trying. But Morris' great strength is its fortifieds. The finest has to be the 25-30 year old Show Muscat, whose intense, rich rancio and raisin palate makes it a four-star wine. Humbler offerings at reasonable prices include the tawny, tea-leaf-like Liqueur Tokay and the Liqueur Muscat whose pale brown, yellow-edged colour is backed up by a rich, nutty, raisiny taste.
   ♀ Star buy: Morris Liqueur Muscat

MOUNT AITKEN   CV
Calder Highway, Gisborne, VIC 3437

w, r, ft, sp   *

Roger McLean makes table, fortified and sparkling wines here from 8 acres (3 ha) at Gisborne and 40 acres (16 ha) at Heathcote.

MOUNT ANAKIE   GL
130 Staughton Vale Road, Anakie, VIC 3221

w, r   *→

Mount Anakie, owned by Otto and Bronwyn Zambelli, was one of the first vineyards to be planted in Geelong in 1968. There are now 55 acres (22 ha) of vines, producing 4,000 cases a year of table wines including, unusually, Dolcetto. As the winery experiments with ageing wines in French, German and American oak, a restoration programme in the vineyard is increasing fruit yields and quality.

MOUNT AVOCA   PR
Moates Lane, Avoca, VIC 3467

w, r   *→

John and Arda Barry planted their vineyard in 1970, completing the winery in 1978. A range of table wines are made at this 50-acre (20-ha) property, entirely from its own grapes. Mount Avoca's Hermitage accounts for almost half of its 11,000-case output and the Trebbiano-based Pyrenees Dry White is its most popular white. Quality here has much improved of late, an 87 Sauv Blanc attracting wide applause.

MOUNT CHALAMBAR WINES GW
Tatyoon Road, Ararat, VIC 3377

w, sp *

Trevor Mast and his family make table wines here and an admired Chardonnay-based Brut Sauvage sparkler, fermented in bottle.

MOUNT DUNEED GL
Feehans Road, Mount Duneed, VIC 3216

w, r, sp *

Chief executive Ken Campbell and wine-maker Peter Caldwell make small amounts of table and sparkling wines from 8 acres (3 ha) of vines.

MOUNT IDA CV
147 High Street, Heathcote, VIC 3523

r *→

Jeff Clarke of **Tisdall**, the contract wine-maker here, makes well-thought-of Shiraz and Cab Sauvignon. Like other wineries in the region, Mount Ida's vines were badly damaged by the 1987 bushfires.

MOUNT LANGI GHIRAN GW
Warrak Road, Buangor, via Ararat, VIC 3377

w, r *→

Ian Menzies and Trevor Mast bought Langi Ghiran (aboriginal for "home of the Yellow-tailed Black Cockatoo") in 1988 from the Italian Fratin brothers. With it came 52 acres (21 ha) of vines and a reputation for some of the best Rhône-style Shiraz wines in Australia. Its Shiraz plantations, at 1,500 feet (450 m), are turned into 3,000 cases of the "black pepper-capsicum flavour wine characteristic of this vineyard". A further 3,000 cases are produced of Bordeaux-inspired red, made from Cab Sauvignon, Cab Franc and a touch of Merlot. Mount Langi buys in Pinot Noir fruit from Ballarat and Ararat to make another 500 cases of wine. The rest of its range comes entirely from home-grown fruit.

MOUNT MARY YV
Coldstream West Road, Lilydale, VIC 3140

w, r *→**

Dr John Middleton bought Mount Mary with his wife Marli in 1971. Mount Mary now has 20 acres (8 ha) of hillside vines in the Yarra not far from **St Huberts**. This small, quality-minded and somewhat idiosyncratic winery produces just 3,000 cases a year, mostly of Chardonnay and a Bordeaux-style Cabernet blend rounded off with Cab Franc, Merlot and Malbec; tiny amounts of a new Sauvignon (actually a Graves-style Sauvignon/Semillon/Muscadelle blend) and Pinot Noir are also made. Middleton's traditional approach has many fans: all his wines (which need bottle-ageing to show at their best) sell out within a fortnight of their release. With wines such as the splendid, full, herbaceous 82 Cabernet, the rich, chunky, blackcurrant 85 Mount Mary blend, the light, strawberry and liquorice-like 82 Pinot Noir and the vibrant, racy 82 Chardonnay, it is easy to see why.

MOUNT PRIOR NE
Howlong Road, Rutherglen, VIC 3685

w, r, ft *

This 125-acre (50-ha) estate used to produce a wide range of table and fortified wines, but has changed hands.

MURRAY VALLEY WINERY MR
Fifteenth Street, Mildura, VIC 3500

w, r, ft *

George Kalamistrakis is in charge of the Greek-influenced table and fortified wine production here.

MURRINDINDI VINEYARDS CV
Murrindindi, VIC 3717

w, r *

Hugh Cuthbertson is wine-maker at this small family-owned place producing small amounts of Chardonnay and Cab Sauvignon.

NICHOLSON RIVER WINERY
Liddell's Road, Nicholson, VIC 3882

EG

w, r ★

Ken and Juliet Eckersley's winery, founded in 1978, now has 10 acres (4 ha) of vines. Just 800 cases are made of "very distinctive individual styles", such as Riesling oak-aged *sur lie*. Bought-in grapes go into Montview, a second label.

OAKRIDGE ESTATE
Aitken Road, Seville, VIC 3139

YV

r ★←→

Founded in 1982, Oakridge is run by partners Jim and Irene Zitzlaff, whose Roseworthy-trained son Michael is wine-maker. With just 12 acres (5 ha) of vines producing some 3,000 cases annually, there are only two wines on offer – a straight Cabernet and a Cab Sauvignon/ Shiraz/Merlot blend, made using traditional Bordeaux methods and 50% of new oak each year. The 86 Oakridge Cab Sauvignon was full of powerful herbaceous, grassy, capsicum flavours. A new 8-acre (3-ha) plot should increase production shortly.

OSICKA'S VINEYARD
Major's Creek Vineyard, Graytown, VIC 3608

GV

w, r ★

Wine-maker Paul Osicka and his family manage 40 acres (16 ha) of vines, planted to Shiraz, Cab Sauvignon, Chardonnay and Rh Riesling. Wines vary from year to year but recent offerings have included Major's Creek Vineyard Cab Sauvignon and Hermitage.

PARISH WINES
Valencia-Briagolong Road, Briagolong, VIC 3860

EG

w, r ★

Gordon McIntosh, the wine-making partner at this 5-acre (2 ha) concern, makes just 400 cases of Pinot Noir and Chardonnay.

PASSING CLOUDS
Kurting Road, Kingower, VIC 3517

CV

w, r ★

This wonderfully named winery, so-called because of the infrequency of summer rain in this area, was founded in 1980. Its 15 acres (6 ha) of vines are run by Graeme Leith and Sue Mackinnon. Passing Clouds buys in half of its fruit, scraping by with 2,500 cases of only one Shiraz/ Cabernet blend most years. Occasionally a straight Cabernet is also produced. White wines here are made in conjunction with **Monichino** of the Goulburn Valley.

PFEIFFER
Distillery Road, Wahgunyah, VIC 3687

NE

w, r, sw, ft ★

Christopher and Robyn Pfeiffer manage 35 acres (14 ha) of Murray River/Sunday Creek flood plain vines and produce around 3,000 cases of wines. About a third of these are fortifieds such as port and Muscat. Also produced are a carbonic maceration Gamay wine and a late harvest Auslese Tokay.

PHILLIPS' GOULBURN VALLEY WINERY
52 Vaughan Street, Shepparton, VIC 3630

GV

w, r, ft ★

This small operation, managed by Don Phillips, has had its problems. Wine-maker Brendan Darvenizanow produces a short list of table and fortified wines here.

PRINCE ALBERT VINEYARD
Waurn Ponds, VIC 3221

GL

r ★

In 1975, the Hyett family re-established the original Prince Albert Vineyard (dating from 1857) here. Nearly 5 acres (2 ha) of vines are turned into just 750 cases of Pinot Noir.

READS   NE
Pound Road, Oxley, VIC 3678

                                                           w, r, ft   ★

Kenneth Read makes small amounts of table wines and a vintage port
here from King Valley grapes.

RED HILL ESTATE   MP
41 Red Hill, Red Hill South, VIC 3937

                                                              w, r   ★

With just four vintages released, Dr Roger Buckle and wine-maker Tom
Dexter of **Elgee Park** are already doing well. There are 6 acres (2.5 ha)
of Cab Sauvignon, Cab Franc, Merlot and Chardonnay here.

REDBANK   PR
Sunraysia Highway, Redbank, VIC 3478

                                                           w, r   ★→

Neill and Sally Robb founded this traditional winery north of Avoca in
1973. They have 40 acres (16 ha) of vines, mostly planted to Cab
Sauvignon, and also buy in local fruit to make their numerous other
wine-styles. The lion's share of Redbank's 3,000 cases is taken up by
Long Paddock, a concentrated Cab Sauvignon-based blend topped up
with Merlot: the 85 yielded a quirky, oaky, eucalyptus-like palate. Other
reds include Sally's Paddock, a blended wine whose 86 vintage had an
odd, hefty, oak-influenced taste, and Redbank, a straight Cabernet.
Redbank's heavily oak-influenced wines need lengthy ageing. The only
white is the Alexandra Kingsley Chardonnay. The Robbs are currently
developing a Pinot Noir style called Huw Hamilton.

ROBINVALE WINES   MR
Block 436, Sea Lake Road, Robinvale, VIC 3549

                                                        w, r, ft, sp   ★

Robinvale's George, Steven, William and Stavroula Caracatsanoudis
have owned 60 acres (24 ha) of vines here since 1976. A wide range of
varieties, including Touriga, are grown and a little Shiraz is bought in
locally. Among the 3,000 cases made are Greek-inspired table wines,
sparklers and fortifieds. Kosher wines and juice are also produced.

ROMANY RYE VINEYARDS   CV
Metcalfe Pool Road, Redesdale, VIC 3444

                                                           w, r, ft   ★

Rod Hourigan looks after the 18 acres (7 ha) of vineyards here,
producing table and fortified wines; most are sold at the cellar door.

ROMSEY VINEYARDS   MC
Glenfern Road, Romsey, VIC 3434

                                                        w, r, ft, sp   ★

Having founded this business in 1977, the Cope-Williams family used to
sell its wine range under the Cope-Williams label. Owner/wine-maker
Gordon Cope-Williams has 27 acres (11 ha) of cool, close-planted
vineyards (soon to double), from which he makes 3,500 cases. Romsey's
range includes Pinot Noir and Chardonnay, blended red and white
wines, *méthode champenoise* sparkling wines and a few fortifieds.
Gordon has sold fruit to **Domaine Chandon** in the past.

ST ANNE'S VINEYARD   GW
Western Highway, Myrniong, VIC 3341

                                                              w, r   ★

Wine-maker Alan McLean and family make 15,000 cases of red and
white table wines from 50 acres (20 ha) of vines.

ST HUBERTS WINES   YV
St Huberts Lane, Coldstream, VIC 3770

                                                        w, r, sw, sp   ★→

With an annual production of 15,000 cases, St Huberts is the largest
concern in the Yarra. Chief wine-maker Brian Fletcher, formerly with
Seppelt, makes 55 acres (22 ha) of Yarra fruit into a long list of varietal
table wines in two ranges: a humble blended wine selection and a

premium range. The winery also produces the Andrew Rowan range, made partly from local grapes and partly from Lyndoch fruit. The talents of its founders (now at **Lillydale** and **Diamond Valley**) ensured that St Huberts, founded in 1968, enjoyed commercial success from the start. Now run by Garry King, St Huberts and its somewhat makeshift winery are entering a new era. A further 10 acres (4 ha) have been planted, partly to Rousanne. Andrew Rowan's 87 Chardonnay, with its pleasant light, oaky, pineappley palate, is worth buying but ignore the coarse, burnt, inky 88 Pinot Noir and the curious, sweet, herbaceous 86 Cabernet. St Hubert's own 87 Pinot Noir has a dull, leafy-gamey palate, the 85 being sappier and more liquorice-like, and the richer, berry-fruit 84 Cabernet, though better, is still ordinary. Expect to see a Chardonnay and Pinot Noir-based sparkler from St Huberts shortly.

ST LEONARDS
St Leonards Road, Wahgunyah, VIC 3687

NE

w, r, sw, sp *

The first vines were planted here in 1860 by James Scott, who named the estate after his Scottish birthplace. By 1900, St Leonards had 100 acres (40 ha) under vine and was producing 200,000 litres of robust reds and fortifieds. Phylloxera, the depression and the war brought an end to St Leonards' prosperity and by 1960 it had ceased wine production altogether. Vineyards were replanted in 1972 on slopes overlooking an attractive lagoon. Now partly owned by **Brown Brothers**, the new operation here concentrates on premium red and white table wines, mostly for cellar-door sales. With a wide range of premium varietals such as Cab Sauvignon and Chardonnay, St Leonards is plainly a quality operation. About 10,000 cases are made each year, mostly under Chenin Blanc and Chardonnay labels, with 1,200 cases each of ripe alcoholic Shiraz and Cab Sauvignon wines. Watch out too for St Leonards' dry rosé and "Loire-style" *méthode champenoise* fizz.

SEPPELT GREAT WESTERN   See Seppelt (SA).

SEVILLE ESTATE
Linwood Road, Seville, VIC 3139

YV

w, r *

Peter McMahon, another former doctor, and his family have 10 acres (4 ha) of vines at the southern end of the Yarra Valley. From this they make 1,500 cases, mostly of Cab Sauvignon and Chardonnay, together with a little Pinot Noir, Shiraz and Riesling.

SEYMOUR VINEYARDS
1 Emily Street, Seymour, VIC 3660

GV

w, r, ft, sp *

This estate, run by chief executive/wine-maker Maurice Bourne, has 50 acres (20 ha) of vineyards at Seymour and Northwood. The wide range of table wine grapes grown are mostly sold to **Mitchelton** and the remainder made into table, fortified, flavoured and sparkling wines.

STANTON & KILLEEN
Murray Valley Highway, Rutherglen, VIC 3685

NE

w, r, ft *→

Founded in 1875, S & K is one of the few Rutherglen concerns that have remained under single-family ownership. Some 50 acres (20 ha) of fortified vines such as Muscat, Muscadelle, Durif and Touriga provide enough fruit to make 8,000 cases a year. Rich, smoky-raisiny Liqueur Muscat, Tokay, and vintage port are the three big sellers.

STONIER'S MERRICKS VINEYARD
52 Thompsons Lane, Merricks, VIC 3916

MP

w, r *

Publisher Brian Stonier runs this pretty vineyard in his spare time with wife Noel. Stonier Merricks, started in 1978, now has 16 acres (6 ha) of vines but no winery, so its 330 cases are made by the **Elgee Park** crew. The Stoniers rate Pinot Noir as their finest wine. The 83 Chardonnay was a fresh, light, pineappley mouthful.

SUMMERFIELD   PR
Main Road, Moonambel, VIC 3478

w, r   *
Ian Summerfield planted 10 acres (4 ha) of vines here as a hobby in
1970. Apart from 1,500 cases of Shiraz and Trebbiano he makes minute
quantities of Chardonnay and Cabernet.

TALTARNI   PR
Moonambel Road, Moonambel, VIC 3478

w, r, sp   *→**
This, the biggest, the best and the most famous of Pyrenees wineries,
has impeccable credentials and a spacious, well-equipped winery – yet
has somehow failed to produce the consistent winners that one might
expect. Taltarni (aboriginal for "red earth") was founded in 1972 by
American John Goelet, owner of Clos du Val in California. Apart from
an early wine-making phase under David Hohnen of **Cape Mentelle**
(WA), it has since been guided by the decidedly French approach of
Montpellier-trained Dominique Portet, whose father was once *régisseur*
at Château Lafite and whose brother Bernard runs Clos du Val.
Taltarni's 290-acre (120-ha) Moonambel plot, which supplies all its
grapes, has large plantings of Chardonnay, Sauv Blanc and Cab
Sauvignon together with a fruit salad of "insurance" varieties including
Merlot and Pinot Noir.

Production, now standing at 40,000 cases plus a year, is divided
equally between sparklers, whites and reds. A Cabernet/Malbec blend
is the bestselling red and Blanc des Pyrenees, an equal three-way blend
of Chardonnay, Sauvignon and Riesling, the most popular white.
Taltarni made a name for itself early on with its oak-aged Sauvignon (or
Fumé Blanc), which Dominic feels is his finest wine: the 84 had an
asparagus scent backed up by young, lively, lemony fruit. Some good
Taltarni Cabernets have also been made, such as the rich, gutsy, cassis-
like 78; the 78 Shiraz boasted a velvety, oaky flavour.

TAMINICK CELLARS   NE
Taminick via Glenrowan, VIC 3675

w, r, ft   *
Chris Booth produces table and fortified wines at this North-East
Victorian winery, most of which are sold at the cellar door.

TAMINICK VALLEY WINES   NE
Taminick Road, Glenrowan, VIC 3675

w, r   *
The Bakers, weekend wine-makers, run this new North-East Victorian
winery and produce small quantities of table wines.

TARCOOLA   GL
Maude Road, Lethbridge, VIC 3221

w, r   *
Wine-maker Alistair Scott grows a range of table grapes here including
the unusual Muller-Thurgau and Chasselas.

TARRAWARRA VINEYARDS   YV
Healesville Road, Yarra Glen, VIC 3775

w, r   **→***
Tarrawarra's modern, high-tech designer winery, set on a small hill
surrounded by landscaped grounds, is reached by a long drive lined
with poplars. The winery cost its owners, Marc and Eva Besen, millions
of dollars to build and equip. Getting a return for this heavy investment
could be difficult as they intend to keep annual production down to just
6,500 cases. The Besens have hired David Wollan, who trained a
Riverina College, as their wine-maker. There are just 18 acres (7 ha) o
hillside Tarrawarra vines, planted two-thirds to Chardonnay and one
third to Pinot Noir. So far only one, expensive, Chardonnay has been
released, causing a storm of publicity. The 86 was fermented in cask
given extended ageing on its lees or yeasty sediment and the end resul
offers full-flavoured yet soft, elegant, melon-like fruit spiked with
attractive spicy cinnamon oak: an impressive first attempt.

TISDALL   GV
Cornelia Creek Road, Echuca, VIC 3564

w, r   *→**

With 320 acres (130 ha) of vineyards, Tisdall is one of VIC's largest
vine-owning wineries. Dr Peter Tisdall and his wife Diana founded the
company in 1979. Since its first vintage in that year Tisdall has churned
out a stream of good wines, currently vinified by Roseworthy-trained
wine-maker Jeff Clarke at its Echuca winery, a former butter factory.
Aiming to produce a top-notch Chardonnay, Tisdall started to look for
a suitable vineyard site in 1974. By 1976 he had found it in the 1,500-
foot (450-m) high foothills of the cool Strathbogie Ranges in Central
Victoria. In addition to these 110 acres (45 ha) of Mount Helen
vineyards, Tisdall has 80 acres (32 ha) of vines at Rosbercon in the
Murray Valley. Wines from this vineyard are sold under the Tisdall,
Hopwood Estate and Peter Tisdall Signature labels. The 5% of Tisdall's
grape needs that are bought in from outside go into Chardonnay and
Shiraz/Cabernet blends. A fresh, apricot and lime-like 88 Chenin Blanc
is also made. Tisdall's finest products are the Mount Helen wines: these
include a sappy, over-oaked 86 Chardonnay and Peter Tisdall's own
favourite, the soft, oaky, blackcurranty 86 Cab Sauvignon/Merlot.
Tisdall's wines have suffered a recent drop in quality.

VIRGIN HILLS   MC
Salisbury Road, Lauriston West, VIC 3444

r=82 83   **→***

Macedon's most celebrated winery, founded in 1968, is owned by
Belgian Marcel Gilbert and its wines are made by Mark Sheppard.
Virgin Hills' plain gold-edged label appears on only one wine – a Cab
Sauvignon-based red topped up with Shiraz, Merlot and a dash of
Malbec. This wine is made from mature fruit grown in the 40 acres (16
ha) of hillside vineyards here, which were bush before the vines arrived.
Virgin Hills is a small traditional operation, with grapes picked by hand
and tiny yields due to poor soil. Hewn out of a hillside, the cramped
earth-floored cellar with its jumble of new and old barrels would look
more at home in, say, Burgundy than high-tech Australia. But no one
could complain about the quality of the wine: the 83 with its rich, full,
cassis-tannin palate and the big, minty 82 with loads of black and green
pepper spice were both first-class wines. The strong eucalyptus, cedary-
spicy, oaky 81 may have spent too long in barrel; like all Virgin Hills
offerings it needs considerable time in the cellar.

WALKERSHIRE WINES   GV
Rushworth Road, Bailieston, VIC 3608

r   *

Yorkshireman John Walker runs this winery and plans to appoint a
fellow wine-maker soon. Walkershire was founded in 1976, but its 50
acres (20 ha) of close-planted vines date from 1891. It also owns the
recently-formed Graytown Wine Company, aiming to produce mainly
white varietals under this label from Central Victorian vines. Walkershire
currently makes some 1,500 cases of a hefty Shiraz/Cabernet, using
only 10% of its own grapes and selling the rest. Walker believes that it
has the potential to produce 25,000 cases.

WANTRINA ESTATE   YV
Bushy Park Lane, Wantirna South, VIC 3152

w, r   *

Founded in 1963, Wantirna is close to, if not yet submerged by,
Melbourne's suburban sprawl and therefore not really in the Yarra. The
Egans, its owners, make just over 1,000 cases of Chardonnay, Pinot
Noir and a Cabernet/Merlot blend from their 10 acres (4 ha) of vines.

WARRAMATE VINEYARD   YV
4 Maddens Lane, Gruyere, VIC 3770

w, r   *

Jack and June Church make 500 cases of Rh Riesling, Cab Sauvignon
and Shiraz at this small winery on a fine 5-acre (2-ha) site sandwiched
between **Yarra Yering** and **Coldstream Hills**.

WARRENMANG   PR
Mountain Creek Road, Moonambel, VIC 3478

w, r *→

Italian restaurateur Luigi Bazzani, who has owned this winery since
1976, intends to turn the site into a restaurant-cum-conference centre.
With 20 acres (8 ha) of new Chardonnay planted and a Roseworthy-
trained wine-maker arriving, Warrenmang's wine-making activities are
being stepped up too. At present 3,500 cases are produced annually –
mostly of Grand Pyrenees, a red blend.

WATER WHEEL VINEYARDS   CV
Calder Highway, Bridgewater-on-Loddon, VIC 3516

w, r, ft *

At Water Wheel, owned by the Pratt family, wine-maker David von
Saldern turns nearly 30 acres (12 ha) of vines such as Hermitage, Rh
Riesling, Cab Sauvignon and Chardonnay into table and fortified wines.

WILD DUCK CREEK ESTATE   CV
Carboons Lane, Heathcote, VIC 3606

r *

The Andersons of Wild Duck Creek produce tiny quantities of a Shiraz-
based wine, made from bought-in grapes.

WYANGA PARK VINEYARDS   EG
Baades Road, Lakes Entrance, VIC 3909

w, r, sw *

Fronting onto the Gippsland lakes, Wyanga hopes soon to incorporate
a wine bar and bistro into its present operation. To produce the annual
2,800 cases of mixed table wines, wine-maker Andrew Smith has access
to 21 acres (8 ha) of vines; the rest of his grapes are bought in.

YARRA BURN   YV
Settlement Road, Yarra Junction, VIC 3797

w, r, sp *

David and Christine Fyffe run a winery with 24 acres (10 ha) of vines
and a handsome restaurant in the extreme east of the Yarra Valley.
Unlike most Yarra concerns, the Fyffes buy in half their grapes locally,
making about 10,000 cases a year. Apart from a Pinot Noir-based
sparkler, Yarra Burn produces Chardonnay, Cab Sauvignon and Pinot
Noir. The 88 Chardonnay was an oily, correct but unremarkable wine
and the 87 Cabernet a spritzy, rustic mouthful.

YARRA RIDGE   YV
Glenview Road, Yarra Glen, VIC 3755

w, r *

The Bialkowers planted the first vines here in 1982 and now have
almost 15 acres (6 ha). Louis Bialkower's early vintages have produced
Chardonnay, Pinot Noir and Cab Sauvignon wines.

YARRA YERING   YV
Briarty Road, Gruyere, VIC 3770

w, r=83 87 78 *→***

Dr Bailey Carrodus founded Yarra Yering in 1969, and his influence on
the development of the Yarra has been great ever since. His earliest
vintage released in 1973 was, along with **Yeringberg's**, the first wine to
be made in the region since 1921. Having bought the neighbouring
Underhill vineyard, whose Shiraz wines will be sold under that second
label, he now has 40 acres (16 ha) of vines on the gentle slopes above
his winery. Dr Carrodus, a research scientist, worked weekends only at
Yarra Yering until 1978, making the vintage during his annual leave. As
such, his winery is designed entirely as a one-man operation: all the
wines have been made in 35 small, square, stainless steel-lined mobile
fermenters, and Carrodus is as clean and methodical as one might
expect a research scientist to be. His life should be easier now that he
has acquired the services of a young Roseworthy-trained wine-maker,
but wines will continue to be made in small batches. About 80% of his
wine is now aged in new oak.

Yarra Yering produces about 3,000 cases of wine a year. These include Cabernet-based Dry Red No 1 blend (blended with Malbec and Merlot), Shiraz-based Dry Red No 2 blend (blended with Marsanne and Viognier), Pinot Noir, Chardonnay and Dry White No 1 Semillon/ Sauvignon blend. The No 1 Red is the winery's biggest seller, and the 78 with its perfumed bouquet and mature, cedary taste was a delight. The 86, with its spicy eucalyptus and berry-fruit mix, is a shade earthy and inky. This characteristic is also evident in No 2 Red blends, such as the robust, farmyardy 86. Carrodus' Pinot Noir is the winning wine. The splendid, savoury 83 offered lots of plum, tobacco, liquorice and rose flavours, while the latest 87 vintage is a soft light, plummy mouthful. An 87 wine made from young Pinot vines is a delicious, classic, young, plum and strawberry-like mouthful.

♀ Star buy: Yarra Yering 87 Young Vines Pinot Noir

YELLOWGLEN
White's Road, Smythesdale, VIC 3551

CV

sp *→

Yellowglen has had several different wine-makers at the helm since grapes were planted here by Ian Home in 1972. The first sparkling wines were made in 1977 and Dominique Landragin (now at **Landragin**) joined as wine-maker shortly after. Yellowglen is now owned by the **Mildara** group. There are 30 acres (12 ha) of vines surrounding the winery with its smart new cellar-door sales facilities for visitors. This acreage supplies just 5% of Yellowglen's needs; the rest comes in "from most of Australia's premium viticultural areas". A massive 130,000 cases of four different *méthode champenoise* sparklers are produced here annually by young Jeffrey Wilkinson the wine-maker; non-vintage Brut no doubt accounts for most of this. The Cuvée Victoria made from partly home-grown Chardonnay, Pinot Noir and Pinot Meunier is Yellowglen's finest offering, though its yeasty-lemony style will not be universally appreciated. This winery's latest offering is Sparkling Liqueur blended with brandy, fortified wines and "natural fruit flavours".

YERINGBERG
Yeringberg, Coldstream, VIC 3770

YV

r=86 80 81, w=87 *→→**

Yeringberg is one of the great Yarra names. Since its foundation in 1862, this historic 1,000-acre grazing estate has remained, remarkably, in the hands of the same de Pury family. The first de Pury came from Neuchâtel in Switzerland in 1851. In their heyday, the vineyards he planted here covered some 80 acres (32 ha). Today, sadly, there are just 5 acres (2 ha) of vines. It was not phylloxera that brought Yeringberg's golden age to an end but lack of sales. Even so, it was one of the last vineyards in the valley to cease production in 1921. The present vineyard was replanted in 1969 on precisely the same plot as the 1860s vines. At Yeringberg the atmosphere of a mid 19th-century Australian winery is still much in evidence. The capacious 1870 gravity-fed winery, complete with its own small railway for moving grapes, and the vast two-tiered 1860 wine cellar are both well worth a visit.

Guill de Pury has no formal wine training but his daughter Helen, now working in the Muscadet region of France, gained her oenological degree from Bordeaux and occasionally helps with the vintage here – as in 1987. The 87 Marsanne has a fresh, waxy scent and light, glacé-fruit flavours. Like the big, rich, plummy, liquorice 86 Pinot Noir and the rich, full, berry-fruit 86 Cabernet (rounded off with Malbec and Merlot), this is an attractive wine. The Cabernet label has now been changed to read simply Yeringberg. A less successful but still worthwhile wine was the ripe, oaky 87 Chardonnay. New Rousanne plantings will be blended in with Marsanne in the Rhône manner to make White Hermitage. Yeringberg produces just 800 cases a year.

ZUBER ESTATE
Northern Highway, Heathcote, VIC 3523

CV

r *

Albno Zuber is wine-maker at this Central Victorian concern. Small amounts of mostly Shiraz-based wines are made elsewhere.

Tasmania

Tasmania is, in the main, an island of apples and not grapes, but its embryonic wine industry has been growing apace as large new vineyards are planted. The first vines were planted close to Hobart in 1823, and the island produced wine earlier than Victoria or South Australia; indeed, it was Tasmanian cuttings that were used to start plantations in both of these mainland states during the 1830s. However, since its climate was totally unsuited to fortifieds and this was then the

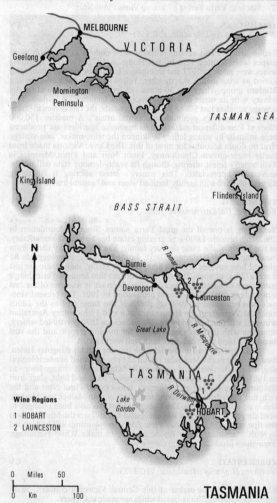

Wine Regions

1 HOBART
2 LAUNCESTON

0   Miles   50

0   Km   100

TASMANIA

fashionable tipple in Australia, Tasmania's vineyards disappeared at the end of the 19th century. However after Jean Miguet, a French engineer, planted vines here in 1959, the promising wines he made persuaded other grape-growers and wine-makers to follow suit.

Although Tasmania cannot compete in size with the other major Australian wine-producing states, it has one great asset – the coldest grape-growing climate in the country. The island's small hillside vineyards produce grapes with an almost European crispness and intensity that other regions find hard to match. This has not escaped outsiders such as Louis Roederer, the champagne house, which has set up a joint operation here with **Heemskerk**, choosing Tasmania in preference to the mainland's larger wine enterprises. Pinot Noir and Chardonnay have both been particularly successful, while good Cab Sauvignon, Rh Riesling and Traminer wines are also made. Mainland wine-makers have learned to value Tasmanian grapes, shipping them across the Bass Strait to Australia.

Wine-producing regions

HOBART (HB)
Situated in the south of the island, this is the older of the two wine-producing regions. The vineyards here, dotted around Hobart on both sides of the wide River Derwent, benefit from a considerably cooler climate than Launceston in the north. Bream Creek, on the east coast to the north of Hobart, now also has a few acres under vine.

LAUNCESTON (LN)
Launceston's vineyards, like Hobart's, are scattered on both sides of the river dissecting the region, in this case the River Tamar. Most of the westerly vineyards lie on the banks of the Tamar; the easterly ones are some distance away at Piper's Brook. The low incidence of frost and reliable rainfall are this region's greatest assets.

Tasmanian wineries

BUCHANAN WINES
Exeter, TAS 7275

LN

w, r *

Buchanan was founded in 1984 by Roseworthy-trained Donald and Judith Buchanan, with Karl Jonsson. They make over 1,000 cases of five premium table wines from almost 30 acres (12 ha) of vines at Loira and Glengarry. They rate Chardonnay and Pinot Noir as their finest wines.

DELAMERE
Bridport Road, Piper's Brook, TAS 7254

LN

w, r *

The Richardson family runs Delamere's 10 acres (4 ha) of vines, leaving the wine-making to Dr Pirie of **Piper's Brook**, whose winery lies just south of this property. Delamere's close-spaced, sloping vineyard is planted mostly to Pinot Noir.

D'ENTRECASTEAUX
Gardener's Bay, TAS 7112

HB

w, r *

This 8-acre (3-ha) estate, situated in an "as yet undiscovered corner of southern Tasmania", was founded in 1985 by Bruce and Jane Gilham, wine-maker and oenologist respectively. Their first vintage was in 1989.

ELSEWHERE VINEYARD
Glazier's Bay, TAS 7112

HB

w, r *

Founded in 1985, Elsewhere is the most southerly winery in the country. Eric and Jette Phillips own 20 acres (8 ha) of vineyards here, planted mainly to Pinot Noir with smaller amounts of Cab Sauvignon and Rh Riesling. The 1988 vintage will be sold by mail order.

FREYCINET   HB
Tasman Highway, Bicheno, TAS 7215

w, r *

Geoff and Suzanna Bull's vines include Chardonnay and Cab Sauvignon. Most of their wines are sold at the cellar door.

HEEMSKERK   LN
Piper's Brook, TAS 7254

w, r *→**

Heemskerk, the island's largest estate, was founded a year after its neighbour and most important TAS rival, **Piper's Brook**. Graham Wiltshire, its owner/wine-maker, planted experimental vines as early as 1966, but Heemskerk did not begin life until 1975. Today there are 75 acres (30 ha) of vines here, more than half of these grown for a joint *méthode champenoise* venture with Louis Roederer, the great champagne house. Current annual production stands at 8,000 cases of Pinot Noir, Chardonnay and Cab Sauvignon, with the first sparkling wines due for release in 1990. Plans include a second 125-acre (50-ha) joint-venture vineyard in the West Tamar area which should boost sparkling wine production considerably.

MARION'S VINEYARD   LN
Foreshore Road, Deviot, TAS 7251

w, r *

Situated on the banks of Launceston's Tamar River at – according to owners Mark and Marion Semmens – "the loveliest vineyard location in Australia", this winery has 17 acres (7 ha) of vines. Just over 1,000 cases of wines are made each year, mostly of Cab Sauvignon and Pinot Noir. A dry Muller-Thurgau white wine is Marion's Vineyard's newest and most popular wine.

MEADOWBANK   HB
Glenora, TAS 7140

w, r *

Founded in 1986 by Gerald Ellis and James Cartledge, Meadowbank is further inland than most TAS wineries. It's 15 acres (6 ha) of vines at Glenora are vinified by Dr Pirie of **Piper's Brook**. Just 200 cases each of Rh Riesling and Cabernet are produced.

MOORILLA ESTATE   HB
655 Main Road, Berriedale, TAS 7011

w, r *→

Moorilla Estate, situated on the banks of the Derwent River and now almost engulfed by the suburbs of Hobart, has been operating since 1958. Moorilla's cloth label, a legacy of its owners' textile background, is one of the most distinctive in Australia. Equally artistic are its unusual fermenters, decorated in the style of Mondrian, Vasarely and Matisse. Claudio Alcorso and his son Julian have 25 acres (10 ha) of vines here and a further 12 acres (5 ha) at Bream Creek on the east coast. Unlike other TAS estates which are happy to grow a variety of vines, Moorilla is now concentrating on Pinot Noir and may well phase out its other vines. This is a pity because it has made some wonderfully rich, velvety, fruit-packed Cabernets.

PIPER'S BROOK   LN
Piper's Brook, TAS 7254

w, r *→**

Dr Andrew Pirie, Piper's Brook's talented and knowledgeable wine-maker, makes his own 5,000 cases of wines and runs a large contract wine-making business. Before planting his vines in 1974, Pirie searched throughout TAS for the right soil and climate, finally choosing this site north-east of Launceston. With 30 acres (12 ha) of vines, Piper's Brook is nowhere near as big as **Heemskerk**. The close-spaced vineyard here produces about 1,200 cases of Riesling and 1,000 of Chardonnay annually, with smaller quantities of a Cabernet blend, Pinot Noir and Traminer; these sell out within a few weeks of their release. Piper's latest project is a 35-acre (14-ha) Chardonnay and Pinot Noir sister vineyard whose wines will be sold under the Pellion label. Pirie's professed aim is "to make wines in the European tradition without compromise on quality". Judging from his elegant (and elegantly labelled), fresh, fruity-buttery 87 Chardonnay, with its steely cool-climate palate, he is succeeding.

POWERCOURT LN
Legana, TAS 7277

r *

Ralph and Roslyn Power own and run Powercourt. With just 5 acres (2 ha) of vines, production is limited to minute quantities of Pinot Noir and Cab Sauvignon sold at the cellar door.

ROTHERHYTHE VINEYARD LN
9 Frederick Street, Launceston, TAS 7250

w, r *

Steve Hyde and family have 13 acres (5 ha) of vines, mostly at Gravelly Beach overlooking the River Tamar. Just 600 cases of Cabernet and 100 cases of Pinot Noir are produced each year. New plantings are expected to come on stream in 1990.

ST MATTHIAS VINEYARD LN
Rosevears Drive, West Tamar, TAS 7250

w, r *

Laurie and Adelle Wing have 20 acres (8 ha) of vines on the banks of the River Tamar. St Matthias is named after the church on the opposite bank, dating from 1835, which also explains its "chapel" tasting room where a wide range of TAS wines can be tasted. The Wings' 2,500 cases of wines, divided between Riesling, Chardonnay, Pinot Noir and a Cab Sauvignon/Merlot blend, are made for them by **Heemskerk**.

ST PATRICK'S WINES LN
Hills Road, Piper's Brook, TAS 7254

w, r *

Leigh Gawith, whose son is a graduate of Roseworthy and whose daughter is assistant wine-maker at **Heemskerk**, founded this place in 1983. The Gawiths have 18 acres (7 ha) of vines here which, from 1990 on, will be vinified at their own winery. Pinot Noir and Semillon are St Patrick's big sellers, with Cabernet close behind. The estate's 1,000 cases of wines are sold under three different brand names: Wattley Creek, Vignette and Montage.

STONEY VINEYARDS HB
Campania, TAS 7202

w, r *

Situated north of Hobart, Stoney's first vines were planted in 1973. Plantings include Rh Riesling and Pinot Noir.

South Australia

South Australia's first vines were planted close to Adelaide in 1837. Today the state produces two-thirds of Australia's wines. Most of this production is taken up by the Riverland region's flood of dreary low-quality flagons and casks, but the remainder represents some of the most magnificent white, red and sparkling wines made in Australia. South Australia's Coonawarra region is the acknowledged home of many of the country's finest reds, while the cooler climate of the Adelaide Hills has produced some first-class Chardonnay and sparkling wines. Clare, situated to the north of the Barossa Valley, also makes some fine Rhine Riesling.

In the past, the big boys of the Riverland have tended to dominate the smaller boutique winery producers. But there are signs now that the small fry are fighting back by joining together to form small wine-makers' groups. Wine-making in South Australia is slowly becoming a more balanced industry. The wineries that appear to have a shaky future are the medium-sized concerns with lists that include pricy boutique offerings as well as cheap cask wines. Because of the low cost of growing grapes there, the Riverland will continue to be Australia's prime cheap flask and cask source. Meanwhile, producers aiming at better-quality fruit – whether they be young wineries such as **Grand Cru** or large Barossa-based firms such as **Yalumba** – will continue to develop higher sites in the Adelaide Hills and the Barossa Ranges.

Wine-producing regions

ADELAIDE HILLS (AH)
The Adelaide Hills are a series of lush green hills starting to the south-east of the city near Mount Lofty, continuing via the Mount Lofty Ranges through the centres of Lenswood, Springton and Eden Valley, and finishing close to Moculta. The altitude, which ranges from some 2,380 feet (726 m) at Mount Lofty down to around 1,250 feet (380 m), is the key to the region's superiority over its neighbours. This factor, together with high rainfall, ensures that the Adelaide Hills forms one of the coolest Australian wine regions, along with TAS and the Yarra Valley (VIC). Other quality factors here include stressed hillside vines.

ADELAIDE PLAINS (AP)
Anyone who has driven from Adelaide to the Barossa Valley will have travelled through parts of the Adelaide Plains where old vineyards have been engulfed by the city's suburban sprawl. All that remains of the fertile plains, apart from **Penfolds'** Magill plot, lies to the north of the city – stretching as far north as the **Roseworthy** vineyards, bounded by the ocean to the west and the Barossa and Adelaide Hills to the east. Also known as the Adelaide Area, the region suffers badly from the heat. Vines have to be irrigated to survive, though cool nights and mid-afternoon sea breezes help a little.

BAROSSA VALLEY (BV)
The Barossa, situated less than an hour's drive north-east of Adelaide, is a valley about 8 miles (13 km) wide by 20 miles (32 km) long. It is rimmed by rolling hills dotted with small Lutheran churches, and the influence of early German settlers from Silesia is still much in evidence. Indeed it is still possible to hear "Barossadeutsch" spoken here. At around 1,970 feet (600 m), the higher-altitude vineyards in the eastern Barossa Ranges produce the region's finest wines; those grown on the hotter valley floor – at around 820 feet (250 m) – are nowhere near as good. There is considerable variation in the Barossa's soils, ranging from light gravel on the hills to the richer red loams of the valley floor. Rhine Riesling is the most important white grape variety, Shiraz and Grenache the most widely planted red varieties.

CLARE (CL)

The long, narrow Clare Valley lies some 62 miles (100 km) north of Adelaide. This attractive region's green valleys, streams and gum trees are protected by the Mount Lofty Ranges on one side and partly by the Camel's Hump Range on the other. The soil is reddish-brown loam over limestone and the climate on the hot side of warm – hotter than North-East Victoria though not as bad as Mudgee or the Hunter (NSW). The region's altitude, ranging from 1,110 feet (340 m) to 1,310 feet (400 m), helps to extend the ripening period. Even so, it is a mystery why Rhine Riesling, Clare's most important variety, does so well here.

COONAWARRA (CW)

Coonawarra (aboriginal for honeysuckle) is Australia's finest red wine region and, indeed, one of the finest in the world. Its curious flat, cigar-shaped strip of superb terra rossa covering deep porous limestone, only 7 miles (12 km) by 1 mile (2 km), has been dubbed Australia's answer to the Médoc. Coonawarra's attributes were recognized as early as the 1890s when vines were first planted here, but by the 1960s economic gloom had reduced the region's vineyards to just 250 acres (100 ha). Now all its central 5,000 acres (2,000 ha) of terra rossa are planted. The region's other great attribute is its climate. Situated some 236 miles (380 km) south-east of Adelaide, Coonawarra is not as cool as the Adelaide Hills, but benefits from its proximity to the sea. Frosts are common and rainfall average. As a result of its ultra-fertile soil and high water table, Coonawarra's greatest problem is too much vine vigour.

Distinctive regional wine-styles

CLARE RHINE RIESLING

Rhine Riesling is recognized as the most suitable variety for Clare, and grows well throughout the valley. Its full style is frequently spicier than other Australian Rieslings and its lime-like flavours are often more delicate too. Be wary of accepting "Clare Riesling" instead of Clare Rhine Riesling; the former is produced from the lowly Crouchen grape and not in the same league.

COONAWARRA CABERNET SAUVIGNON

Coonawarra Cabernet, often rounded off with a little Merlot and Cabernet Franc, is as close as Australia is likely to get to Claret. Its chief characteristics are a rich, cedary-truffley scent and a firm, tannic and herbaceous, yet still fruity, palate – often reminiscent of green pepper, eucalyptus or mint. The Bordelais are right to be concerned: Australia will be their next challenger.

COONAWARRA CHARDONNAY

This style may lack the class of wines produced in cooler regions but if you appreciate fine, melon-like fruit mellowing into rich, buttery, oak-influenced styles – at keen prices – then Coonawarra Chardonnay is the wine-style for you.

COONAWARRA SHIRAZ

Often grafted here onto more fashionable varieties like Merlot, unloved Shiraz makes some fine, peppery-spicy wines whose luscious black fruits-like palate rarely takes on the leathery qualities of the Hunter (NSW) and elsewhere.

LANGHORNE CREEK (LC)

Langhorne Creek, 47 miles (75 km) south-east of Adelaide, comprises around 1,500 acres (600 ha) of vines planted around the River Bremer which flows into Lake Alexandrina. Winter floods necessitate a complicated system of ditches, banks and floodgates to prevent water from washing away the vineyards, but the rich alluvial silt provides vines here with a rich diet.

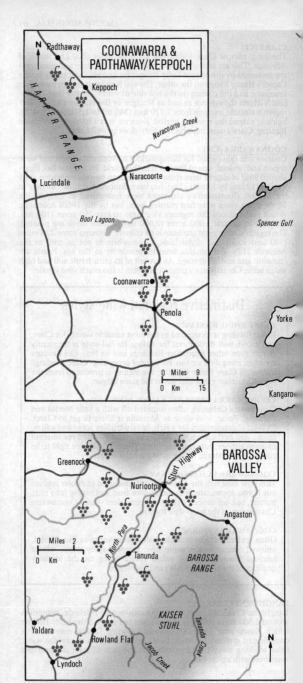

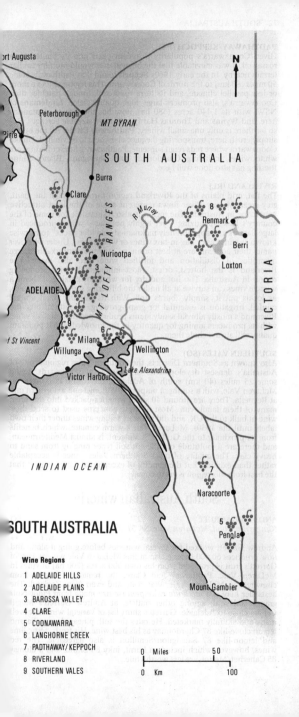

N

ort Augusta

Peterborough

Pirie

MT BYRAN

SOUTH AUSTRALIA

Burra

Clare

BURRA RANGES

4

R Murray

Renmark

8

Berri

Loxton

Nuriootpa

2

3

MT LOFTY RANGES

ADELAIDE

8

VICTORIA

f St Vincent

Milang

6

Willunga

Wellington

Lake Alexandrina

Victor Harbour

INDIAN OCEAN

7

Naracoorte

5

SOUTH AUSTRALIA

Penola

Wine Regions

1 ADELAIDE HILLS
2 ADELAIDE PLAINS
3 BAROSSA VALLEY
4 CLARE
5 COONAWARRA
6 LANGHORNE CREEK
7 PADTHAWAY/KEPPOCH
8 RIVERLAND
9 SOUTHERN VALES

Mount Gambier

0   Miles   50

0   Km   100

PADTHAWAY/KEPPOCH (PA)
Given Coonawarra's popularity in recent years and its limited terra rossa soil, it was inevitable that the big wineries would hunt for similar terrain nearby. In the early 1960s **Seppelt** found it at Padthaway, some 50 miles (80 km) to the north of Coonawarra. This region enjoys a more or less parallel climate, and its terra rossa soil, though patchier than Coonawarra's, also produces large, high-quality yields. **Lindemans** of NSW, with its 1,440 acres (580 ha), now has the largest plantations here, and **Wynns** and **Thomas Hardy** also have sizeable acreages. But so far there is only one small winery: **Padthaway Estate**. All the others simply crush here, transporting the juice elsewhere to be vinified. Unlike Coonawarra where reds reign supreme, Padthaway's finest offerings are white wines including Chardonnay and Sauvignon Blanc. Rhine Riesling has also done well here.

RIVERLAND (RL)
The flat, arid plains of the Riverland region through which the giant, grey-green Murray River flows represent some of the least attractive winescape in Australia. The region is also responsible for some of the country's least appetizing – yet highly popular – wines, produced in large flagons and appropriately nicknamed "bladder packs" (otherwise known as wine casks, bag-in-box wines or wine boxes). Under whatever name, their contents are at best ordinary, at worst undrinkable. Large quantities of distillation and fortified wines are also made. The Riverland is the hottest, driest, most inhospitable wine-producing region in Australia. Too hot and dry for wheat or grazing, it seems a miracle vines can survive at all under the blistering sun; everything else, as locals put it, simply "burns up". With its pitifully small annual rainfall, irrigation is essential for grape-growing. In spite of this, the Riverland's mostly alluvial sandy loams produce over half of SA's wine, with its producers aiming for quantity in the knowledge that premium quality will always elude them.

SOUTHERN VALES (SO)
Also known as Southern Districts, the Southern Vales region is one of Australia's densest developments of wineries and vineyards. Lying some 25 miles (40 km) south of Adelaide, the region is centred on McLaren Vale, with a southern outpost at Willunga and a northern one at Reynella. There are around 40 small wineries packed into this area, many of them family-run. Most of these concerns used to send their wine in bulk to the UK, and did not start selling wines under their own labels until the 1950s. McLaren Vale's warm climate, which benefits from its proximity to the Gulf of St Vincent, is almost Mediterranean, and there are a multitude of different soil types ranging from sand to heavy clay. The quality of most Southern Vales wines is acceptable rather than exciting, but the handful of exceptional wines suggest that the best from this region is yet to come.

South Australian wineries

ANDREW GARRETT   SO
Kangarilla Road, McLaren Vale, SA 5171

w, r ★→★★

Andrew Garrett worked for several wineries before going it alone and now produces 60,000 cases a year at this McLaren Vale winery. Part of Garrett's fruit is produced from his own 500 acres (200 ha) of vines in McLaren Vale, Padthaway and Clare; the remainder comes from elsewhere in McLaren Vale, Watervale and even New Zealand. The bestseller here is a *méthode champenoise* fizz made from Pinot Noir grapes and sold, among other outlets, at Andrew Garrett's Magill Cellars close to Adelaide. Garrett's short list of varietal wines are well made and skilfully marketed. He rates the soft, pineapple, vanilla and lemon clove-like 87 Chardonnay as his best wine. His fresh, zesty, lime and lemon-like 87 Sauvignon/Semillon is also agreeable. The red wines, however, which include a burnt, inky 85 Shiraz and a clumsy 85 Cabernet/Merlot, are less worthwhile.

ANGLESEY   AP
Heaslip Road, Angle Vale, SA 5117

w, r   *

Founded in 1969, this 45-acre (18 ha) estate is situated just south of
the Gawler River. Anglesey's specialities – inexpensive, easy-to-drink
blends – are made for John Minnett and his co-owners by consultant
Lindsay Stanley. Among the red wines are a straight Cab Sauvignon
and Anglesey QVS, a popular Cabernet/Shiraz/Malbec blend, which is
given 18 months ageing in small oak casks. Other red blends include
Cabernet/Malbec, Shiraz/Cabernet and Cabernet/Merlot. White wines
include a blended QVS, a "Chablis-style" Semillon/Chenin blend and
Anglesey's straight varietal versions of Chardonnay, Semillon, Chenin
Blanc and Sauv Blanc.

ANGOVE'S   RL
Bookmark Avenue, Renmark, SA 5341

w, r, ft   *→

Angove's was set up in 1886 by Dr William Angove, who came to
Australia to practise medicine. He started making wine for his patients
until eventually it absorbed all his time. His descendants still own the
business. Angove's, with its 1,200 acres (490 ha) of vines close to
Renmark, is one of the better Riverland producers. Around two-thirds
of its wine is made from its own vines; most bought-in grapes are turned
into bulk wines or its popular St Agnes brandy. Angove's even makes
Stone's Ginger Wine under licence from the UK company, as well as its
own Marko vermouth. Cheaper blended wines are sold under the
Paddle Wheel and new Misty Vineyards labels. Opt instead for the
varietal range, which is well regarded by Australian judges. Its finest
offerings include Sauvignon, Chardonnay, Cab Sauvignon and a new
Pinot Noir. French Colombard is the bestseller here. Visitors are
welcome Mon-Fri, 8.30am-5pm.

ASHBOURNE WINES   AH
Lenswood, Ashbourne, SA 5157

w, r   *→**

Knowledgeable Geoff Weaver, head of white wine production at
Thomas Hardy, is one of many moonlighting SA wine-makers who, in
addition to their daytime duties at a large winery, find time to run their
own place. Founded in 1980, Ashbourne has 20 acres (8 ha) of young
Riesling, Chardonnay, Cabernet and Merlot vines at Lenswood, not far
from Mount Lofty. More plantings are envisaged if sales continue at
their present rate. Both quality and quantity have been improving with
each vintage and Weaver is optimistic about the future. Current annual
production stands at some 2,000 cases, made using the facilities at
Petaluma. Weaver, like Petaluma's Brian Croser, does all he can to
manipulate fruit flavour in the vineyard and to preserve this, right
through to the final wine, with careful protective cold-handling. Sadly
for foreigners, Ashbourne wines are obtainable only in Australia.

BAROSSA SETTLERS   BV
Trial Hill Road, Lyndoch, SA 5351

w, r, ft   *

Howard and Joan Haese, fourth-generation Barossa settlers, founded
this winery in 1983. From their 65 acres (26 ha) they make 1,500 cases
of single varietal wines and a tawny port.

BAROSSA VALLEY ESTATES   BV
Heaslip Road, Angle Vale, SA 5117

w, r, sp   *→**

Although based in the Adelaide Plains, most of this producer's wines
are made from Barossa fruit. **Berri-Renmano** owns the business,
producing two different ranges here: the up-market Lauriston selection,
made from grapes grown all over SA and beyond, and the Barossa
Valley Estates (BVE) wines. So far, Lauriston has released 5,000 cases
of Sauvignon, Chardonnay, *méthode champenoise* fizz and blended
red – all well received in Australia. The comprehensive BVE collection
of red and white table wines has done much to popularize the quality of

Australian wines abroad. Try the delicious fresh, zingy, flowery, lime-like 87 Riesling, the zesty, peachy 88 Semillon/Chenin Blanc or the soft, peppery 86 Shiraz/Cabernet. They are well-made wines and they are great value for money.

🍷 Star buy: All Barossa Valley Estates wines

BASEDOWS **BV**
161-165 Murray Street, Tanunda, SA 5352
w, r, ft ★→★★

Founded in 1896, Basedows has no vines of its own. Wine-maker Douglas Lehmann, son of **Peter Lehmann**, makes almost 40,000 cases of wine out of fruit bought in from the Barossa and elsewhere in SA. The wood-aged Semillon (sold as White Burgundy in Australia), with its fine, fresh, citric and apricot-like fruit, is Basedows' best wine; the pleasant, leafy, peppery 85 Cab Sauvignon should not be ignored either, but the 85 Shiraz, with its sweet, peppery taste, is less worthwhile.

BERESFORD WINES **SO**
22 Reynell Road, Reynella, SA 5161
w, r ★→

Robert and Bronwyn Dundon's 10,000 cases consist of four easy-to-drink wines made entirely from bought-in McLaren Vale, Padthaway and Coonawarra fruit. Beresford Chardonnay is oak-fermented and the Pinot Noir undergoes part carbonic maceration. Robert, formerly with **Thomas Hardy**, is consultant wine-maker to 14 other SA concerns.

BERNKASTEL **BV**
Langmeil Road, Tanunda, SA 5352
w, r, ft, sp ★

The Fassinas make a traditional range of Barossa table, fortified and sparkling wines at this winery.

BERRI-RENMANO **RL**
Berri, SA 5343
w, r, ft ★

Quantity, not quality, is the Berri-Renmano watchword. Anyone visiting these two Brobdingnagian-sized "juicing factories" in the Riverland, with their acres of tank "farms" and gigantic fermenters capable of handling the 65,000 tonnes of grapes bought in every season, will see that wine production can be a grim, depressing business. Having said that, and given the Riverland's climate, the quality of some of their 55 million bottles is surprisingly good. Renmano, established close to Renmark in 1916 as a brandy distillery, was Australia's first co-operative. By 1970, it had switched most of its production from fortified wines to table wines. Berri, established in 1922, had a later start but by the late 1950s it was clear that the company would dominate the Riverland wine scene. Berri and Renmano joined forces in 1982 as Consolidated Co-operative Wineries, growing bigger still in 1984 with the acquisition of **Barossa Valley Estates**. Combined output now accounts for over 15% of Australia's annual wine production.

Berri-Renmano own only 20 acres (8 ha) of vines; the rest of their fruit is supplied by their many grape-growing shareholders or members. A wide selection of unexciting wine casks (ranging from 2 to 15 litres) are produced which, together with bulk wines, constitute most of the output. Ignore the fortifieds, carbonated Passionwine and other Berri offerings, and choose wines instead from the carefully crafted Renmano Chairman's Selection – such as the buttery-sappy 87 Chardonnay, the lime juice-like 86 Rh Riesling or the luscious, peachy, aniseed-like 85 Traminer. The 85 Berri Estates Cabernet/Shiraz's sturdy, spicy cassis and black pepper mix, although a touch jammy, is also a good buy.

BETHANY WINES **BV**
Bethany Road, Tanunda, SA 5352
w, r, ft ★

Six generations of the Schrapel family have grown grapes here. In the past, most Bethany grapes were sold to **Kaiser Stuhl**, but when it was taken over in 1977 the Schrapels started to make their own wines.

About 5,000 cases are made each year from the 60-acre (24-ha) vineyards – mostly of single varietal wines, but white port and Old Quarry Tawny Port are also produced.

BLEASDALE LC
Wellington Road, Langhorne Creek, SA 5255

w, r, sw, ft, sp *→**

Bleasdale's heritage is proudly proclaimed on every label: "Frank Potts first arrived in 1836 on board HMS Buffalo from Portsmouth. He was the founder of Bleasdale and one of Australia's pioneers". It was 14 years before Frank could afford this naturally-flooded estate, and another decade before he planted a vineyard. Today fifth-generation Michael Potts is the wine-maker. His 100 acres (40 ha) of vines consist of table and fortified wine grapes. Fortifieds such as Palomino and Verdielho (sic), together with ports and sherries, account for some 20% of Bleasdale's 30,000-case annual production. Sparkling wines, such as Spumante Moscato, are also produced. Bleasdale feels that its 16-year-old blend Verdielho is its finest wine. This wine's smoky-raisiny style and orangey-brown colour turning yellow at the edges indicates large quantities of old wines in the blend.

BONNEYVIEW WINES RL
Sturt Highway, Barmera, SA 5345

w, r, ft *

Wine-maker Robert Minns produces just over 3,000 cases from 6 acres (2.5 ha) of vines next to the winery, not including his 2-litre flagons of port and Muscat. Home fruit supplies Bonneyview with half its needs; the rest comes from elsewhere in the Riverland. Apart from its Chardonnay, Bonneyview's whites and reds are all blends; the newest wine is a Cabernet/Petit Verdot mix. The big seller here remains the sweet Frontignac Blanc. All wines are sold at the cellar door.

BOWEN ESTATE CW
Naracoorte Road, Penola, SA 5277

w, r *→

Tucked away at the southern end of the Coonawarra strip is this small family-owned winery, run by Roseworthy-trained Douglas and Joy Bowen. The 60 acres (24 ha) of prime Coonawarra vineyards provide all their fruit, but it is debatable whether the estate is making the most of its soil. Currently only half its vines are producing; the other half, mostly reds, should come on stream over the next three years. There are at present four Bowen wines: Rh Riesling, Chardonnay, Shiraz and a Cab Sauvignon blend rounded off with 10% Merlot. A fifth grape variety, Cab Franc, will eventually be blended in with the Cabernet/Merlot. The Bowens consider the Cab Sauvignon to be their best wine, though others prefer the Shiraz.

BRANDS LAIRA CW
Naracoorte Road, Coonawarra, SA 5263

w, r *→**

Captain Stentiford, a retired sea captain, planted the first vines here in the 1890s, calling the place "Laira" after a favourite ship. Situated in the centre of the terra rossa strip, Brands' quality is good, rather than great. Try the pale garnet-red 84 Cabernet/Merlot blend with its delicate tea-leaf scent, light tobacco spice and somewhat sinewy fruit on the palate. Shiraz, Malbec, Cab Franc, Chardonnay and Rh Riesling varieties are also grown here.

BREMER LC
Wellington Road, Langhorne Creek, SA 5255

w, r, sw, ft *

Wine-maker William Davidson produces a wide range of table and fortified wines from Bremer's 12 acres (5 ha) of Shiraz, Cab Sauvignon and Rh Riesling vines. A restaurant at the winery is open to visitors most days for lunch.

BRIDGEWATER MILL See **Petaluma**.

CAMBRAI   SO
Hamilton's Road, McLaren Flat, SA 5171

w, r, sp, ft ★

Graham Stevens is in charge of this 21-acre (8-ha) estate. As well as the
more usual grape varieties, Cambrai's vines include varieties rare in this
region – such as Muller-Thurgau, Sylvaner, Gewurztraminer and
Zinfandel. Sparkling and fortified wines are also made.

CARRINGTON   See **Orlando**.

CHALK HILL   SO
Brewery Hill Road, McLaren Vale, SA 5171

w, r, ft ★

Nancy Benko started this place in 1973. Together with her architect
husband who designed the cellar, she produces a range of table and
fortified wines from 50 acres (20 ha) of vines at Chalk Hill and 27 acres
(11 ha) at McLaren Flat.

CHAPEL HILL WINERY   SO
Chapel Hill Road, McLaren Vale, SA 5171

w, r, ft ★

This winery, owned by the Gerard family, takes its name from the
converted 1865 Methodist chapel which houses its tasting room and
port storage. The wine-maker, Bevan Wilson, has acquired the services
of wine consultant Pamela Dunsford, no doubt partly to help with
future sparkling wine production. For this project, 35 more acres
(14 ha) are being planted and a new stone winery and underground
cellars built. At present, however, there are just 15 acres (6 ha) of vines
here, supplying two-thirds of Chapel Hill's needs; the rest is bought in.
Annual production is 5,000 cases – mostly Cab Sauvignon, followed by
Shiraz and Grenache-based tawny port.

CHARLES MELTON   BV
Krondorf Road, Tanunda, SA 5352

w, r, sp ★

Graeme Melton is the wine-maker at this new Barossa estate, which
produces small amounts of table and sparkling wines.

CHATEAU DELROSA   RL
Loveday, SA 5345

w, r, sw, ft, sp ★

This 74-acre (30-ha) Riverland property makes a wide range of table,
fortified, flavoured and sparkling wines, mostly sold at the cellar door.

CHATEAU DORRIEN   BV
Sturt Highway, Dorrien, SA 5352

w, r, ft ★

Fernando Martin has turned this century-old winery into a tourist
attraction, with shops made from converted fermentation tanks and
other such gimmicks. A full range of table and fortified wines are made,
on sale only at the cellar door.

CHATEAU YALDARA   BV
Gomersal Road, Lyndoch, SA 5351

w, r, sw ★

Visitors can take conducted tours around this fancy German stone
"château" owned by the Thumm family and admire its paintings and
other *objets d'art*. They can also see films on wine-making and visit the
winery. Greater emphasis is now being placed on the wines themselves.

CHATTERTON'S WINE CELLARS   BV
Barritt Road, Lyndoch, SA 5351

w, r, ft ★

These small cellars in the Barossa, run by the Chatterton family, make
table wines and port for sale at the cellar door.

COOLAWIN   See **Norman's**.

CORIOLE SO
Chaffey's Road, McLaren Vale, SA 5171

w, r *→**

Coriole's first vines were planted in 1918 and the even older house and barn here, dating from 1860, are still used for tastings. Stephen Hall and Mark Lloyd make about 11,000 cases of wine, 90% produced from Coriole's 50 acres (20 ha) of vines. Most of this output consists of straight varietals but they also produce a 50/50 Cabernet/Shiraz and, unusually, a Sangiovese wine. The first Chardonnay was made in 1988. Try the light, appley-flowery 88 Chenin Blanc. Coriole's bestseller, the peppery scented 86 Shiraz, is less impressive.

COUNTY HAMLEY RL
Bookmark Avenue, Renmark, SA 5341

w, r, ft *

County Hamley in the Riverland produces a small range of red and white table wines and fortifieds.

CRANEFORD AH
Williamstown Road, Springton, SA 5235

w, r *→

Colin and Jenny Forbes are joint chief executives here, with Colin responsible for wine-making. Craneford was founded in 1978 and now has 15 acres (6 ha) of fine Chardonnay, Rh Riesling, Cab Sauvignon, Merlot and Cab Franc vines just north of Springton. These supply half the fruit needed to make 3,000 cases; the rest is bought locally.

CURRENCY CREEK SO
Winery Road, Currency Creek, SA 5214

w, r, sw, ft, sp *→

Once known as the Santa Rosa Winery and now owned by Wally, Rosemary and Phillip Tonkin, Currency Creek is situated some way to the south of the main Southern Vales region. Its 42 acres (17 ha) produce about 9,000 cases of straight varietal wines, made by outside wine-makers. The fresh, flowery, elegant 88 Semillon is its chief wine; the grassy 88 Sauvignon is not so impressive. A Shiraz-based port is also produced, as well as Muscats, vermouths and sparkling wines.

D'ARENBERG SO
Osborn Road, McLaren Vale, SA 5171

w, r, sw, ft *

Roseworthy-trained Chester and Francis d'Arenberg Osborn own this winery situated in the Seaview Hills. D'Arenberg has 150 acres (60 ha) of vines and produces 42,000 cases a year. About two-thirds of its grapes are bought in locally. Apart from an inexpensive single varietal range, it makes blended wines such as the bestselling Dry Red and Dry White, several botrytised styles, ports and Muscats.

DENNIS DARINGA CELLARS SO
Kangarilla Road, McLaren Vale, SA 5171

w, r *

Peter Dennis, founder and wine-maker here, recently began marketing his wines under the "Dennis of McLaren Vale" label. With 33 acres (13 ha) of vines, he has enough grapes to make 7,500 cases of wines.

DONOLGA SO
Main South Road, Aldinga, SA 5173

w, r, ft, sp *

The Girolamo family originally made wine here as a hobby, but now produces table, sparkling and fortified wines commercially.

DUNCAN ESTATE CL
Spring Gully Road, Clare, SA 5453

w, r *

The family-owned Duncan Estate, a few miles to the south of Clare, has 20 acres (8 ha) of vines at its winery, together with three dams to alleviate water stress in the summer. Like most Clare producers, the

Duncans use only their own fruit, keeping enough to make 1,000 cases of wine and selling the rest locally. But unlike other Clare wine folk, who tend to specialize, they produce a wide, cheap range including Riesling and Traminer in both dry and late-picked styles, besides straight Shiraz and Cabernet. In addition they make Shiraz/Merlot and Shiraz/Cab Sauvignon blends.

DYSON WINES   SO
Sherriff Road, Maslin Beach, SA 5170

w, r, sp   *

Allan Dyson's 15 acres (6 ha) of vines, planted in 1977, are situated about as far west in the Southern Vales as you can go, just inland from the beach. His 2,000 cases are all single varietal wines, apart from a *méthode champenoise* fizz made from Pinot Noir and Chardonnay. Dyson rates his Cab Sauvignon as his best wine.

EDEN SPRINGS WINE ESTATE   AH
Boehm Springs Road, Springton, SA 5253

w, r   *

This new, idyllic-sounding estate in the Adelaide Hills has something of a commercial bent. Popular red and white table wines such as Chablis, White Burgundy, Rh Riesling, Eden Ridge Claret and a Shiraz/Cabernet blend are made here by Lindsay Stanley, a well-known wine-maker from the Barossa Valley.

ELDERTON WINES   BV
3 Tanunda Road, Nuriootpa, SA 5355

w, r, sp   *

The Ashmeads, owners of Elderton, make a small range of white, red and sparkling wines, including a Nouveau style.

FAREHAM ESTATE   CL
Main North Road, Watervale, SA 5452

w, r, sp   *

Fareham's 20 acres (8 ha) lie at the southern end of Clare, close to Watervale. Wine-maker Peter Rumball shares his duties with Debbie Saegenschnitter and Stephen Elliott, his partner. Founded in 1976, Fareham is still little known but its new champagne cellar and *méthode champenoise* fizz should earn it a higher profile. Some 25,000 cases of sparkling wine are made, mostly from bought-in fruit. Fareham Brut (a Pinot Noir, Chardonnay, Riesling, Sauv Blanc and Ondenc wine) is the big seller; also made are Shiraz-based sparkling Burgundy and 85 Cuvée Deluxe (50/50 Pinot Noir/Chardonnay). Table wine production appears to have ceased.

GENDERS MCLAREN PARK VINEYARD   SO
Recreation Road, McLaren Vale, SA 5171

w, r, ft   *

Keith Genders and family founded this winery in 1969. Just 2,500 cases of Shiraz and Cab Sauvignon are made, partly from their neighbour's grapes. Wines are not released until five years old or "mature". Vintage port is also produced and a Chardonnay is on its way.

GEOFF MERRILL   SO
Pimpala Road, Reynella, SA 5161

w=84 86, r=80 82 86   *→******

Blessed with handlebar moustaches that Hercule Poirot would have died for, Geoff Merrill has bags of personality. He is also a highly talented wine-maker. Merrill was once chief wine-maker at **Thomas Hardy** and started this place as a side venture in 1983. Set on top of Mount Hurtle, a small hill overlooking 4 acres (1.5 ha) of vines and a dammed pond, the pretty winery now takes up all his time. Merrill stylishly rebuilt the original winery which dated from 1897, adding a long jarrah-wood tasting bar and a restaurant. He hopes to plant another 50 acres (20 ha) here in 1990 which, when bearing, will supply about 80% of his grapes. Until then, he will continue to buy fruit from McLaren Vale, Coonawarra and the Barossa.

Half of Merrill's 12,000-case output is divided equally between the Geoff Merrill Cabernet and Chardonnay. The remainder is taken up by his Mount Hurtle label, consisting mainly of a Cabernet, with large quantities of Sauv Blanc and a little Grenache also made. The Mount Hurtle wines are made entirely from McLaren Vale fruit, but sources for the Geoff Merrill duo vary. The delicious, perfumed, oaky 86 McLaren Vale Chardonnay has some 19% Barossa Chardonnay in the mix, while the aromatic, truffley, rose-scented and cassis-palated 86 Cabernet is a blend of Coonawarra Cab Sauvignon lightened with McLaren Vale Cab Franc. The rich velvety, yet restrained blackcurrant fruit of the 85, roughly the same blend, is as good but needs time to develop. By comparison, Merrill's Mount Hurtle 86 Cabernet is a grassy, vibrant, redcurrant and raspberry-like mouthful and his 88 Sauvignon is also fresh and grassy. Merrill achieves his aim – "a more restrained European style, full on the middle palate but with elegance too".
♀ Star buy: Geoff Merrill label wines

GNADENFREI ESTATE — BV
Seppeltsfield Road, Marananga, SA 5360

w, r, ft ∗

Close to **Seppelt**, this estate is run by Malcolm Seppelt who broke away from the family firm when it was taken over. Table wines, sparkling wines and ports are made here from 25 acres (10 ha) of vines.

GORDON GRANT — See **Ryecroft**.

GORDON SUNTER — AP
(No permanent address)

w, r, ft ∗

This well-thought-of label is made from Adelaide Plains fruit by wine-maker Stuart Blackwell. So far 1,000 cases have been made at various SA wineries. Cab Sauvignon is the best of a small range that includes port.

GRAND CRU — AH
Ross Dewells Road, Springton, SA 5235

w, r ∗

This boldly-titled winery is owned and run by Karl Seppelt, who courageously left a rather more sedentary Managing Director's seat at **Seppelt**, his family firm, when it was taken over. Situated just south of Springton, Grand Cru now has 20 acres (8 ha) of mostly Chardonnay and Cab Sauvignon vines which supply half its fruit. Rh Riesling and Hermitage (Shiraz) grapes are bought in from the Eden Valley. All this is made into 4,000 cases of varietal wines including a *méthode champenoise* Chardonnay. Started in 1981, Grand Cru's first vintage was in 1985. To tide him over, Seppelt buys finished wines from other wineries. The 85 Chardonnay was made for him by **Petaluma**.

GRANT BURGE — BV
Barossa Way, Jacob Creek, Barossa Valley, SA 5352

w, r, ft ∗

Grant Burge, astute marketing man and wine-maker, runs this small show-piece winery with its vineyard network of 350 acres (140 ha). He intends to sell almost 10,000 cases of Burge's Best, a short list of single varietals such as the rich, spritzy, vanilla-like, wood-matured 88 Semillon and the gutsy, lemon clove-like 88 Chardonnay. Other products will include more traditional Barossa fare such as tawny port, Liqueur Frontignac and a Merlot blend topped up with Cab Sauvignon and Cab Franc. Until the winery is ready, these will be made at **Basedows** and at **Ryecroft**, Burge's other SA interest.

GRAZIANA — RL
1 Scott Road, Berri, SA 5343

w, r, ft ∗

Established in 1975 by the Graziana family, this small Riverland winery produces table and fortified wines.

HEGGIES VINEYARD — See **Yalumba**.

HENSCHKE   AH
Moculta Road, Keyneton, SA 5353

w=87, r=87 82, sw   **∗∗→∗∗∗∗

Situated well to the east of the Barossa Valley in the southern Mount
Lofty Ranges, award-winning Henschke's climate has less in common
with the Barossa's heat than the relative chill of the Adelaide Hills. At
around 1,300 feet (400 m), it is significantly higher than the Barossa,
most of which is about 850 feet (260 m). The Henschke family, like
many others in this area, came originally from Silesia. Johann Christian
Henschke planted vines here in the early 1860s and today the family
business continues in its fifth generation under Stephen Henschke and
his viticulturist wife Prue. Henschke's 200 acres (80 ha) of vineyards,
which supply 80% of its grapes, are scattered throughout the Adelaide
Hills. These include newly-acquired Lenswood in the Eden Valley and
two ancient Shiraz plots – Hill of Grace at Moculta, which has century-
old vines, and Mount Edelstone at Keyneton, with 70-year-old vines.
The Henschkes also own vines in the Barossa Valley. A third of their
annual 35,000 cases are Rh Riesling and almost a further third Shiraz.
The other wines consist of various whites and 2,000 cases of Cyril
Henschke Cab Sauvignon.

Reds are still made in the traditional manner here with open
fermenters and a submerged cap, but the whites owe all to modern
technology. Henschke's reputation is borne out by wines such as the
light, lemony-gold, buttery-oaky 87 Eden Valley Chardonnay or the
steely 87 Eden Valley Rh Riesling with its flowery scent and fresh, zesty,
lime-like palate. The 85 Merlot/Cabernet, a luscious, ripe, cedary-
blackcurranty 60/40 blend from Keyneton, is finer still. Stephen rightly
regards the Hill of Grace Shiraz as his finest wine; the stunning 85 is an
intense, blackberry, loganberry and cassis-packed mouthful. Half a
notch down in quality, but still a four-star wine, is the soft velvety,
cedary-leathery 85 Mount Edelstone.
  ♀   Star buy: Henschke Hill of Grace & Mount Edelstone Shiraz

HERITAGE WINES   BV
Seppeltsfield Road, Marananga, SA 5352

w, r   *

Heritage, founded in 1984, is run by wine-maker Stephen Hoff. Some
2,500 cases of table wines are made from bought-in Clare and Barossa
grapes. The latest venture is a Clare Valley Cab Franc.

HIGH WYCOMBE WINES   BV
Bethany Road, Bethany, SA 5352

w, r, ft   *

High Wycombe's Angela and Colin Davis have 30 acres (12 ha) of vines,
from which they make table and fortified wines.

HILL-SMITH ESTATE   See **Yalumba**.

HOFFMAN'S NORTH PARA WINES   BV
Para Road, Tanunda, SA 5352

w, r, ft, sp   *

Table, fortified and sparkling wines are made at this Barossa winery
from a variety of grapes.

HOLLICK   CW
Racecourse Road, Coonawarra, SA 5263

w, r   *→

Ian and Wendy Hollick founded this winery in 1982. Ian, who worked
at **Mildara's** Coonawarra estate, was joined as wine-maker early in
1989 by Pat Tocaciu, formerly with **Penfolds**. Hollick's 65 acres (26 ha)
of vines surrounding the winery provide all the fruit for its 11,000-case
production. Cab Sauvignon, which accounts for most of this, is blended
with Merlot (15%) and Cab Franc (5%) *à la Bordeaux*. The other
Hollick wines – including Shiraz, Pinot Noir, Chardonnay and Rh
Riesling – are varietal wines. New developments at Hollick include
macerating part of the Pinot Noir to make a lighter, more vibrant wine
and treating Shiraz as a separate varietal. Hollick's Chardonnay is

barrel-fermented and the management trio think it their best-value wine. The 88 with its spicy scent and light, fresh, lemony palate was not, however, especially exciting. Nor was the light, young, somewhat jammy 86 Cabernet/Merlot which they rate as their finest. Australian judges are keener, for Hollick's Cabernet has won the prestigious Jimmy Watson Trophy. Visitors can taste here daily in the attractive timber-slab cottage, 9am-5pm.

HOLMES SPRINGTON   AH
Main Street, Springton, SA 5235

w, r, ft, sp *

This winery and adjoining restaurant is run by Leon and Leonie Holmes. They make a wide range of table, sparkling and fortified wines from 37 acres (15 ha) of Rh Riesling, Cab Sauvignon, Shiraz and Pinot Noir. Among these are a Sherlock Holmes Port and a Dr Watson Claret, produced for the Sherlock Holmes Appreciation Society of Australia.

HUGO   SO
Elliott Road, McLaren Flat, SA 5171

w, r, ft *

The Hugo family owns 65 acres (26 ha) of McLaren Flat vines and aims to produce 10,000 cases a year. As well as tawny port, four single varietal table wines are made, including a full-bodied Shiraz.

INGOLDBY   SO
Ingoldby Road, McLaren Flat, SA 5171

w, r, sw, ft *

Walter and Kerry Clappis own Ingoldby's 50 acres (20 ha) and are about to plant 70 acres (28 ha) more. They occasionally buy in grapes from elsewhere in McLaren Vale to make up their 11,000 cases of mostly single varietal wines. Their biggest seller and finest offering is Cab Sauvignon; the 88 is an ordinary peachy-palated wine.

JAMES HASELGROVE   CW
Naracoorte Road, Coonawarra, SA 5263

w, r, sw, ft, sp *

James Haselgrove's 40 acres (16 ha) of vines are situated in Coonawarra and McLaren Vale. Having no winery, his Coonawarra Rh Riesling, Shiraz, Chardonnay, Gewurztraminer, Malbec and Cab Sauvignon grapes are sent to **Mildara** (VIC) to be vinified, while the Rh Riesling and Shiraz from McLaren Vale are sent to **Thomas Hardy**. These two sources provide Haselgrove with just over 8,000 cases of 14 different and unusual wines which he markets himself. The range includes Coonawarra Nouveau, an admired botrytis-affected and wood-aged Rh Riesling sold under the Julianne Classic label, ports, *méthode champenoise* sparkling wines and *auslese* Rieslings.

JEFFREY GROSSET   CL
King Street, Auburn, SA 5451

w, r *→**

This most southerly of Clare wineries was founded by Catherine and Jeffrey Grosset in 1981. They now have 12 acres (5 ha) of vines at Mount Horrocks, the highest point in Clare. But as the vineyard is not yet in production their Riesling, Chardonnay and Cab Sauvignon (blended with a dash of Cab Franc) wines are made from bought-in Clare grapes. The quality-minded Grossets sell more of the light, pineapple and lemon clove-like 87 Chardonnay than their other wines, which include the 88 Polish River Riesling with its peachy, spicy, raisiny palate and the elegant, grassy-minty 86 Cabernet. To make ends meet, they act as consultants and contract wine-makers.

JIM BARRY WINES   CL
Main North Road, Clare, SA 5453

w, r, ft *→

After nursing 44 Clare vintages into life, Jim Barry is now a famous wine-maker in the region. Graduating from Roseworthy in 1947, he spent much of his career working for others before setting up his own winery in 1968 at the northern end of the Clare Valley. He is ably assisted by his three sons and three daughters; Mark, the eldest son, is the wine-maker. With 260 acres (100 ha) of vines and annual production standing at 25,000 cases of well-made wines, Barry's is one of the larger Clare concerns. White wines consist of dry and late harvest Rieslings, Sauv Blanc and Chardonnnay, reds of Cab Sauvignon, a 60/40 Cabernet/Merlot blend and a new Shiraz-based wine, the Armagh. It was the quality of the 20-year-old Shiraz vines in Barry's flat, sunny Armagh vineyard that persuaded him to produce a special wine, described as "black essence of Shiraz"; priced at $30 it ought indeed to be special. The winery buys in 5% of its needs from elsewhere in Clare, most of this no doubt going into the popular Watervale Riesling. It also produces the wonderfully-named Sentimental Bloke vintage port.

JUD'S HILL
Farrell Flat Road, Clare, SA 5343

CL

w, r   *

Jud's Hill wines feature the name of "chief wine-maker" Brian Barry in large letters on the label, together with details of his impressive wine-judging career. In spite of that he does not make his own wines, sending his grapes instead to **Wirra Wirra**. The business was founded in 1977 and Barry now has 61 acres (24 ha) at Jud's Hill, the vast majority Rh Riesling vines. In addition to 5,000 cases of this wine he makes 1,000 cases of Cab Sauvignon and 2,000 of a 80/20 Cab Sauvignon/Merlot blend. Barry rates the Jud's Hill Rh Riesling as his best. Watch out for a Merlot/Cab Franc blend soon, and eventually perhaps a Chardonnay.

KAISER STUHL
Sturt Highway, Nuriootpa, SA 5355

BV

w, r, ft, sp   *→→**

One of the great old Barossa Valley names, the giant Kaiser Stuhl ("emperor's throne") winery, named after a local hill, now belongs to **Penfolds**. Lutheran traditions have remained strong here since its foundation in the 1930s: the gothic script on its labels and indeed, to some extent, the style of its wines reflect this. Certainly the vast Teutonic Kaiser Stuhl Chateau, built in 1972 on the outskirts of Nuriootpa, would look entirely at home in Germany. Kaiser Stuhl's long rows of tanks are capable of handling an awesome 30,000 tonnes of grapes from some 1,500 acres (600 ha) of vines. In spite of this quantity, the quality of much of its output is worthwhile. There is a full range of table, fortified and sparkling wines, the latter sold under both the dull Kaiser Stuhl and the sweet, cloying, carbonated Summer Wine labels. Ignore shameless Teutonic imitations such as the Black Forest crock and bin bottles, and dive straight into the 85 Red Ribbon Shiraz, with its splendid scented, spicy, cinnamon-like style or the pleasant fresh, citric Green Ribbon Riesling.

KARLSBERG WINES
Gomersal Road, Lyndoch, SA 5351

BV

w, r   *

Karlsberg, not to be confused with the beer, was founded in 1972 by the Cimicky family. A range of varietal table wines are made here.

KATNOOK ESTATE
Penola Road, Coonawarra, SA 5263

CW

w, r   **→→***

With 860 acres (350 ha) of vines at the southern end of Coonawarra and plans for a further 340 acres (136 ha), Katnook is the second-largest landowner in the region after **Wynns**. Varieties grown here include Cabernet, Shiraz, Pinot Noir and Merlot for the reds, with Chardonnay, Sauv Blanc and Riesling for the whites. These are turned into some 12,000 cases annually by Wayne Stehbens and David Thompson, though outside wine-making help has always been employed as well. An impressive collection of single varietal wines are vinified in the old winery, part of which was a sheep-shearing shed built in 1867 by John Riddoch, Coonawarra's wine pioneer. In addition, Katnook sells grapes, juice and wine to wineries desperate for a touch of Coonawarra class in their blends. Katnook's first wines were released in 1980. It now produces two ranges: the superior Katnook Estate selection and the well-thought-of Riddoch Estate range. Since the beginning, the star of the Katnook selection has been the Sauv Blanc, whose tremendous punch of zingy flowering currant and gooseberry fruit makes it easily as good as European equivalents. Not quite in the same league, but very good nonetheless, was the 85 Katnook Coonawarra Estate Cabernet with its peppery scent and gutsy, herbaceous palate. The Riddoch Estate Cabernet/Shiraz won the Jimmy Watson Trophy in 1987.

KAY BROTHERS' AMERY VINEYARDS   SO
Kays Road, McLaren Vale, SA 5171

w, r, sw, ft ★

Hubert and Frederick Kay bought this 320-acre (130-ha) estate in 1890, when it had just 5 acres (2 ha) under vine. They soon expanded the vineyard and built a winery, but it was not until 1970 that the Kay family started to bottle under its own label. Today, third-generation Colin Kay, trained at Roseworthy, makes a long list of inexpensive table and fortified wines from 17 acres (7 ha) of vines, buying in two-thirds of his needs from neighbours. Kay's Block 6 Shiraz is made from vines planted in 1892. The family rates its Liqueur Muscat highest.

KELLERMEISTER WINES   BV
Barossa Highway, Lyndoch, SA 5351

w, r, ft, sp ★

Kellermeister is a traditional Barossa concern with a vast range of table, fortified and sparkling wines on sale mostly at the cellar door.

KIES ESTATE   BV
Hoffnungsthal Road, Lyndoch, SA 5351

w, r, ft, sp ★

This Barossa property was once known as the Redgum Vineyard. Now owned by the Kies family, its 150 acres (60 ha) of vines are turned into numerous single varietal table wines, sparklers and fortifieds by winemaker Nigel Logos.

KILLAWARRA   See Seaview.

KINGSTON ESTATE WINES   RL
Sturt Highway, Kingston on Murray, SA 5331

w, r, sw ★

Bill Moularadellis and family run the 30 acres (12 ha) of fruit that go into Kingston Estate Wines, founded in 1979. Their own Gordo, Doradillo, Mataro and other grapes contribute just 10% of Kingston's 16,000 cases; the rest comes from other local estates. Moularadellis regards Cab Sauvignon and Colombard as his finest wines.

KRONDORF   BV
Krondorf Road, Tanunda, SA 5352

w, r ★→★★

Krondorf, situated some way off the Sturt Highway in the Barossa Hills, was originally established as Falkenberg in the 1860s by a Silesian immigrant of that name. The name changed in the early 1970s, but it was not until 1978, when **Grant Burge** and Ian Wilson bought this run-down winery, that Krondorf began to shine. Backed by the pair's clever wine-making and marketing skills, Krondorf leapt into the limelight – not just in Australia but also in the UK. The business is now owned by **Mildara** (VIC), but the approach remains the same. Krondorf buys fruit from all over SA to supplement its 60 acres (24 ha) of Barossa fruit at Lyndoch. Its 150,000-case output is 80% white to 20% red and, unlike its competitors, includes only two styles – a basic range and a superior Show Reserve level. Although best known for its Chardonnays, such as the rich, perfumed, buttery-oaky 87 Show Reserve and the light, soft, lemony 88 Limited Edition Chardonnay, Krondorf is also proud of its ultra-popular 88 Chablis whose sweet, peachy palate has wide appeal. Reds include the truffley, farmyardy 84 Cab Sauvignon and the far superior toasty, raspberry and myrtille-like 85 Cab Franc.

LADBROKE GROVE   CW
Millicent Road, Penola, SA 5277

                                                                  w, r   *

Peter McDonald, owner of this small winery, makes Cab Sauvignon,
Hermitage (Shiraz) and other wines, sold mostly at the cellar door.

LAURISTON   See **Barossa Valley Estates**.

LECONFIELD   See **Richard Hamilton**.

LEO BURING   BV
Chateau Leonay, Para Road, Tanunda, SA 5352

                                                               w, r   *→**

Hermann Paul Leopold Buring was born in Australia in 1876. After
training at Roseworthy and Geisenheim, he worked first as a wine-
maker and then as a Sydney wine merchant. His selections went down
so well in Australia and abroad that in 1945 he was able to build his
own winery and plant vineyards. Just north of Tanunda in the Barossa
he redesigned an original 1897 winery in what he imagined to be the
"style of a Flemish château". The Buring business did well. Today it is
part of the **Lindemans** group and has an 89-acre (36-ha) vineyard –
planted to Rh Riesling, Cab Sauvignon and Chardonnay – surrounding
the Tanunda winery and Hunter River (NSW) vines too. Grapes are
also bought in from elsewhere in SA.

Like other wineries in the Lindemans group, Buring is coy about
revealing output, but it processes 10,000 tonnes at Tanunda and makes
five ranges of wines: drinkable but uninspiring 3-litre wine casks;
beverage table wines such as the bestselling 88 Liebfrauwine, which
vies with **Houghton's** (WA) White Burgundy as the most popular white
bottled wine in Australia; ordinary vintage varietal wines, the best bet
being the rich, juicy, bramble-like 86 Shiraz; worthwhile bin wines,
including the 87 Coonawarra Rh Riesling DWQ19 with its intense,
aromatic, spicy-flowery palate and the rich, robust, cassis-fruit 85
Coonawarra/Barossa Cab Sauvignon Bin DR488; and finally aged
Reserve Bin or Museum wines, such as the 73 Watervale Rh Riesling
DWC14, with its deep buttercup-gold colour and butterscotch palate.

MAGLIERI WINES   SO
Douglas Gully Road, McLaren Flat, SA 5171

                                                          w, r, sw, ft, sp   *

Founded in 1972 by Steve Maglieri, this 53-acre (21 ha) estate now
employs John Loxton as wine-maker. Maglieri's acreage yields a quarter
of its total fruit needs; the rest is bought in. Its popular range includes
Lambrusco, Hock Lime & Lemon, Muscats, ports and coolers.

MANNING PARK   SO
Chalk Hill Road, McLaren Vale, SA 5171

                                                                w, r, ft   *

This new operation in McLaren Vale produces a range of red and white
table wines and fortifieds.

MARIENBERG   SO
Black Road, Coromandel Valley, SA 5051

                                                                  w, r   *

Ursula Pridham, one of Australia's pioneering female wine-makers, was
born into an Austrian wine family and married Geoff Pridham when
she emigrated to Australia. Together they bought Marienberg in 1966,
producing their first wines in 1968. In addition to their Coromandel
vines, they own a 40-acre (16-ha) vineyard close to McLaren Vale.
Ursula believes that her Austrian origins are reflected in her short list of
table wines and admits to enjoying "a touch of sweetness".

MASTER BLENDERS   RL
(No permanent address)

                                                                     sp   *

This is the new face of Steve and Monique Lubiana's old Lubiana label.
Just 500 cases of Baronet, a *méthode champenoise* fizz, are produced.

MAXWELL   **SO**
24 Kangarilla Road, McLaren Vale, SA 5171

w, r, sw, ft   *

Mark Maxwell makes the wines at this family concern in the heart of McLaren Vale. About 40% of Maxwell's 4,000-case production comes from its 21 acres (8 ha) of vines; the rest is bought-in. In addition to a short list of cheap varietal wines, Maxwell makes tawny port and Adelaide Nouveau, and is the largest Australian producer of mead.

MERRIVALE   See **Rovalley**.

MINTARO CELLARS   **CL**
Leasingham Road, Mintaro, SA 5415

w, r   *

This most westerly of Clare wineries, situated in historic Mintaro, is also one of the newest. James Pearson, its Roseworthy-trained wine-maker, produces Rh Riesling and Cab Sauvignon.

MITCHELL CELLARS   **CL**
Sevenhill, via Clare, SA 5453

w, r   *→**

Established in 1975, this winery is owned by Andrew and Jane Mitchell. Andrew is the wine-maker, though Jane has also studied wine-making. Together they turn 65 acres (26 ha) of their fine Clare fruit into 12,000 cases of well-made wines. Half of this consists of Watervale Rh Riesling, a further quarter of their Peppertree Vineyard Shiraz. Also made are Wood-Aged Semillon and a Cab Sauvignon, the latter mixed with smidgens of Cab Franc and Merlot. The 88 Watervale Riesling has an appealing spicy, youthful, pear-drop character, the 84 being rather more sherbetty and Muscat-like. Mitchell's 87 Peppertree Shiraz, though not in the same league, offered a big, rich, peppery scent and taste.

MOCULTA WINE COMPANY   **AH**
Truro Road, Moculta, SA 5353

w, r, ft   *

At this small, remote winery John Doughty produces a range of table wines under the Attunga Hill label and ports under the Parrot Hill label.

MOUNT HORROCKS   **CL**
Mintaro Road, Watervale, SA 5452

w, r   *→**

Named after John Horrocks, Clare's first white settler, Mount Horrocks was founded in 1981 by Trevor, Lyall and Rodger Ackland. **Jeffrey Grosset** makes their wines for them from 105 acres (42 ha) of vines, producing 1,000 cases each of Rh Riesling, Wood-Aged Semillon, Chardonnay and Cabernet/Merlot. The herbaceous 87 Watervale Wood-Aged Semillon and the luscious, minty, blackcurrant pastille-like 86 Watervale Cabernet/Merlot are both good buys.

MOUNTADAM   **AH**
High Eden Ridge, Eden Valley, SA 5253

w, r, sw, sp   *→**

Talented, bullish Adam Wynn's unglamorous but well-equipped winery was set up in 1972 with help from his father David, with whom he planted SA's first Chardonnay vines here. Adam's departure from the family firm (**Wynns**) was something of a break with tradition, as was his decision to take a wine course at Bordeaux (in preference to Roseworthy), where he graduated top of his class. Mountadam's 70 acres (28 ha) of vines are all sited around the winery at an altitude of about 1,970 feet (600 m). More than two-thirds are planted to Chardonnay but small quantities of Pinot Noir and Riesling are grown too, with just a little Cab Sauvignon. Some 10,000 cases of wine, including late harvest Riesling, are made from Mountadam fruit. Grapes are also bought in from elsewhere in the Eden Valley to produce 5,000 cases of David Wynn second label Chardonnay, Shiraz and Riesling. **Roseworthy** made the 79-83 vintages, but all wines from 1984 on have been Adam Wynn's work. He describes his wine-making techniques as "basically ancient French but applied in a modern and clean context". Filtration and other treatments are kept to a minimum, with wines given a year in French Tronçais barrels before bottling. Adam's latest baby is a Chardonnay/Pinot Noir fizz. Try the 87 Chardonnay, with its smoky-herbaceous scent and firm, oaky-fruity palate.

NOON'S WINERY   SO
Rifle Range Road, McLaren Vale, SA 5171

w, r, sw   *

Situated in the south of the Southern Vales region, this winery is run by David and Nerida Noon. David turns its 6 acres (2.5 ha) of Grenache grapes together with some outside fruit into about 2,000 cases of wines a year, including Shiraz/Cabernet and Traditional Red, all of which are sold at the cellar door.

NORMAN'S   AH
Grants Gully Road, Clarendon, SA 5157

w, r, sp, ft   *→→*

This family-owned firm in the southern Adelaide Hills overlooking McLaren Vale was founded by Jesse Norman in 1851. There are now 150 acres (60 ha) of vines, the best of which is the Chardonnay plot adjacent to the Clarendon winery. Norman's other vineyards are in the Adelaide Plains. To achieve its annual 150,000-case production, Norman's also uses grapes from McLaren Vale, some of which go into its Coolawin wines. Chief wine-maker Brian Light makes an extensive range of table wines, sparkling wines and ports. According to Light, the buff-coloured Chais Clarendon labels form "the pinnacle of our production". Recent innovations include the arrival of Norman's New Shiraz, a light red once sold as "Beaujolais". Norman's plans to step up production over the next three years and break into the export market with wines such as the robust, peppery white label 87 Fine Hermitage. Quality here is good without being spectacular.

OLIVERHILL   SO
Seaview Road, McLaren Vale, SA 5171

w, r, sw, ft, sp   *

Vincenzo Berlingieri, who founded Oliverhill in 1972, has just 3 acres (1 ha) of vines. By buying in 95% of his grapes from elsewhere in McLaren Vale he produces 3,000 cases of table and fortified wines a year. He also runs the Victor Harbour Winery at Middleton.

ORLANDO   BV
Barossa Valley Highway, Rowland Flat, SA 5352

w=86 80, r=86 82, ft, sp   *→→***

Among the Barossa's most pleasing developments in 1988 was the news that Orlando's senior staff, including chief wine-maker Robin Day, had bought back the company (along with **Morris** in VIC) from Reckitt & Colman, its increasingly uninterested owners. Pernod-Ricard has now made a large investment in the firm. Orlando began life in 1847 when Johann Gramp, a Hamburg-born German émigré, established a vineyard on the banks of Jacob Creek in the Barossa, releasing a Hock-style wine in 1850. Gramp's son Gustav expanded the business and moved it to its present site, where it became known as Orlando. Further generations of Gramps nursed it through the depression and the difficult war years, when anti-German feeling ran high even in the Barossa. But it was the post-war introduction of two wines made in a new Geiss pressurized fermentation tank – the revolutionary, ultra-fruity 53 Riesling and the 56 "Barossa Pearl", Australia's first *cuve close* sparkler – that pushed Orlando into the big league. Since then quantity and quality have climbed steadily: the 88 releases were Orlando's best yet.

Like most big Australian firms, Orlando sources its grapes from all over SA, its own vineyards lying in the Barossa and Eden valleys and at its vast Ramco site in the Riverland. A further 100 acres (40 ha) have just been planted to supplement its existing 500 acres (200 ha) or so, but it is content to rely on large quantities of bought-in grapes. What is truly astonishing about Orlando, considering the 50 million litres it produces annually, is the quality and good-value of its wines – from the humble

4-litre Coolabah wine casks up to the superb new Jacaranda Ridge Coonawarra Cabernet. It is Orlando's superior technical expertise that distinguishes this winery. Coolabah, which has 25% of the Australian cask market, may not thrill discerning palates but few would grumble at the value of the 88 Jacob's Creek Semillon/Chardonnay (sold as Chablis in Australia) with its light, fresh, peachy fruit or the floral, sherbetty 88 Rh Riesling. The truffley, liquorice-scented 86 Jacob's Creek Shiraz/Cabernet (sold as Claret in Australia) with its robust, berry-fruit palate is the country's biggest-selling bottled red.

The Orlando RF Chardonnay and Cab Sauvignon twins have also improved. The light, elegant, pineappley 88 Chardonnnay benefits from cooler-climate fruit and part fermentation in oak, while the soft, ripe cassis-fruit of the 86 RF Cabernet is finer than its predecessors. Next up is Orlando's Saints range, introduced in 1983. This includes the fine 86 St Hilary Chardonnay, whose spicy cinnamon scent and luscious pineappley fruit is worthwhile, and the aromatic, floral 88 St Helga Riesling, with a rose scent reminiscent of Traminer. The robust beef tea and chocolate-like 86 St Hugo Cabernet is, however, eclipsed by the magnificent 82 Orlando Jacaranda Ridge Coonawarra Cabernet with its distinguished oriental spice box of a bouquet leading onto a luscious velvety palate; verging on four-star quality, this wine has won Orlando considerable glory at shows. Ports, coolers, non-alcoholic Maison wines and well-made Carrington sparklers complete the range.

℞ Star buy: Orlando RF Chardonnay & Cab Sauvignon

PADTHAWAY ESTATE   PA
Padthaway, SA 5271

w, r, sp   *

A trio of white and pink sparklers are produced at this solitary winery from Chardonnay and Pinot Noir grapes, with table wines based on the same varieties. Its wines are made by **Thomas Hardy**.

PATRITTI   AP
13 Clacton Road, Dover Gardens, SA 5048

w, r, sw, ft, sp   *

Peter and Geoffrey Patritti own 200 acres (80 ha) of vines – half of them planted at Aldiga on the coast south of Adelaide, the rest at Blewitt Springs east of McLaren Vale. A large quantity of table, fortified, sparkling and flavoured wine is made, much of it sold in bulk.

PAULETTS   CL
Polish Hill River Road, Sevenhill, SA 5453

w, r *→

Neil Paulett is the wine-maker at this family-run concern started in 1982. His Rh Riesling is popular in Australia, a good example being the big fresh, passion fruit-like 84. Reds are also produced.

PENFOLDS   AP
Penfold Road, Magill, SA 5072

w=78 84 88, r=71 82 86, ft, sp   *→*****

Penfolds' Grange Hermitage, the company's and the country's greatest red wine (or so they say), is no longer made here but produced at the vast Nuriootpa complex in the Barossa Valley. Nevertheless, it is at Magill that the heart of Grange lies and with it the heart of the company. Christopher Rawson Penfold planted vines here on the eastern outskirts of Adelaide in 1844, having bought the land before he left England for Australia. Although a doctor by profession, Penfold's winery soon eclipsed his medical practice. After his death in 1870, his wife Mary continued to acquire more wineries and vineyards, as did subsequent generations of Penfolds. Today Penfolds is the biggest wine firm in Australia, owning **Wynns**, **Kaiser Stuhl**, **Tollana** and **Seaview** in SA, as well as **Tulloch** in NSW. All told, the group has 5,000 acres (2,000 ha) of vines which provide about a quarter of its fruit.

The Penfolds flotilla of wine-makers, led by John Duval, makes 100 million bottles a year. Penfolds' Grange Hermitage remains the flagship of the firm and has attracted much controversy since it was created by Max Schubert in 1951. On a visit to Bordeaux, Schubert had been bowled over by the style and longevity of first-class Clarets aged in small new oak barrels. Returning home, he selected the best Shiraz or Hermitage grapes he could find (Australia in those days lacking sufficient Cabernet), and then fermented and aged them in small new oak hogsheads, hoping to produce "a big full-bodied wine . . . something different and lasting": he got it. Grange is an extraordinary wine – an intense, burnt, port-like mouthful with overtones of leather, herbs, creosote and tar, backed up by an enormous thwack of luscious blackberry and blackcurrant-like fruit. Once tasted, its character is never forgotten. Although initially unsuccessful, Grange eventually got the acclaim it deserved. Over the years, the wine has become a shade lighter and more approachable, although John Duval dismisses this as "nothing more than vintage variations". Try the truffley, burnt, cedary 81 or the finer seductive port, cedar and cassis-like 82.

Penfolds produces plenty of other great red wines. St Henri Claret (or Cabernet/Shiraz), Grange's closest relative, suffers from comparison, its charred, oak-like 84 needing more in bottle yet. But the rich, velvety, blackcurranty-cedary fruit of the 85 Penfolds Cab Sauvignon Bin 707 is very fine indeed. The new Magill Estate, a Shiraz wine made from the hallowed Magill vines, is close to Grange in style; the 86 boasted a delicious ripe blackberry taste tinged with charred oak. Penfolds' Bin 389 Cabernet/Shiraz is aged in the previous Grange vintage's casks and the warm, rich, spicy eucalyptus fruit of its 85 vintage makes a fine glass; so too does the spicy, but more full-bodied Barossa Shiraz-based 85 Kalimna Bin 28. The 85 Coonawarra Shiraz-based Bin 128 with its rich, scented berry-fruit was much more fragrant and feminine in style. However, the gutsy, chunky 87 Koonunga Hill and Dalwood Shiraz/ Cabernet blends are not in the same league. Up with the rest of the Penfolds greats is the Clare Estate red, a predominantly Merlot wine with a good dollop each of Malbec, Cab Franc and Cab Sauvignon. The result is an ultra-stylish plummy, velvety, spicy four-star wine.

The Penfolds white wines never quite reach the heights of the reds, but the best – the 87 Chardonnay – has a fragrant, luscious, cinnamon style. Penfolds also makes a light, grassy 87 Fumé Blanc, a vanilla-like 87 Semillon/Chardonnay blend, an unusual spicy, grapey Bin 202 Traminer/Riesling blend and ordinary Minchinbury sparklers.

♀ Star buy: Penfolds 85 Cab Sauvignon Bin 707 & 86 Shiraz Bin 128

PENOWARRA   CW
Naracoorte Road, Coonawarra, SA 5277

w, r, ft   ∗

Ken Ward turns 20 acres (8 ha) of Shiraz, Cab Sauvignon and Rh Riesling into table and fortified wines for owner Raymond Messenger.

PETALUMA   AH
Lot 6, Spring Gully Road, Piccadilly, SA 5151

w=80 87 86, r=86 85 79, sw, sp   ∗∗→∗∗∗∗

No one has done more for the fame of the Adelaide Hills than Brian Croser of Petaluma, variously and somewhat lavishly known among Australia's wine fraternity as "god" and "genius". Like all Australian tall poppies he collars his share of criticism, but even his keenest opponents have to admit that this single-minded, globe-trotting dynamo squeezes more into a year than many fit into five. Besides producing his own first-class wines, Croser appears to advise half the industry and make wine for the other half. Yet he still finds time to judge at major wine shows, run the Australian Wine-makers' Forum which he set up, visit his sparkling wine vineyard in Oregon and enjoy a new role as restaurateur at his imaginative Bridgewater Mill complex.

Having eased his way through the Adelaide "Uni" Ag Science course with financial help from **Thomas Hardy**, followed by a stint with his patrons, Croser spent 18 months at Davis, California's top wine school. Back at Thomas Hardy he produced the revolutionary and much admired 75 Siegersdorf Rh Riesling from humble Barossa fruit. Bored with the constraints of a large firm, Croser left Thomas Hardy and helped set up the respected wine course at Riverina College in Wagga Wagga (NSW). There he made his first 76, 77 and 78 Petaluma late-picked Rh Riesling wines from bought-in fruit, choosing the name

"Petaluma" at random from the California page of an atlas. Buying land in the Adelaide Hills with the help of his mentor, expert wine man Len Evans, and financier Peter Fox, he produced Petaluma's first home-made vintage in 79. Croser's wine-making philosophy has influenced a whole generation of Australian wine-makers. Although it has shifted slightly over the years, the central theme remains the same: that "the real quality of a wine is directed in the vineyard and all the techniques we have established are to protect that fruit flavour". Anyone visiting his highly practical winery, surrounded by 150 acres (60 ha) of hand-manicured, close-spaced vines, can see the Croser techniques at work.

Croser buys in grapes from Coonawarra and Clare to supplement his 100 acres (40 ha) of Coonawarra vines (mainly Cab Sauvignon and Merlot) and his predominantly Rh Riesling vines in Clare. These are turned into 35,000 cases of first-class wines. Rh Riesling is the biggest seller; the fresh, flowery, restrained lime juice style of the 87 is what a classic Clare Riesling is all about. Croser has also made some impressive botrytis Rieslings. Petaluma's Chardonnay is now sleeker and more restrained than the fat, buttery Cowra-influenced 82: try the splendid 86, whose fragrant, cinnamon oak is balanced with a mix of fine lemon clove-like Chardonnay. Croser's favourite table wine is the Coonawarra Cabernet and, apart from the delectable "Croser" itself, it is his finest wine. The 82 has now turned into a rich, silky mouthful, reminiscent of blackberries and truffles, albeit with a chocolatey note on the finish from its 12% Shiraz. The 85, with 30% Merlot in the mix, has a youthful herbaceous scent toned down by a robust, blackcurranty palate. The 87, with its opaque-purple-black, intense, complex fruit and truffle-packed palate, looks set to become the best Coonawarra Cabernet vintage yet.

Petaluma's sparkling wine project is Brian Croser's most ambitious. Bollinger bought a part-share in Petaluma in 1985 and now owns 37% of the firm, but it leaves the decisions to Croser and his young, talented wine-making team. The 15,000 cases of top-quality Croser bubbly are usually made from a Piccadilly Hills blend of two-thirds Chardonnay to one-third Pinot Noir, though the proportions vary from year to year according to fruit quality. Discerning Australians rate the seductive, creamy pinhead bubbles of the 86 Croser as their finest fizz. Vinified at Petaluma, the bubbly is transferred for two years' ageing on lees and second fermentation to Bridgewater Mill. This converted 1860 flour mill, complete with restaurant, wine bar and shop (open daily, 11am-5.30pm), is the name on Croser's excellent-value second label, of which a further 15,000 cases are made. Try the rich, fruity cassis style of the 85 Cabernet or the stylish 86 Sauvignon, redolent of gooseberries.
℘ Star buy: Bridgewater Mill range, esp 86 Sauvignon & 85 Cabernet

PETER LEHMANN   BV
Para Road, Tanunda, SA 5352

w, r ✴→✴✴
After working at both **Yalumba** and **Saltram**, Peter Lehmann founded his own Barossa winery in 1980. The three other wine-makers here help Lehmann to select grapes (bought exclusively from Barossa grape-growers) and vinify some 100,000 cases of wine a year. Besides a wide range of table wines including the cheaper Masterson range, Lehmann produces sparkling wine and vintage port. The bestselling 88 Dry Semillon, with its zesty apricot-like palate and pleasant aperitif style, shows that he knows what he's doing – as does the well-made elegant, smoky 86 Rh Riesling. Reds are not quite so successful: an 85 Shiraz/Cabernet was too jammy and the bestselling 85 Shiraz Dry Red offered pleasant, spicy, but dull fruit. The 85 Pinot Noir from the Lehmann Premium Range is a light, palatable, minty-tobacco mouthful.

PEWSEY VALE   See Yalumba.

PIKE'S POLISH HILL RIVER ESTATE   CL
Polish Hill River Road, Sevenhill, SA 5453

w, r ✴→✴✴
The Pike family has owned this well-thought-of winery since 1984. Roseworthy-trained brothers Neil and Andrew, who work full-time at **Mitchell Cellars** and **Penfolds** respectively, are in charge. It says much

for their energy that they find time to make good Sauv Blanc, Shiraz and Chardonnay as well as even finer Rh Riesling and Cab Sauvignon (blended with a little Cab Franc and Merlot). About half of their fruit comes from Pike's 30 acres (12 ha) of vines, the rest from elsewhere in Clare. Annual production is 6,000 cases, with Riesling accounting for half. Try the peachy, palatable 88 Chardonnay, the agreeable minty-chunky 87 Cabernet or the rather more jammy 87 Shiraz.

PIRRAMIMMA   SO
Johnston Road, McLaren Vale, SA 5171

w, r, ft ★

This winery's romantic name, dreamt up by the founder of the Johnston family business in 1892, is derived from two aboriginal words – *pirra* meaning moon, and *mimma*, stars. Today, third-generation Geoff Johnston is the wine-maker here. Trained at Riverina, he has 136 acres (55 ha), most of them planted in 1988. Like many McLaren Vale concerns, Pirramimma's wines originally went overseas; wine was not bottled under its own label until 1965. A 10,000-case range of table and fortified wines are made, including a lively Rh Riesling, an oaky Chardonnay and a Hillsview carbonic maceration Cabernet.

PRIMO ESTATE   AP
Old Port Wakefield Road, Virginia, SA 5120

w, r, sw ★→→

Drive 16 miles (25 km) due north from Adelaide and just north of Virginia you will come across Primo Estate. The first vines were planted here by Primo Grilli in 1973, but it was his son Joseph and daughter-in-law Dina, the present proprietors, who founded this estate in 1979. Joe Grilli, the talented Roseworthy-trained wine-maker, makes about 8,000 cases of varied table wines, mostly from the 34 acres (14 ha) of vines surrounding the winery. Apart from these, Grilli makes *auslese* and *beerenauslese* styles of botrytis Riesling by injecting grapes with a botrytis culture. In true Italian style, he also produces an "Amarone"-style Cab Sauvignon, drying the grapes for a fortnight before fermentation. He hopes eventually to round off his finest wine, the new double-pruned "Joseph Cabernet", with a good dash of Merlot and Cab Franc *à la Bordeaux*. Quality here is surprisingly high for the Adelaide Plains – perhaps, as the Grillis believe, because of Primo's proximity to the sea.

QUELLTALER ESTATE   See Wolf Blass.

REDMAN   CW
Naracoorte Road, Coonawarra, SA 5263

r ★→→★

Owen, Edna, Bruce and Malcolm Redman started this estate in 1966, a year after they sold **Rouge Homme** to **Lindemans**. Until they built their winery in 1969, wines were made at nearby **Brands Laira**. Redman has 80 acres (32 ha) in the heart of Coonawarra, where it grows mostly Shiraz, some Cabernet and a smidgen of Merlot, not yet bearing. Using "traditional techniques", Bruce Redman turns this into just over 16,000 cases of Shiraz-based Redman Claret (sold as Redman Shiraz in some countries). This accounts for three-quarters of production, Cab Sauvignon for the rest. Europeans will appreciate the fine, rich, velvety, oaky-fruity style of the 84 Redman Cab Sauvignon, but they will be less enamoured of the chunky, earthy, leathery 84 Shiraz. Tradition notwithstanding, Redman uses mechanical harvesting and crushes its grapes in the vineyard, but wines are bottled in Adelaide.

RENMANO   See Berri-Renmano.

RICHARD HAMILTON   SO
Main Road, Willunga, SA 5172

w, r ★

In 1837, Dr Richard Hamilton's great-great-grandfather founded the famous Hamilton Ewell vineyards, forming SA's first winery. Today his descendant runs two wine empires – Willunga, with its 40 acres (16 ha) of vines, and Leconfield in Coonawarra, which has 80 acres (32 ha).

Leconfield, acquired in 1981, is the red wine headquarters, while most of the whites are produced at Willunga; no outside fruit is used. The 7,000 cases produced at Leconfield include straight and late harvest Rieslings in addition to Cab Sauvignon, Shiraz and a recent offering – Cabernet/Merlot. Leconfield's new vineyards to the south are a mix of Cab Sauvignon, Cab Franc and Chardonnay. Of the 10,000 Willunga cases the soft, biscuity, but somewhat boring 87 Chardonnay accounts for about half. Sizeable quantities are also made of racy, clean 87 Semillon and oak-influenced "Fumé-style" Sauv Blanc, as well as a little Chenin Blanc and Cab Sauvignon.

THE RIDGE WINES   CW
Naracoorte Road, Coonawarra, SA 5263

                                                          w, r *
Suzie and Sid Kidman have run this winery, just north of Coonawarra, since 1984. Sid makes about 1,000 cases of wines from Ridge's 5-acre (2-ha) plot, divided almost equally between Cab Sauvignon, Rh Riesling and Shiraz, the newest offering; most of this is sold at the cellar door.

ROBERT HAMILTON & SON   AH
Springton Winery, Hamilton's Road, Springton, SA 5253

                                                          w, r, ft *
Robert Hamilton and Son, run by another great-great-grandson of SA's wine pioneer Richard Hamilton, should not be confused with the dynasty's other strand – the **Richard Hamilton** winery. The original Hamilton Ewell vineyards, which had been bought by **Mildara** (VIC) in 1979, were bought back by the family concern in 1981. Some 60 acres (24 ha) of vines are turned into just over 4,000 cases of table wine, including dessert wine-styles and ports, by wine-maker Maurice Ou.

ROCKFORD WINES   BV
Krondorf Road, Tanunda, SA 5352

                                                          w, r, ft *
The O'Callaghans make a range of table and fortified wines here from their own Rh Riesling and bought-in grapes.

ROSENBERG CELLARS   CL
Main North Road, Watervale, SA 5452

                                                          w, r *
Historic Rosenberg is one of the original Clare Valley wineries. Its small quantities of popular wines are made by **Sevenhill**.

ROSEWORTHY   BV
Roseworthy, SA 5371

                                                          w, r, ft, sp *
Roseworthy, founded in 1883, is Australia's most important wine school. In spite of attracting occasional criticism for its "recipe wine-making" techniques, it has produced generation after generation of competent wine-makers. A wide range of table, fortified and sparkling wines made here every year by the students are sold at the cellar door and throughout Australia.

ROUGE HOMME   CW
Naracoorte Road, Coonawarra, SA 5263

                                                 w, r=78 76 85   *→****
Rouge Homme was founded in 1908 by Bill Redman (hence its name) and passed down in the Redman family. Like everyone else in the 60s, the Redmans found wine-making a financial strain and they sold out to **Lindemans** in 1965. Lindemans preserved the Rouge Homme name and vineyards intact. Today, there are 320 acres (130 ha) in central Coonawarra, planted to Rh Riesling, Sauv Blanc, and Chardonnay for the whites, with Shiraz, Cab Sauvignon and Pinot Noir for the reds. The Chardonnay has been available for some time, but the Estate Dry White, a blend mainly of aromatic Rh Riesling and Sauv Blanc, was launched in 1988 following UK demand for a Coonawarra white. Rouge Homme's only other blended wine – an 80/20 Shiraz/Cabernet, sold in Australia under the Claret label – is its bestseller.

Greg Clayfield, Rouge Homme's award-winning wine-maker, makes consistently good wines. The fresh, flowery, lime and oak-influenced 88 Estate white is palatable, although not especially exciting. The same can be said for the peachy, but slightly oily 87 Chardonnay. Equally pleasant is the 87 Shiraz/Cabernet, whose black pepper spice and blackberry-like palate lacks a little weight. The stars in this range are the Rouge Homme Cabernets. The current 85 release boasts a cedary scent and a rich, firm, beefy, yet almost velvety palate, which still needs time. Finer still is the 78 Cabernet, a Classic Wine Release or "exceptional wine" that Lindemans has kept back to sell at its peak. This wine's intensely rich, herbaceous-cedary, velvety palate is what a great Coonawarra Cabernet is all about. Forget the steep price, just buy it.

ROVALLEY   BV
Sturt Highway, Rowland Flat, SA 5352

w, r, ft, sp   *
Owner/wine-maker Dean Lieblich is assisted here by Christopher Schmidt, just as he is at Merrivale. Both outlets produce a small, inexpensive range of flagons, fortifieds, sparklers and table wines.

RYECROFT   SO
14 Ingoldby Road, McLaren Flat, SA 5171

w, r   *→
Founded in 1888, Ryecroft was one of the original wineries in this region. Like many other local concerns, it did not sell wines under its own label until 1956. Gradually the Ryecroft name became better known, and by the mid-60s its mostly sweet fortified wines were selling well overseas. However, the bottom dropped out of this market and it went through several changes of ownership. Ryecroft's future now looks assured as it was recently bought by a consortium which includes several wine men involved in the success of **Krondorf**. The vineyards, replanted in 1981, have about 124 acres (50 ha) of Chardonnay, Cab Sauvignon, Malbec and Merlot, which will gradually be increased.

Apart from the premium single varietal reds and whites sold under its own label, Ryecroft is home to a number of other wines. The consortium has just bought the Middlebrook winery and its wines will all be made here. In addition, Ryecroft produces Gordon Grant wines, a competitively-priced varietal and blended wine label launched in 1986 and popular in the USA. Try the fresh, grassy 87 Chardonnay or the fleshy, robust 86 Cab Sauvignon. **Grant Burge**, a fellow member of the consortium, vinifies some of the grapes from his Barossa estate at Ryecroft. To confuse matters further Nick Holmes, the group's wine-maker, also has his own well-thought-of Shottesbrooke label, producing only a Sauv Blanc/Cab Sauvignon/Cab Franc/Merlot blend, whose 1987 vintage was a toasty-oaky wine. In spite of the members' individual interests, 20,000 cases are sold under the Ryecroft label itself. These include a rich, hefty, buttery 88 Chardonnay and a chunky, inky, cassis-like 86 Cab Sauvignon.

ST FRANCIS   SO
Bridge Street, Old Reynella, SA 5161

w, r, sw, ft, sp   *
Owned by David Ward and Pompey Donato, St Francis was founded in 1970 on the site of an 1852 brandy distillery. The on-site restaurant near the main road south of Adelaide attracts visitors to taste the St Francis varietal and regional range, and the new, cheaper, blended Governor Phillip selection. About 35,000 cases are made here by wine-makers Jim Irvine and Rob Dundon, all from bought-in fruit. The winery is due to be relocated shortly and replaced by a motel complex.

ST HALLETT'S   BV
St Hallett's Road, Tanunda, SA 5352

w, r   *
Founded in 1944 by the Lindner family, St Hallett's owns 180 acres (70 ha) of Barossa vines. Annual production is 8,000 cases, half made from its own fruit, the rest from elsewhere in the region. The winery has just switched from 80% port production, so there are only six wines.

SALTRAM   BV
Angaston Road, Angaston, SA 5353

w, r, ft *→**

Founded in 1859 by English émigré William Salter, this winery is now owned by Seagram, the giant American wines and spirits conglomerate. Like other large Barossa concerns, Saltram buys in most of its grapes; its own 70 acres (28 ha), planted equally to Cabernet, Rh Riesling, Chardonnay and Shiraz, supplies only a tiny portion of its needs. Lowest of Saltram's five wine ranges is the basic Hazlewood collection, followed by the finer Saltram varietal range, including the unusual Pinot Noir Nouveau. Higher up in quality are the fine oaky-toasty 87 Mamre Brook Chardonnay (sourced from McLaren Vale and the Hunter), a delicious rich, spicy-fruity 84 Cab Sauvignon/Shiraz blend (made from Barossa fruit) and Metala, a Cabernet/Shiraz mix (based partly on Langhorne fruit). Saltram's most expensive range of wines is the Pinnacle Selection, which includes Coonawarra Cabernet and a Gewurztraminer. Among the fortifieds made here is the well-thought-of Mr Pickwick's Particular Port.

SCARPANTONI ESTATES   SO
Scarpantoni Drive, McLaren Flat, SA 5171

w, r, sw, ft *

Domenico and Paula Scarpantoni run this place together with their two sons. They produce almost 5,000 cases of a long list of table wines entirely from the estate's 70 acres (28 ha) of vineyards. The Scarpantonis use modern equipment yet favour traditional methods, admitting that they do most of the hard vineyard work themselves. In addition to inexpensive table wines, they make vintage port, Liqueur Riesling and a carbonic maceration wine sold under the Premier label.

SEAVIEW   SO
Chaffey's Road, McLaren Vale, SA 5171

w, r, ft, sp *→**

Since **Penfolds** bought Seaview in 1985, this winery's importance has diminished – but its wines go from strength to strength and now form the biggest-selling table wine range in Australia. The grapes used here come from all over SA as well as its own McLaren Vale vineyards, but good, inexpensive Seaview wines do exist. Try the 86 Coonawarra Shiraz with its luscious blackberry palate. The 88 Traminer/Riesling with its light, sweet, spritzy, rose-scented style and the citric, floral 88 Riesling are both pleasant and popular. However, the vanilla and lemon curd-like 88 Chardonnay is somewhat ordinary, as are the firm, berry-fruit 86 Cabernet/Shiraz and the better, oakier, blackberry-like 86 Cab Sauvignon. The Seaview wines to seek out are the *méthode champenoise* sparklers. The flagship fizz is "Edmond Mazure", an 80/20 Pinot Noir/Chardonnay blend; its fresh but subdued 85 vintage was disappointing. Opt instead for the 85 Pinot Noir/Chardonnay (75/25 Pinot Noir/Chardonnay) bargain bubbly, whose rich, biscuity scent and palate is given three years on yeast. Ports are also produced at Seaview: look out for the fresh, light Killawarra range, acceptable both in bottle and box.

SEPPELT   BV
Seppeltsfield, SA 5352

w=84 87, r=80 82 84, ft, sp *→**

Seppelt, with its annual production of 30 million bottles, is another Australian wine giant. It operates at three different wineries, two of them – Chateau Tanunda, the Seppelt table wine GHQ, and Seppeltsfield, chiefly a fortified wine producer – in the Barossa. The third, Seppelt Great Western's sparkling wine centre, is in VIC. Historic Seppeltsfield is a must for any visitor to the Barossa. Its majestic avenues of palm trees, family mausoleum (for male Seppelts only), handsome 1878 port store and ingenious 1888 gravity-fed vintage cellar are well worth seeing. Its founder was wealthy, feudal-minded merchant, Joseph Ernst Seppelt, who left Silesia in 1849 with 13 families and nine single men intent on building a new life for himself and his workers. He started Seppeltsfield in 1851, making his first wine in the dairy before building the winery, which was later extended by his son Benno. With its small captive community, the firm and village thrived. During the economic gloom of the 1930s Benno's son Oscar provided jobs for the locals by planting great palm trees on every Seppelt property. Today, with two members of the family still involved in the firm, Seppelt has 3,700 acres (1,500 ha) of vines close to its wineries. In addition, it owns vast tracts at Padthaway, Dorrien, Qualco in the Riverland and Partalunga, as well as its Barooga vineyards (NSW) and others at Drumbourg (VIC). Seppelt also has larger plantings of fashionable Chardonnay than any other estate, but it still has to buy in fruit from all over Australia.

Seppelt is not involved in the cask trade and its whole product line was rigorously rationalized several years ago. Even so, it has plenty of inexpensive wines to cater for this end of the market. The big low-cost brand is the Queen Adelaide range, which became part of the Seppelt portfolio when it bought Woodley Wines in 1985. The 88 Rh Riesling in this range offers simple tropical fruit flavours, and the 88 Chardonnay is similar but has peachy-pineappley overtones. Both wines are on sale at a knock-down price, together with Seppelt's robust, peppery 86 Queen Adelaide Claret. The next step up is the Gold Label range which includes the full, tropical-pineappley 88 Barooga Chardonnay. Seppelt's top Show Chardonnay is bigger, richer and more buttery, but with lychee-like tropical fruit creeping in. The Black Label range is superior to the gold, featuring wines such as the 85 Black Label Hermitage with its blackberry jam flavours and the firm, herbaceous, blackcurranty 86 Black Label Cabernet. Top of the Seppelt chart are the Individual Vineyard table wines. These include the astringent, yet chocolatey 84 Drumbourg Cabernet and the finer 84 Drumbourg Riesling.

Seppelt's Great Western sparklers are also admired – especially the Pinot Noir/Chardonnay *méthode champenoise* Salinger, whose 84 vintage was rich, full and biscuity. The fortifieds here are some of the best in Australia, and the Show Tawny Port enjoys the distinction of being the most awarded wine in the country. A little of the amazing 1878 Para Liqueur Port, blended from original 19th-century stocks, is also sold each year. Its extraordinarily intense flavours of sweet roses, liquorice and caramel are worth the equally extraordinary price of $1,500 per bottle. What you are drinking is Seppelt's history.

THE SETTLEMENT WINE COMPANY   SO
Settlement Road, McLaren Flat, SA 5171

w, r, ft, sp   *

Dr David Mitchell owns this winery. His range of table, fortified and sparkling wines – including Plasma Port and Koala Port sold in appropriate gift packs – are not for serious wine drinkers.

SEVENHILL   CL
College Road, Sevenhill via Clare, SA 5453

w, r, ft   *

Sevenhill, established by the Jesuits in 1851 and still run by them, is the oldest winery in Clare and the only Australian winery run by a religious order. The production of sacramental wine remains its main function, but in the last three decades the Brothers have branched out into ordinary table wines and fortifieds. Brother John May and his team produce 8,000 cases a year from 130 acres (52 ha) of vines here. Among the wide range of wines sold are Rouge Nobel (made from Touriga port grapes), Traminer Frontignac and College White. The latter, a blend of Pedro Ximenez, Clare Riesling (Crouchen) and Rh Riesling, is the best-seller. Fortifieds include Shiraz-based Tawny Port and Liqueur Tokay. Visitors are welcome daily, 8.30am-4.30pm, at this historic estate.

SHEPPARD'S HUTT RIVER ESTATE   CL
Main North Road, Clare, SA 5453

w, r   *

This winery, across the Hutt River from **Jim Barry**, is owned by Frank and Barbara Sheppard, who used to run the country's largest wine transport business. Founded in 1985, their new estate produces small quantities of table and fortified wines.

SHOTTESBROOKE   See Ryecroft.

SIMON HACKETT SO
McMurtrie Road, McLaren Vale, SA 5171

w, r ★

Simon Hackett's wines are made at various wineries in the Southern Vales region, from a number of different grape sources. Hackett himself hopes that this site will be his permanent home.

SKILLOGALEE CL
Skillogalee Valley Road, Sevenhill, SA 5453

w, r, ft ★

Wine-maker Andrew Mitchell from the nearby **Mitchell Cellars** winery makes about 5,000 cases a year of a range of red and white table wines and fortifieds for Skillogalee.

SOUTHERN VALES SO
151 Main Road, McLaren Vale, SA 5171

w, r, ft ★

Southern Vales has recently undergone a major change, for Jane Paull is now the wine-maker and its new owners are a group of grape-growing shareholders. This co-operative was founded in 1901 and, although its range of wines is currently being revised, it is likely to continue producing table, fortified and bulk wines. Premium table wines here are sold under the Tatachilla label.

S SMITH & SON See **Yalumba**.

STANLEY WINE COMPANY CL
7 Dominic Street, Clare, SA 5453

w, r, sw ★→★★★

Thomas Hardy bought this operation in 1987 and has tried so far (as it has tried with **Houghton** in WA) to keep the identity of the Stanley Leasingham label separate from its mother company. Indeed, Thomas Hardy recently bought the Clarevale Co-operative from **Penfolds** specifically to boost Stanley's production. The Stanley Wine Company, founded in 1894 to capitalize on a glut of grapes in Clare, is one of the great names in Australian wine history. The company has had its share of family disputes and financial problems over the years, Heinz rescuing it from the latter in the 1970s before selling out to Thomas Hardy. Stanley has long been known for the quality of its Rh Rieslings as anyone who has tasted the luscious, smoky, lime-like 73 Bin 7 Riesling can testify: truly a three-star wine. The 600 acres (240 ha) of vines here provide just over a third of Stanley's needs. The winery also buys in vast quantities of Sunraysia grapes, mostly made into 6 million Stanley Leasingham 4-litre wine casks.

Stanley's 100,000 cases of bottled wines are headed by a wine-makers' selection range (with non-consecutive bin numbers, omitting those that failed to make the grade). Bin 14 Chablis, of which 30,000 cases are sold annually, is the bestseller; Bin 5 Riesling and Bin 68, a rich, soft, minty 80/20 Cabernet/Shiraz blend, are also big money-spinners. The range is completed by Bin 3 White Burgundy, Bin 56 Cabernet/Malbec, Bin 49 Cab Sauvignon, Bin 7 Rh Riesling, a light, spicy Chardonnay and a delicate, grassy Fumé Blanc. The early harvest Bin 7 Riesling and Bin 56 Cabernet-Malbec with its soft, restrained, herbaceous, Bordeaux-like flavours are deemed by the current Stanley wine-maker – and Australian judges – to be the top wines. But the special-release 85 Cabernet Mick Knappstein (named after one of Stanley's most important wine men), with its rich, ripe, chocolatey, earthy style, is definitely worth tasting. If the 85 vintage is anything to go by, even the humble Spring Gully Riesling can come up with delicious, lime-like flower scents and flavours.

♀ Star buy: Stanley Wine Company 85 Spring Gully Riesling

TARANGA SO
Main South Road, McLaren Vale, SA 5171

w, r, ft, sp ★

Noel Sibley produces a range of table, sparkling and fortified wines at this McLaren Vale winery.

TARCHALICE BV
Research Road, Tanunda, SA 5352

w, r, sw, ft *

Born into an old Barossa grape-growing family, owner/wine-maker Christopher Schmidt makes 2,500 cases, partly from his own 6 acres (2.5 ha), but buying in three-quarters of his needs. He produces a short varietal list, with tawny and Pioneer port on the side.

TAYLORS CL
Mintaro Road, Auburn, SA 5451

w, r *

This large, functional winery is one of the most southerly in Clare and one of the largest with 750 acres (300 ha) under vine. It started life in 1969 when the Taylor family, originally Sydney wine merchants, planted a large plot of Cab Sauvignon vines here. Further plantings in 1981-82 brought the vineyard up to its present size. Apart from Cabernet, wine-maker Andrew Tolley now grows Chardonnay, Shiraz, Rh Riesling, Crouchen and Pinot Noir. Roughly 200,000 cases are produced here, partly from bought-in Clare grapes. An inexpensive premium single varietal range accounts for the lion's share, but an even cheaper Bin range is also available. The Taylors did not release their first Chardonnay until 1985 and they feel it ranks with the Cabernet as their finest wine. Further plantings are due in 1990. The quality here is acceptable rather than exciting: the 88 smoky-biscuity Chardonnay tastes a shade over-oaked and the 86 Cabernet, also in the premium range, is rich and robust but rather too rustic.

TEMPLE BRUER LC
Milang Road, Angas Plains, SA 5255

w, r, sw *→→*

This winery, named partly after its owners and partly after a ruined 12th-century Lincolnshire monastery of the same name, is sometimes grouped with the Adelaide Hills wineries. In fact, it lies close to Strathalbyn which is the entrance to the Langhorne Creek region. Barbara and David Bruer, both ex-Roseworthy chemistry teachers, own the winery and run a large vine nursery here. Half of their 20 acres (8 ha) of vines are planted to Cab Sauvignon which, together with smaller amounts of Shiraz, Merlot, Cab Franc and Malbec, supply almost all of Temple Bruer's grape needs. Botrytis-attacked Riesling grapes are bought in from a neighbour whose vineyards, like Temple Bruer's, abut onto the River Angas. The winery's 70/30 Cabernet/ Merlot and 70/30 Hermitage/Malbec blends account for most of its annual 4,000 cases. The 85 Temple Bruer straight Cab Sauvignon boasted a simple soft, minty, berry-like scent and taste.

THOMAS FERN HILL ESTATE SO
Ingoldby Road, McLaren Flat, SA 5171

w, r, ft *

Wayne Thomas, owner/wine-maker here, has just 1 acre (0.5 ha) of Cabernet vines. The other 95% of his fruit is bought in from McLaren Flat and Blewitt Springs. Thomas produces 5,000 cases a year of table wines and port here, making the red wines traditionally in open fermenters. Cab Sauvignon and Rh Riesling are the big sellers, but Thomas regards the Shiraz as his finest wine.

THOMAS HARDY & SONS SO
Reynell Road, Reynella, SA 5161

w=80 82 86, r=80 82 87, ft, sp *→****

Now the second-largest wine group in the country after **Penfolds**, Thomas Hardy & Sons owns the **Stanley Wine Company** in Clare and **Houghton** in WA. The company is headed by the urbane Sir James Hardy, perhaps better known as a yachtsman than as Thomas Hardy's Chairman, and five members of the Hardy family still occupy key company positions. Thomas Hardy, a 20-year-old Englishman from Devon, emigrated to Australia in 1850. After working for John Reynell just south of Adelaide, he tried his luck with the Victorian gold prospectors, returning several years later to plant his own vineyard and make wine at Bankside, to the west of Adelaide. So successful was this venture that, by 1859, he was exporting wine to England. Further expansion was rapid and, by 1894, Hardy's was the largest wine-maker in Australia. Thomas Hardy died in 1912, but subsequent generations of Hardys continued to build up the firm. Having already bought land in McLaren Vale and the Riverland, it bought the Barossan Siegersdorf winery in 1921, 825 acres (330 ha) at Padthaway in 1969, Houghton in 1976 and the Stanley Wine Company in 1987. Perhaps most satisfying of all for the family was the acquisition in 1982 of Chateau Reynella, where Thomas Hardy first started work. The handsome cream Reynella homestead, dating from 1842, has been painstakingly restored.

In total, the Hardy group produces some 19 million bottles and 7 million casks annually. Besides sparkling wines and ports, there are four quality table wine ranges (the cheaper end of the market being catered for by the Stanley Wine Company's casks). At the lower end are wines such as the 88 Old Castle Riesling with simple peachy, lime juice style and the ordinary 86 St Thomas Burgundy. Hardy's bestseller, the pleasant, appley-citric 87 Siegersdorf Rh Riesling, is roughly at this level too – some way below the brilliant Bird Series of single varietal and blended wines. The Bird Series labels, which include informative coded back labels, are some of the best in the world. The 87 Bird Series Chardonnay has a pleasant, smoky-pineappley scent but a light palate. The new blended Stamp Collection's fresh, zesty lemon and lime 88 Premium Classic Dry White and ripe, blackcurranty 86 Dry Red are of comparable quality.

The next range up, sold at roughly twice the price, is the Hardy Collection. The 87 Padthaway Chardonnay's fresh, pineappley fruit is enhanced with delicate, cinnamon-like oak. Of the white wines, the 87 Semillon/Sauvignon is equally good, its elegant, flowering currant-like bouquet backed up by a honeyed citric palate. The Hardy Collection reds are worthwhile too. Try the fine 86 McLaren Vale Cabernet, with its light, fresh, redcurrant and blackcurrant style, or sweet wines such as the luscious apricot and butterscotch 85 Rh Riesling Beerenauslese. Finest of all is the Eileen Hardy range, named after Thomas Hardy's mother. The 87 Eileen Hardy Padthaway Chardonnay boasts a delicious trio of rich vanilla, pineapple and butter flavours. Visitors are welcome daily at this historic winery, 10am-4pm.
℗ Star buy: Thomas Hardy Bird Series wines

TIM ADAMS
CL
Wendouree Road, Clare, SA 5453

w, r   *→

Tim Adams, once wine-maker at the **Stanley Wine Company**, has started his own Clare winery close to **Wendouree**. Try his fresh, lively, citric 88 Semillon or his robust, grassy-peppery 87 Shiraz.

TIM KNAPPSTEIN
CL
2 Pioneer Avenue, Clare, SA 5453

w, r   *→→***

Tim Knappstein, whose family is associated with the **Stanley Wine Company**, trained at Roseworthy before founding his own firm in 1976, initially called Enterprise after the handsome 1878 Enterprise brewery building which it occupies. Tim Knappstein's fine wines and handsome labels have always stood out from the Clare crowd; even his early Enterprise releases were head and shoulders above local competition. The zappy, flowery, lime-like 84 Riesling and the early, grassy Fumé Blanc Sauvignon were both excellent, and the 80 Cabernet, with its luscious cassis and blackberry flavours, was a three-star wine. Although **Wolf Blass** bought the majority shareholding of this firm in 1986, the Knappsteins still own the vineyards and Tim remains firmly in charge. Most of his 115 acres (56 ha) are in Clare, but he also owns vines in the Adelaide Hills at Lenswood. These vineyards provide about two-thirds of his grapes, the rest coming from elsewhere in Clare. Some 35,000 cases are produced of six different wines. Rh Riesling is the big seller, followed by Fumé Blanc (which Knappstein claims to have introduced to Australia), Cabernet/Merlot, Chardonnay and Cab Sauvignon. Much smaller quantities of Gewurztraminer are also produced.

Knappstein is a clear-thinking, down-to-earth wine-maker who likes to point out that Australia's heat is not dissimilar to that of North Africa. To counteract this he refrigerates from crushing right through to storage, whether in or out of oak. About a third of new French oak, and some American, is used here each year. Knappstein believes firmly in the Bordeaux-inspired approach and his Cabernet is rounded off with 10% each of Merlot and Cab Franc. The 1986 vintage of the 85/15 Cabernet/Merlot blend is a pleasing, gutsy, herbaceous wine, but it is eclipsed by the big, rich, robust 86 Cab Sauvignon which has a fine liquorice-like palate. The steely, elegant 88 Chardonnay is also worth seeking out. Knappstein's Fumé Blanc, a 55/45 Sauvignon/Semillon mix, is his bestselling wine, although the pear drop and barley sugar flavours of the 88 need time to come round. Look out for a new Lenswood Pinot Noir and the occasional sweet botrytis release.

TINLIN'S WINERY   SO
Kangarilla Road, McLaren Vale, SA 5171

w, r, ft ⋆

The Tinlins own 200 acres (80 ha) of vines at this Southern Vales winery. Most of their fruit is made into bulk wine, though Dry Red, Dry White, and Tawny Port are also made.

TOLLANA   BV
Sturt Highway, Nuriootpa, SA 5355

w, r ⋆→⋆⋆⋆

Tollana, owned by the **Penfolds** group, lies just over the road from its mother company and neighbouring **Kaiser Stuhl**. Its numerous acres of winery installations in the Barossa give chief wine-maker John Duval plenty to do, but quality here is way above expectation for a big wine conglomerate. Established in 1888 as Tolley, Scott & Tolley, a brandy distillery, it did not concentrate on wine until 1966, its first vintage emerging in 1969. After buying vineyards at Waikerie in the Riverland, a further 370 acres (150 ha) in the Eden Valley were purchased in 1975, principally for Rh Riesling. Tollana's well-made red wines include the excellent 85 Eden Valley Hermitage (Shiraz), whose velvety mouthful of black pepper spice is definitely worth seeking out, as is the moreish 82 Eden Valley Shiraz/Cab Sauvignon. Less impressive is the jammy, charred 84 Cab Sauvignon. Of the whites, the 88 Chablis, with its zesty, peachy-flowery quality, is one of the better "Chablis" made in Australia; the smoky-grassy 88 Sauvignon is acceptable. Tollana's best white is its 87 Eden Valley Riesling, whose attractive, aromatic kerosene scent and peachy palate will develop in bottle.
♀ Star buy: Tollana Eden Valley Shiraz/Cab Sauvignon & Shiraz

TOLLEY'S PEDARE   AF
30 Barracks Road, Hope Valley, SA 5090

w, r, sw, ft, sp ⋆→⋆⋆⋆

Situated in the sprawling north-eastern suburbs of Adelaide, Tolley's Pedare is a shining example of what Australia makes so well: fine flavoursome wines at low prices. This family-owned firm was founded in 1892 by Douglas Tolley. The Pedare part of its title is an acronym taken from the names of Douglas Tolley's grandsons (PEter, DAvid and REg Tolley), but it is Chris Tolley who is now the wine-maker. With 500 acres (200 ha) of vines in the Barossa and Hope valleys supplying 60% of its fruit, Tolley's Pedare is a substantial operation. The rest of its grapes come from Coonawarra, the Southern Vales, Clare and the Riverland. These are turned into a wide range of dry red and white table wines, sparkling wines, sherries, ports, Muscats and vermouths. What is remarkable about the Tolley's Pedare wines is their consistently good, sometimes superb quality, and their excellent value for money. Even the humble selected harvest wines, such as the delicious rose petal-scented and sweet grapey-palated 88 Late Harvest Muscat (Spatlese Frontignac in Australia), can rise above two stars for a ridiculously low price. Try the fine, spicy-grapey 88 Gewurztraminer too or the zesty, lime-like 88 Rh Riesling. Tolley's Pedare's finest table wine offerings are sold under its Cellar Reserve labels.
♀ Star buy: Selected Harvest range, esp Late Harvest Muscat

TORRESAN   SO
Manning Road, Flagstaff Hill, SA 5159

w, r, sw, ft, sp   *

Founded in 1960, this winery was originally known as G. Torresan & Sons. It was incorporated into the Happy Valley Winery in 1974, and Torresan is the name that now appears on about 14,000 cases of the 58,000 made by Amelio Torresan each year. The rest is sparkling wine and bulk sales. Torresan's wines are mostly single varietal McLaren Vale offerings but it also makes Godfather port and a cheaper "white label" range which includes wines such as Chablis.

VERITAS WINERY   BV
94 Langmeil Road, Tanunda, SA 5352

w, r, ft   *

Rolf Binder is owner/wine-maker of this 4,000-case winery founded in 1955. Its 85 acres (34 ha) of Barossa vines are vinified traditionally into a long list of wines, including fortifieds.

VICTOR HARBOUR WINERY   See **Oliverhill**.

WARD'S GATEWAY CELLARS   BV
Barossa Valley Highway, Lyndoch, SA 5351

w, r, ft   *

The Ward family makes table and fortified wines from 5 acres (2 ha) of vines situated at the entrance to the Barossa Valley.

WATERVALE CELLARS   CL
North Terrace, Watervale, SA 5452

w, r, sw   *→**

English ex-lawyer Robert Crabtree and his wife Elizabeth have owned Watervale Cellars since 1977. Their own 30 acres (12 ha) of vineyards provide about half their fruit; the rest is bought in from other Clare growers and Watervale. Helpfully, they list their grape sources on the back labels of all their wines. Two-thirds of their annual 3,000-case production is divided between a Riesling and a 70/30 Shiraz/Cab Sauvignon blend. A little Semillon and Muscat are also made. The Crabtrees follow what they describe as "fairly old production techniques", such as a basket press for the reds and barrel fermentation for Semillon. Their 88 Semillon is a straightforward leafy, herbaceous wine and their 86 Shiraz/Cabernet a big, rich, minty-chunky mouthful. Visitors are welcome daily, 10am-5pm.

WEIN VALLEY ESTATES   RL
Nixon Road, Monash, SA 5342

w, r, sw, ft, sp   *

Otto Konig looks after the Wein Valley consortium's 3,000 acres (1,200 ha) of Riverland vines. A wide range of table, fortified, sparkling and bulk wines are made here, as well as an ouzo. A Melbourne bottling plant buys 6 million litres of the consortium's wines to sell under the Langwarra Wines label. Moselle and Tawny Port are Wein Valley's own biggest selling wines.

WENDOUREE   CL
Spring Farm Road, Clare, SA 5453

w, r, ft   *→

A P Birks Wendouree, to give this place its full title, was founded in 1895 and bought by the Liberman family in 1972. Wine-maker Anthony Brady, Liberman's son-in-law, has continued the Birks tradition of specialization in hearty red wines and chunky fortifieds, with Shiraz accounting for 500 of his 2,000 cases; Cab Sauvignon, a big, blackcurranty Cabernet/Malbec and a Shiraz/Mataro blended wine also feature heavily. Wendouree Pressings is a speciality – made, as the name suggests, from the pressed wine of various grapes. Its hefty, full-bodied style is perhaps as near as modern Australia gets to the 19th-century original. Wendouree's 25 acres (10 ha) of vines, averaging 64 years old, also produce Rh Riesling, Muscat of Alexandria and vintage port. Seek out the 88 Malbec made from an 1898 planting.

WILSFORD WINES   **BV**
Gomersal Road, Lyndoch, SA 5351

w, r, ft   *

The Burge family owns this Barossa outlet (which has nothing to do with **Grant Burge**). Table and fortified wines are made here from a variety of different grapes.

THE WILSON VINEYARD   **CL**
Polish Hill River Road, Sevenhill, SA 5453

w, r   *→

Once known as Polish Hill River Vineyards, this concern was started in 1974 and had its first commercial vintage in 1980. Dr John Wilson, a "one-man-band" wine-maker as he puts it, runs this family partnership in the spare time he has from medicine. To supplement his 20 acres (8 ha) of vines here, he buys in 15% of his needs from an adjoining vineyard. Rh Riesling accounts for most of the 3,000-case production, together with straight Cab Sauvignon and a Cabernet/Shiraz/Malbec blend. Tiny amounts of Pinot Noir and Chardonnay are also made, as well as – of all things – a Late Harvest Zinfandel, which Dr Wilson believes is the only example of this wine in the country.

WIRRA WIRRA   **SO**
McMurtrie Road, McLaren Vale, SA 5171

w, r, ft   *→**

Brothers Greg and Roger Trott run this high-quality label, using grapes from their two separate vineyards to make Wirra Wirra's 20,000-case range of premium quality table wines. To top up their own vines, the Trotts buy in grapes from the Adelaide Hills, Clarendon and Coonawarra. Wines are made in a new fermentation cellar built into the hill behind the old cellar with the help of wine-making consultant, Oenotec. Wirra Wirra's best wines are a stylish, classic, zesty Sauvignon and an appealing Church Block Cabernet/Merlot blend. The full, soft, fruity, black pepper spice of the 87 Church Block Cabernet (blended with Shiraz and Merlot) and the smoky-toasty, flowery 86 Chardonnay are worth experiencing. Finer still is the Cab Sauvignon with its rich, ripe, velvety style. Small quantities of port are also made.

WOLF BLASS   **BV**
Bilyara Vineyards, 97 Sturt Highway, Nuriootpa, SA 5355

w, r, ft, sp   *→**

Love him or loathe him, it is impossible to ignore the diminutive, bow-tied form of Wolfgang Franz Otto Blass. No one in Australia has promoted himself or his wines more assiduously over the last 20 years. His brash, kitsch, unorthodox style may shock the die-hards, but few can match his track record. Founded in 1969 and floated in 1986, Blass' winery has won 2,000 wine gongs and annual production now stands at 500,000 cases. He also owns his own bottling company, half-owns Remy Blass, a joint distribution company with the French Rémy Martin group, has recently acquired **Tim Knappstein** and Quelltaler in Clare, and is currently involved in a joint New Zealand vineyard venture with **Corbans**.

Wolf Blass was born in Germany in 1934. He came to Australia with wine-making experience, working at first for **Kaiser Stuhl** and **Tollana**, with a period in between as a freelance wine consultant; at the same time he blended and sold his own Bilyara label wines. After striking out alone, Blass initially made red wines only, but he anticipated the Australian trend to whites and now makes more white than red. He is certainly worthy of his German *kellermeister* diploma, for his wines are clever, heavily-oaked blends that have great appeal to Australians but less to European palates. Although he has yet to repeat his hat trick of the mid-1970s, when he won three successive Jimmy Watson Trophies at the Melbourne Show, Blass still clocks up vast numbers of medals for his early-maturing wines.

Although it owns just 14 acres (6 ha) in the Barossa, the firm now has a vast vineyard site in Clare and 35 acres (14 ha) in the Eden Valley. Blass' purchase of Quelltaler's 360 acres (150 ha) in 1987, and the first release in 88 of three wines from here under the Eaglehawk label further strengthens his portfolio. It will be intriguing to see what happens to the 30-year-old Quelltaler Semillon vines, responsible for such three-star treats as the great Wood-Aged Semillons (known as White Burgundy in Australia). The 87 Gold Label Rh Riesling is one of Australia's most popular wines: with its soft, sweet, sherbetty style it is easy to see why. The sweet, pineappley 87 Chardonnay was equally commercial. Blass' reds are an acquired taste for Europeans, as shown by the strong, oaky, eucalyptus-like 85 Yellow Label Cab Sauvignon. Blass rates the perfumed, oaky 84 Black Label President's Selection Cab Sauvignon as his best wine. It is a distinct improvement on the 83 vintage, whose excessive, high-toned essence of sandalwood, mint and eucalyptus was hard to stomach.

WOODSTOCK   SO
Douglas Gully Road, McLaren Flat, SA 5171

w, r, sw, ft *→

Woodstock was named after the English town in Oxfordshire by Arthur Townsend, who settled here in 1859. The winery, founded by the Collett family in 1974, did not sell wines under its own label until 1982. The 60 acres (24 ha) of vineyards here are planted in almost equal proportions to Shiraz, Cab Sauvignon, Chardonnay, Riesling and Grenache; about a third of the Collett needs are bought in from elsewhere in McLaren Vale. Scott Collett, the acclaimed Roseworthy-trained wine-maker, turns these into a neat 30,000-case range of single varietal table and fortified wines. Woodstock's buttery 87 Chardonnay and agreeable fruity Cabernet spend some time in new oak, unlike its peppery Shiraz. The most admired wine is the rare Woodstock 85 Noble Dessert Wine, a *trockenbeerenauslese* style made mainly from Rh Riesling and Chenin Blanc: an intensely sweet pudding wine. The Colletts recently opened the "Coterie", a handsome rammed-earth building complete with restaurant facilities.

WYNNS   CW
Memorial Drive, Coonawarra, SA 5263

w=82 87, r=86 85 84 *→→***

Samuel Weintraub (the name means literally "wine grape") emigrated from Poland to Australia in 1863. Changing his name to Wynn, he set up a wine merchants and blending business in Melbourne. It was his son David, pioneer of the wine flagon and developer of the wine cask, who bought a sizeable chunk of Coonawarra's terra rossa in 1951. Under David's aegis, the famous Wynns label – still Australia's most stylish – was devised: the distinctive Coonawarra Estate black and white woodcut depicting a trio of monkey puzzle trees and the three-gabled cellar built by John Riddoch in 1891. Riddoch first spotted the potential of the terra rossa here and divided it into blocks which he sold as vineyard land. His vast, handsome old cellar is still used by Wynns today. Despite the obvious quality of its wines, Wynns had problems during the 60s like everyone else in the wine business. Going public in 1970, it eventually became part of the **Penfolds** group.

Wynns is the largest owner of Coonawarra's terra rossa and must now account for a third of the region's vines. Surprisingly, it is not Cabernet that has the lion's share of production, but Rh Riesling. The finesse of the 87, with its greeny-gold colour and fine light, spritzy lemon and lime taste, is worth experiencing; so too is the powerful, rich lime juice character of the 75, although this wine is now drying out. Wynns' straight Cabernet has in its time provided tastes as disparate as the chocolatey 72, the big, rich, green pepper-like 75, the luscious, spicy, eucalyptus-like 78 and more recently the fine sweet, cassis-like 84 or the voluptuous, velvety 85. But the finest offering is its John Riddoch Cabernet: the ripe, concentrated, blackcurrant pastille-like 82 and the complex, gutsy 86 are both three-star wines; the cedary, eucalyptus-like 85 is not far behind. Wynns' Coonawarra Chardonnays are also worth looking out. The rich, buttery-lemony 82 is still going strong, while the lighter, toasty cinnamon fruit of the 87 demonstrates the lighter oak-influenced approach that Wynns is now adopting with this grape. Wynns' Coonawarra Shiraz may not be as fine as its Cabernet but wines such as the scented, spicy, black fruits-like 86 should not be ignored;

neither should the more rustic, ripe, burnt, briary 82 Wynns Ovens Valley Shiraz, made from North-East Victorian grapes. Don't bother with the disappointing Cabernet/Shiraz wines. Remarkably, Wynns recently came up with a more than passable rich minty-plummy 86 Pinot Noir. Coonawarra's extraordinary terra rossa is capable of much.
♀ Star buy: Wynns Coonawarra Cabernet

YALUMBA   BV
Eden Valley Road, Angaston, SA 5353

w = 73 84 86, r = 86 84 87, ft, sp   ∗→∗∗

Samuel Smith, an English brewer, founded Yalumba (aboriginal for "all the land around") in 1849. With the aid of a small gold strike at Bendigo in 1852 his vineyard thrived and, by 1900, S Smith & Son had 120 acres (48 ha) of vines. The imposing turretted Yalumba building and clock tower, built from local "blue quartz", was completed in 1911. The family business prospered and, at some point, the Smiths became Hill-Smiths. Today, this 415,000-case winery is owned entirely by one half of the family, with young Robert Hill-Smith at the helm. The others, headed by Master of Wine Michael Hill-Smith, his brother Matthew and father Mark, have left to start up their own concern.

Yalumba's belief in the importance of the vineyard is as strong today as it was in Samuel Smith's time. It now has over 1,000 acres (400 ha) of vines. Fruit from the main Oxford Landing Estate site in the Riverland ends up principally in casks and the cheaper Country and Gourmet ranges. Yalumba also owns the Hill-Smith Estate vineyard in the eastern Barossa Ranges and further acres in the Barossa itself. But it is the higher, cooler Pewsey Vale and Heggies vineyards nearer the Adelaide Hills that provide the company with the cream of its crop. Besides vinifying its own grapes Yalumba buys in from some 60 SA growers. There is a continual process of vine selection work and grape quality assessment here, with frequent vinification trials carried out in the large and well-equipped laboratory.

The Pewsey Vale and Heggies selections are made exclusively from these vineyards. Try the luscious, ripe, lime-like 84 Pewsey Rh Riesling or the 87 Heggies Rhine with its fresh, flowery, citrus palate. The finest wine to date is the splendid 86 Cabernet/Merlot with its fine eucalyptus and blackcurrant pastille-like fruit. Current Hill-Smith Estate wines are not very exciting; nor are the Yalumba Signature Series wines. What are worth looking out for are the Yalumba sparklers, such as the transfer-method Angas Brut in both its elegant, appley straight and sappy-fruit rosé versions. "Yalumba's D" was originally a joint venture with the Deutz champagne house which aborted early on. The toasty *méthode champenoise* Pinot Noir/Chardonnay-based 86 offers broad biscuity flavours. Yalumba's ports, such as the rich, raisin and tea-leaf-like Galway Pipe are worth tasting. The Hill-Smiths also have a venture in the North Island of New Zealand, called Nautilus, which produces Chardonnay as well as a somewhat overwhelming verdant, herbaceous Sauvignon; a Nautilus Pinot Noir is also expected soon.

For a firm so committed to wine quality, the wines here are not as consistently impressive as they might be. Anyone tasting a cross-section of the Yalumba range will encounter some fine wines, but will also see room for improvement. With talented Brian Walsh as the new chief wine-maker, expect to find richer, fruitier Yalumba wines in the future.
♀ Star buy: Yalumba Pewsey Vale & Heggies Rh Riesling

ZEMA ESTATE   CW
Naracoorte Road, Coonawarra, SA 5263

w, r   ∗

These 20 acres (8 ha) of vines in central Coonawarra are run by the Zema family, Matteo Zema sharing the wine-making with Ken Ward. About two-thirds of the hand-picked vines are Cab Sauvignon, with Shiraz accounting for the rest. In order to make a third wine, the estate buys in Rh Riesling grapes from elsewhere in Coonawarra. It has just purchased another 62 Coonawarra acres (25 ha).

Western Australia

Western Australia's wineries owe their appearance on the world's fine wine map to the Margaret River region. This is not to say that good wine is not made elsewhere in the state, nor that bad Margaret River wine does not exist. But it is the combination of this region's conducive climate for viticulture and the wide impression made by its articulate wine-makers that has gained remote, little-visited Western Australia its growing reputation for fine wine.

If antiquity is anything to go by, "WA" (as Australians refer to the state) should be better known for wine than either Victoria or South Australia; its first vineyard, planted in 1829 in the Swan Valley, predates this easterly opposition by several years. It is possible to see the cellar where Western Australia's first wines were made still in use today at **Olive Farm Wines**. Although vineyards were later established elsewhere in the state, the Swan remained its chief centre of production until the early 1970s. At one stage, there were almost 10,000 acres (4,000 ha) of vineyards in Western Australia, mainly in the Swan, but as the fortifieds which predominated there became unfashionable, many declined. It was Dr John Gladstone's enthusiastic 1965 report on vine-growing in south-west Australia that gave birth to the new wine regions, especially the Margaret River and Mount Barker/Frankland River. In spite of rapid expansion over the last two decades, Western Australia can boast only half its former acreage of vines today.

The chief constraint on the whole of the south-west is lack of water. Yields in Western Australia are about half those of the eastern states. It is only recently that vignerons have realized that their stressed, sun-baked vines need irrigation and in many cases nutrition. Irrigation systems are being installed, but there are continuing problems with salinity. Better yields should mean that more, finer wines become available at cheaper prices.

Wine-producing regions

DARLING RANGES (DR)
Situated in the Perth Hills some 20 miles (30 km) east of the city, the Darling Ranges is a small, new and little-known region. This narrow 9-mile (15-km) wide strip benefits from its 1,000 feet (300 m) of altitude and, although cooler than the Swan, is warmer than the Margaret River. **Darlington Vineyard** is the largest producer.

MARGARET RIVER (MA)
The Margaret River, a region of lush, green vineyards set with tall jarrah and marri gums, is generally regarded as the jewel in WA's crown. But this 56-mile (90-km) long projection between Cape Naturaliste and Cape Leeuwin, some three hours' drive south from Perth, is not the viticultural paradise that it is sometimes made out to be. Although its clay terrain overlaid with gravelly, sandy soils is well-suited to vines, the region suffers from a lack of irrigation and soil nutrition, and from its exposure to salty sea breezes. Contrary to what many maintain, it is not a cool-climate region; its climate is mild or Mediterranean, with rain in the winter, droughts in the summer and few frosts. The Margaret River's problems are, however, being rapidly eradicated by its talented vignerons. The first wine-makers here were medical men who planted vines in 1967 in response to Dr Gladstone's report. In the last two decades, the Margaret River has gained a high profile, and some 1,700 acres (700 ha) are now under vine. Apart from Rhine Riesling, the fine fruit here has shown gloriously intense varietal flavour. Semillon, Sauvignon and Chardonnay vines have all done well, as have Cabernet Sauvignon, Shiraz, Merlot and even the occasional Pinot Noir. With present problems overcome, the next generation of Margaret River vine-growers and wine-makers will be hard to beat.

N

| Miles | 0 | 25 |
| Km | 0 | 50 |

R Swan

Upper Swan

Wanneroo

PERTH

Fremantle

Mandurah

Pinjarra

R Murray

Harvey

INDIAN OCEAN

Bunbury

Cape Naturaliste

Capel

Donnybrook

R Capel

Busselton

R Margaret

Bridgetown

Margaret River

R Blackwood

WESTER

Manjin

Cape Leeuwin

Pemberton

DARLING RANGE

Wine Regions

1 DARLING RANGES
2 MARGARET RIVER
3 MOUNT BARKER/FRANKLAND RIVER
4 SOUTH-WEST COASTAL PLAIN
5 SWAN VALLEY

WESTERN AUSTRALIA

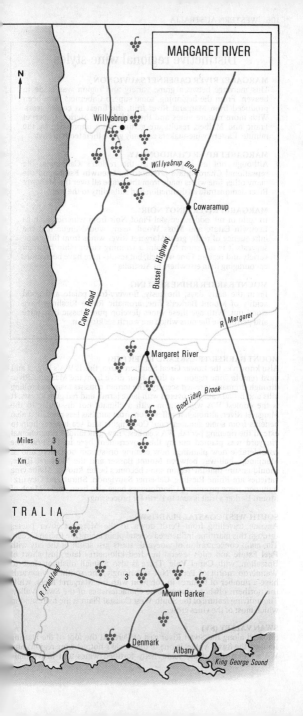

Distinctive regional wine-styles

MARGARET RIVER CABERNET SAUVIGNON
This marriage between grape variety and region was made in
heaven. From the beginning, some superb Cabernets have been
produced from Margaret River fruit, the finest in cooler years.
With more mature vines and the addition of Merlot, Cabernet
Franc and Malbec, results are getting more impressive by the
minute. Eastern wine-makers can only grind their teeth in envy.

MARGARET RIVER CHARDONNAY
Although not as impressive as the region's Cabernets, the
sensational Chardonnays produced by **Leeuwin Estate** and the
many other fine wines made from this grape all over the Margaret
River demonstrate its distinction and suitability to the soil.

MARGARET RIVER PINOT NOIR
In spite of the odd successful Pinot Noir from wineries such as
Leeuwin Estate and **Moss Wood**, many would argue that the
infrequency of really great Margaret River wines from this grape
suggests it is too soon to claim a winning partnership between
variety and region. Time will tell, but results here have been more
encouraging than elsewhere in Australia.

MOUNT BARKER RHINE RIESLING
From the early days, the zesty, flowery-fruit palate and good
acidity of Mount Barker's fine, aromatic Rhine Rieslings have
stood out. With age these wines develop pure classic lime juice
and petrol-like flavours which are worth seeking out.

MOUNT BARKER/FRANKLAND RIVER (MB)
Also known as the Lower Great Southern Area, this is WA's largest and
most remote wine region – a three-hour drive from the Margaret River
through dramatic forested scenery. The terrain consists mainly of rolling
hills and broad valleys, covered with large jarrah and red gum forests. It
is the coolest WA wine region with a climate not dissimilar to the
Margaret River, although it suffers from frost and has less rainfall; it also
benefits from some summer rain. Cool nights and sea breezes help to
extend the ripening period. WA's earliest "new generation" experimental
vineyard was planted out by the Government here in 1965-66. The
considerable new plantings now coming on stream both here and at
Manjimup, half-way between Mount Barker and the Margaret River,
should ensure that the region soon becomes better known. Major vine
varieties are Rhine Riesling, Cabernet Sauvignon, Shiraz and Gewurztraminer; some promising Chardonnays have also been made. Much of
Mount Barker's fruit is sent to Perth for processing.

SOUTH-WEST COASTAL PLAIN (SW)
Anyone travelling from Perth down to the Margaret River passes
through this maritime-influenced coastal plain facing the Indian Ocean.
The main concentration of vineyards starts just south of the city with
Peel Estate and ends several hundred kilometres later, just short of
Busselton, with **Capel Vale**. There is also a small offshoot close to
Wanneroo, north of Perth. Not surprisingly, the southern vineyards
have a number of features in common with the Margaret River, while
the northern offshoot shares some characteristics of the Swan Valley.
The unifying feature of the South-West Coastal Plain is the tuart sand in
which most of the vines grow.

SWAN VALLEY (SV)
Situated along the Swan River east of Perth at the foot of the Darling
Ranges, the Swan Valley is one of the world's hottest wine regions and
WA's oldest. For many years, hefty fortified wines and heavy table

wines were all it could produce – a style relished by the Yugoslav families who settled in the valley during the early 20th century and whose presence is still strong. The Swan's vineyards suffer from an arid terrain and hot easterly winds. Reasonably heavy winter rainfalls do help to alleviate its stressed vines but irrigation, now on the increase, is the only real answer. Frosts are rare. Thanks, among other innovations, to cold fermentation technology, the Swan now makes some palatable Chenin Blanc, Chardonnay, Verdelho and Semillon white wines – for example **Houghton's** White Burgundy – and some decent Cabernet Sauvignon. Traditional Swan producers continue to make earthy table wines and the once-loved fortifieds.

Western Australian wineries

ADRIATIC WINES

SV

Great Northern Highway, Herne Hill, WA 6056

w, r, ft *

The Jurjevich family makes table and fortified wine here from Chenin Blanc, Shiraz, Pedro, Grenache and Muscat grapes. Founded in 1954, this traditional winery sells all its wines at the cellar door.

ALKOOMI

MB

Manjimup Road, Frankland, WA 6396

w, r *→**

Alkoomi, aboriginal for "a place we chose", is the first winery you come to driving into the Mount Barker/Frankland River region from Perth. Mervyn and Judy Lange, its friendly owners, run a large sheep and grain farm as well as their 32 acres (13 ha) of vines, planted in 1971. Alkoomi is worth visiting for its handsome winery, built from local stone and set partly into the hillside with fine views over the Frankland River. Kim Hart, the Roseworthy graduate recently appointed as wine-maker, will no doubt continue the Alkoomi tradition of producing whites that are appealing, though dumb when young, and firm, gutsy, long-lived reds which also need time. The Langes worried for a while that their wines were not getting the recognition they deserved, but these worries have been allayed by a series of local wine awards.

Alkoomi whites include a Rh Riesling in both straight and late harvest versions, as well as a little Semillon and Sauvignon. The 84 Rh Riesling had an attractive, lively, citrous character and fine, lime-like flavours on the palate; its late harvest sister showed some agreeable fresh apricot-like sweetness. The Alkoomi reds, which are superior to the whites, are led by Cab Sauvignon, with a little Malbec and Merlot. The Malbecs are not easy on European palates, but no one would grumble about the Cabernets. The hefty, peppery-earthy style of the 82, with mint and eucalyptus in the mix, shows Alkoomi's expertise; so too does the 77 with its big, mature, cedary and cinnamon-like taste.

AMBERLEY

MA

Wildwood and Thornton Roads, Yallingup, WA 6282

w, r *

No wines have yet been released at this new vineyard, planted to Chardonnay, Sauv Blanc, Semillon and Chenin Blanc white varieties, with Shiraz, Cab Sauvignon, Cab Franc and Merlot for the reds.

ASHBROOK ESTATE

MA

Harman's South Road, Willyabrup, WA 6284

w, r, sw *→**

Ashbrook is very much a family estate. Since its foundation in 1975, all the Devitts have done their share: organic chemist Brian Devitt and his wife live here and manage the estate; Brian's brother Tony, a WA Government viticulturist with Roseworthy training, travels down from Perth every weekend with his wife Marnie, who runs the cellar-door sales; and the Devitt parents also help out whenever they can. Tucked away in the middle of a red gum forest and reached by a long, winding track edged with "black boy" ferns, Ashbrook is worth the detour. This is a 500-acre (200-ha) estate, but with only 30 acres (12 ha) of vines, one-third just planted. Chardonnay and Semillon account for half of these vines; Verdelho and Cab Sauvignon make up another quarter, with small amounts of Riesling, Sauv Blanc, Cab Franc and Merlot; a quarter of Ashbrook's fruit is bought in locally. The Devitts believe in simple, careful wine-making techniques.

Recent tastings have seen some dramatic improvements in quality here, partly helped no doubt by more mature vines. The Devitts now make a very presentable 88 Semillon with a fresh, young, barley sugar taste, good structure and bite. The crisp, flowery 88 Sauvignon is good too and now has a pleasing snap of spicy oak. The late-picked 88 Gold Label Rh Riesling is better still – fresh, peachy and citrous. The 88 Chardonnay's deliciously rich, buttery flavour of oak and pineapple makes it their best wine. Ashbrook's whites sell out within a year of their release, but reds like the 84 Cabernet take longer. This seductive, cassis-scented wine now contains a 16% dollop of Cab Franc and Merlot in its mix, and benefits from two years in classy French oak. However, its taste is still a shade grassy, chewy and austere. A large new winery extension with a cool cellar down below and more wine-making space above will give the Devitts more room to manoeuvre. With the Ashbrook vineyard now fully irrigated and receiving proper nutrition, their hard work should pay off with some decent crops. Cellar-door sales operate on weekends and public holidays, 11am-5pm.

BANARA WINES   SV
Banara Road, Caversham, WA 6055

ft   *

The Knezovics, a family of Yugoslav descent, founded Banara in 1937. They concentrate on fortified wines, including Muscats and ports.

BASSENDEAN ESTATE   SV
147 West Road, Bassendean, WA 6054

w, r, ft   *→

The vineyard here, first planted by Laurie Nicoletto in 1939-40, was replanted in the 60s. As its original name, Riverside Estate, suggests it is on the banks of the Swan River. Bassendean's reds are well thought of in Australia, and Nicoletto gives them considerable bottle age before release. His range includes Burgundy, Cabernet/Shiraz and Shiraz.

BLACKWOOD CREST WINES   MB
Chamber's Road, Boyup Brook, WA 6244

w, r, ft   *

The Fairbrass family founded this 10-acre (4-ha) estate in 1976. The wide spectrum of wines made here includes Cab Sauvignon, Rh Riesling, Sauv Blanc, Shiraz, Semillon and Chardonnay, as well as pink wines and port; each style is made in minute quantities.

BOLGANUP WINES   MB
Bolganup Homestead, Porongurup, WA 6324

r   *

David McNamara is the wine-maker of this small concern. As yet only Cab Sauvignon has been grown here; 1986 was the second vintage.

BONANNELLA & SONS   SV
3 Pinjar Road, Wanneroo, WA 6065

w, r, ft   *

Immacolata Bonannella produces a range of table and fortified wines made from Muscat and Grenache grapes.

CAPE CLAIRAULT   MA
Henry Road, Willyabrup, WA 6284

w=88 87 85, r=86 85 82, ft   *→***

Cape Clairault, which advertises itself somewhat coyly as "the great little tucked-away winery", makes some of the finest wines in the Margaret River and charges reasonable prices for them too. Only just over 2,000 cases are available annually. Remarkably, wine-maker Ian Lewis is entirely self-taught – modest too, for he dismisses his ability by stating simply, "I drank enough of the good stuff to know what it should taste like". Ian, an ex-geologist, and his South African wife Ani (hence the winery's Cape Dutch frontage) came to the region in 1976, "looking for a change in life style". Cape Clairault was chosen for its soil and slopes, and from the beginning the winery was a success. 1981 was the first commercial vintage. With their 82 Cabernet the Lewises won the first of many trophies at the leading Canberra wine show, and drove across Australia to receive it.

There are 18 acres (7 ha) of vines here and, following Ian's purist line, no grapes are bought in. He uses organic fertilizer and is currently installing a new trellising system to allow more sun onto the vines, increasing yields and improving fruit flavour. Cab Sauvignon, Sauv Blanc and a wood-matured Semillon/Sauvignon blend are the three main wines. Rh Riesling is also grown, as well as a little Merlot and Cab Franc; these last two reds will be blended with the Cabernet from 1990. Cellar-door sales offer straight and late harvest Rh Rieslings, a medium-dry white, a vintage port and Claireau, a liqueur-style wine.

Ian Lewis describes his wine-making technique as a "unique blend of traditional/technological gentleness, attention to detail and tender loving care". Certainly anyone tasting his zesty, flowering currant-like 88 Sauvignon or his well-made 87 Classic Dry White with its pleasing fresh, leafy-flowery style would not find fault with his wine-making techniques. Ian understands how to handle white wine and wood. His splendid 88 Semillon/Sauvignon (just 10% Sauv), which spends three months in oak, boasts an intriguing mango and tropical fruit salad scent and a fine balance between fruit, oak and acidity. With age this wine, as the 85 showed, develops a deliciously rich, waxy, honeyed style. Ian Lewis is as good at making reds as he is at whites, and his intense, ripe cassis and mulberry-like 85 Cabernet is a delight; so too is the 86, which is more herbaceous, but with tremendous cherry and plum-like flavours. Visitors are welcome here every day, 10am-5pm.

♥ Star buy: Cape Clairault 88 Sauvignon & 87 Classic Dry White

CAPE MENTELLE   MA
Wallcliffe Road, Margaret River, WA 6285
                    w=85 88, r=84 82 86 88   ∗→∗∗∗∗

David Hohnen is a new-generation Australian wine-maker *par excellence*. After taking the ultra-practical wine course at California's Fresno State University, Hohnen first became vineyard manager at **Taltarni** (VIC), where he met and studied the methods of Dominique Portet. Armed with this experience he sped off to work on a vintage at California's Clos du Val, run by Dominique's brother Bernard. By 1976, when David Hohnen arrived in the Margaret River with his brother Mark to found Cape Mentelle, he had absorbed three different wine cultures: his own native Australian and those of California and France. It was to prove a powerful combination. Cape Mentelle's first vintage was in 1977. Five years later, Hohnen walked off with the major wine awards at the Melbourne Show, including the prestigious Jimmy Watson Trophy. The following year he did the same again.

Hohnen now has 100 acres (40 ha) of vines, planted one-third to Cab Sauvignon and one-quarter to Semillon, with lesser amounts of Sauv Blanc, Merlot, Chenin Blanc, Cab Franc, Shiraz and Zinfandel (a Californian inspiration). The entire crop is machine-harvested, making it possible to pick the white grapes at night. No doubt because of the region's low yield, he has to buy in about a fifth of his fruit. Annual production now stands at 15,000 cases, one of the largest in the region, but Hohnen intends to double this. He uses traditional Bordeaux techniques for his Cabernet but adopts a more American approach to his Zinfandel and Shiraz. Not content with his Australian enterprise, Hohnen also owns 100 acres (40 ha) of vines at **Cloudy Bay** in New Zealand, where results have been equally impressive.

Hohnen's Shiraz wines boast big, peppery, liquorice-like flavours which in top years such as 84 tone down into elegant, irresistible layers of black pepper spice, mint, eucalyptus and cassis. The spicy, perfumed 84 Zinfandel is also a fine wine, but Cape Mentelle's Cabernets are its finest offerings. Anyone who has tasted a range of recent vintages can see the impressive leaps in quality from year to year. Hohnen favours his herbaceous-blackcurrancy 86 and his pleasant, herbaceous 82, but

the 84 with its delicious rich, perfumed, cassis style could be the finer wine. Watch out for the first releases of the 88: it is superb. Hohnen also produces a white blend made from two-thirds Semillon to one-third Sauvignon; the refreshing, uncomplicated, grassy-leafy 87 needs to be drunk young. The CM Dry White and Dry Red blends are worthwhile too. Cape Mentelle welcomes visitors every day, 10am-4.30pm.
℣ Star buy: Cape Mentelle CM Dry White & Dry Red

CAPEL VALE WINES SW
Lot 5, Stirling Estate, Capel North West Road, Capel, WA 6271

w, r, sp   **→***

Capel Vale's record at wine shows must be one of the best in the West: every wine it made in the period 1983-86 won a medal. Basking in this glory is Dr Peter Pratten, the director and major shareholder, his wife Elizabeth and wine-maker Alan Johnson. They achieved this impressive run by rejecting disappointing vats in order to keep quality high and by pursuing improvements from vintage to vintage. They also hired high-tech Oenotec, the wine consultancy firm, from 1983 until 1986. Johnson, a Roseworthy graduate, joined Capel Vale in 1985.

Situated half-way between Bunbury and Busselton, this cool winery overlooks the pretty Capel River – a wildfowl reserve, home to the shell duck featured on the Capel Vale label. Medical man Pratten set up Capel Vale in 1973, after catching the wine bug at Sydney University. He sees wine and medicine as logical bedfellows and points in evidence to WA's numerous other medical wine folk. Pratten is a firm believer in blending batches of the same grape, and occasionally different grapes, to achieve first-class quality. He takes parcels adding up to 20% of his needs from all over the region in order to do this; the other 80% comes from 50 acres (20 ha) close to Capel.

In fact, the only Capel wine made exclusively from home vines is Chardonnay. The Prattens hope that by 1991 this will account for 12,000 cases of a projected 30,000 cases. Other whites include Rh Riesling, Gewurztraminer, a Sauv Blanc/Semillon blend and a *méthode champenoise* Chardonnay/Pinot Noir blend. Reds on offer include Cab Sauvignon, Shiraz and Merlot. Dr Pratten is very proud of his Bordeaux-style blend of Cab Sauvignon, Shiraz, Merlot and Cab Franc. This small *barrique*-aged red is known as Baudin after the French explorer who charted the coastline close to where the grapes were grown. First released in 1985, Baudin varies each year according to grape quality. It will always, however, be Capel Vale's best red wine. Pratten believes that the Chardonnay is his finest wine. It would indeed be hard to beat the structured pineapple, melon and peach charms of the 87.
℣ Star buy: Capel Vale 87 Chardonnay

CAROSA VINEYARD DR
Lot 3, Houston Street, Mount Helena, WA 6555

w, r, sp   *

Carosa's Jim Elson was formerly wine-maker at **Darlington Vineyard**. His Chardonnay, Cabernet (blended with Merlot), Rh Riesling and sparkling wines are all from the 1988 vintage.

CASTLE ROCK ESTATE MB
Porongurup Road, Porongurup, WA 6330

w, r   *→

Founded in 1982, Castle Rock takes its name from an odd-looking rock formation nearby which is featured on its labels. Angelo and Wendy Diletti's 20-acre (8-ha) plot, perched high on the side of this low mountain range, escapes frost and enjoys a cool, long-growing season which produces some fine grapes. Castle Rock wines are made with the help of Kim Hart at **Alkoomi**. There have been three releases: a well-regarded Rh Riesling, a late harvest Riesling and a Cab Sauvignon.

CHAPEL VIEW MB
St Werburgh's Road, Mount Barker, WA 6324

w, r   *

Goundrey Wines makes a range of red and white table wines for Chapel View, including a successful Cab Sauvignon.

CHATEAU BARKER MB
Redmond West Road, Redmond, WA 6327

w, r ∗

The Coopers, who founded this winery in 1973, have recently sold their Mount Barker vineyard though happily not the business. Instead they are concentrating on developing their other vineyards. Wine-maker James Cooper, the son of the founders and a Roseworthy graduate, makes seven different wines: Quondyp Rh Riesling, Gewurztraminer, Fumé Blanc, Tiger's Eye Pinot Noir, Pyramup Cab Sauvignon, Hermitage (Shiraz) and a Pyramup "Bordeaux-style" blend. So far these have been kept almost exclusively for the home market, which is a pity for foreigners as several have pleased the Australian press.

CHATEAU XANADU MA
Off Wallcliffe Road, Margaret River, WA 6285

w=85 86 87, r=82 84 86 ∗→∗∗

This southern Margaret River winery was named after Kublai Khan's summer palace near Peking and inspired by Coleridge's famous poem, a few lines of which appear on both corks and labels. Literary-minded Dr Lagan and his wife Dr Sheridan came from Ireland in 1968. They have owned and run this winery since 1976, more recently with wine-making help from John Smith and Conor Lagan. The 50 acres (20 ha) of vines here consist mostly of Semillon, Cab Sauvignon, Chardonnay and Pinot Noir, with a small patch of Cab Franc (used to round off Cab Sauvignon wines) and an even smaller patch of recently-planted Pinot Noir. Grapes are also occasionally bought in locally. Annual production at Chateau Xanadu is now almost 7,000 cases.

New temperature-controlled underground storage and wine-making cellars have improved the Xanadu style. Grapes are now chilled for 24 hours prior to crushing and whites fermented in small French oak casks. Semillon is the bestseller, but the Lagans regard the Chardonnay as their finest wine. The weighty 87 Chardonnay with its 14% alcohol won a Gold Medal in the Mount Barker show, but the strong, verdant 87 Semillon is finer than the rich, peachy-pineappley 86 Chardonnay. All wines are aged in oak, apart from the off-dry Semillon 11 which is made in a stainless steel tank to preserve its fruit flavours.

CHATSFIELD WINES MB
34 Albany Highway, Mount Barker, WA 6324

w, r ∗→∗∗

Chatsfield, founded in 1984 and now owned by Waterman & Kyle, hires **Goundrey** to make its wines. Production here is limited to well-thought-of Gewurztraminer, Rh Riesling, Shiraz and Chardonnay.

CHIDLOW BROOK VINEYARD DR
Lakeview Road, Chidlow, WA 6556

w, r ∗

Les Johnston is responsible for the wine-making here. Chardonnay, Cab Sauvignon, Shiraz and Merlot are grown.

CHITTERING ESTATE DR
Chittering Valley Road, Lower Chittering, WA 6084

w, r ∗→

Food and fish industry colleagues, Steven Schapera and George Kailis, started this 62-acre (25-ha) concern some nine years ago. Set high in a cool valley north of Perth, Chittering is one of WA's showpiece estates. Its landscaped winery building, complete with fancy equipment, is an easy hour's drive from Perth and has obvious appeal for day-tripping wine enthusiasts. But Chittering is likely to live up to its handsome setting for Schapera takes wine-making seriously. He attended Davis, California's wine school, and has worked several vintages overseas. Wine-makers and technology from both Old and New Worlds have been brought in to help him get the best from the grapes here. These include Chardonnay, Sauv Blanc, Semillon, Pinot Noir, Cab Sauvignon and Merlot. Schapera hopes his Chardonnay will outshine all WA competitors. Whether it does or not, Chittering Estate is a winery to watch. The first release was in 1987.

COBANOV   SV
Stock Road, Herne Hill, WA 6056

                                                        w, r, ft   *

Steve Cobanov produces and sells bulk white, red and fortified wines at this Swan winery near Perth.

COORINJA VINEYARD   SV
Toodyay Road, Toodyay, WA 6566

                                                           r, ft   *

Established in 1870, Coorinja is one of WA's oldest wineries. The Woods have 37 acres (15 ha) of Shiraz, Pedro, Grenache and Muscat grapes which are turned into table, fortified and flavoured wines.

CULLENS   MA
Caves Road, Cowaramup, WA 6284

                                           w=84, r=86   *→→**

Cullens is everyone's favourite Margaret River winery. This has perhaps rather more to do with the remarkable Cullen family than its wines. **Vasse Felix** and **Moss Wood** may have got their vines into the ground a few years earlier, but the Cullens were no less pioneering for that and they inspired many others to follow their lead. Diana Cullen and her husband Kevin, a doctor, had been living in the Margaret River for some years before they planted a Cab Sauvignon and Rh Riesling vineyard in 1971. Diana ran the wine-making unaided until recently when Vanya, her Roseworthy-trained daughter, came to join her.

Cullens has 53 acres (21 ha) of producing vines, with another 20 acres (8 ha) planted. This may sound a large acreage but the Cullens, like other local vignerons, have had trouble with low yields owing to the lack of topsoil and soil nutrition. Dr Richard Smart, the leading Antipodean viticulturist, has been advising them and new vines, when they come on stream, should help to solve the problem. At present, their plantings consist of Chardonnay, Sauv Blanc, Semillon and Rh Riesling whites, with Cab Sauvignon, Merlot, Cab Franc and Pinot Noir reds. Annual production is 6-8,000 cases. A Cabernet/Merlot blend accounts for the largest share of this, followed by Sauv Blanc, Chardonnay and Semillon, with small quantities of Pinot Noir, Fumé Cabernet and Spatlese Riesling. The Cullens are currently much preoccupied with oak, partly perhaps because Vanya saw Robert Mondavi's oak-ageing programme at first hand in 1985. The three Cullens whites are all fermented in small oak, as is the Fumé Cabernet. All Cullens wines aged in oak carry Ashley Jones' distinctive acorn and oakleaf label.

Over the years, Cullens has made some good Sauv Blanc wines. The best current wine is the fresh, grassy 87 Sauvignon with its oaky bite, derived from a year's ageing in German oak. Both the vanilla-scented 87 Chardonnay with its bitter, oaky finish and Cullens' 88 Chardonnay with its highly aromatic banana-vanillin oak appear to have had too much of a good thing. The fruit on the 86 and 87 Cabernet/Merlot (a two-thirds: one-third blend) also seems overcome with oak; with time, these wines should soften. The Cullens in any case aim to make firm, robust reds capable of ageing. The winery receives visitors Mon-Sat, 10am-4pm. An excellent restaurant serves light meals.

DARLINGTON VINEYARD   DR
Lot 39, Nelson Road, Darlington, WA 6070

                                                           w, r   *

Founded in 1983, Darlington Vineyard lies at the heart of the Darling Ranges. Its owner, who goes by the impressive name of Balthasar van der Meer, has acquired the services of wine-maker/consultant Rob Bowen, previously with **Plantagenet**. Cab Sauvignon has the largest share of Darlington's 20-acre (8-ha) vineyard, followed by Semillon; the remainder is split between Chardonnay, Sauv Blanc, Gamay, Shiraz and Merlot. Extra Cab Sauvignon and Shiraz are grown at a leased vineyard nearby. Darlington is in the early stages of evolution and van der Meer hopes to push current 2,000-case production up to 5,000 cases. Shiraz and Semillon are the bestsellers. Darlington also makes a young, light red wine known as "Vin Primeur". So far quality has been deemed worthwhile, not wonderful.

ELLENDALE ESTATE   SV
18 Ivanhoe Street, Bassendean, WA 6054

w, r, ft, sp *

Once known as Sveta Maria, Ellendale has two vineyards: a principal 64-acre (26-ha) site in the Upper Swan and another small 5-acre (2-ha) vineyard at Bassendean. John and Lyn Barrett-Lennard manage the business and make 28 table, fortified, flavoured and sparkling wines.

EVANS & TATE   SW
Swan Street, Henley Brook, WA 6055

w=88, r=88   *→→**

Now solely owned by John and Toni Tate, Evans & Tate has two grape sources of its own: the 10-acre (4-ha) Gnangara Estate here and the 50-acre (20-ha) Redbrook Estate in the Margaret River; about 10% of its grapes come from elsewhere. Gnangara Shiraz (first produced in 1974) is the bestseller, but it is the Margaret River wines that have picked up the medals. These include Cab Sauvignon, Shiraz, Merlot, Cab Franc, Chardonnay, Semillon and Sauv Blanc. Redbrook was first acquired in 1975 and the Tates have planted more vines since then, Cab Sauvignon taking the largest share. There is a fair amount of blending between properties – all above-board given the 80/20 rule (see Introduction), but it does annoy purists. Even the Gnangara Shiraz gets a dollop of Margaret River Cabernet to add richness and structure.

The first Chardonnay was released in 1986 and the 88 won a double Chardonnay medal at Perth and Mount Barker. Evans & Tate has now produced the lower-quality Two Vineyards Chardonnay to accompany it. The latest release, Margaret River Classic, is a blend of Sauv Blanc, Chenin Blanc and Semillon. The bestselling Gnangara Shiraz is usually an enormous, beefy, burnt wine like the 81 vintage, although the rich, perfumed, spicy 77, consumed a few years back, proves that this wine does soften given long enough. The 81 Margaret River Cabernet, with 16% Shiraz in its blend, boasted a herbaceous and spicy, yet somewhat stalky, flavour – as did the 79. The delicious fragrant, smoky, flowery 83 Semillon, also from this property, was much finer. Equally charming was the 82 vintage whose palate had begun to take on toasty, bottle-aged Semillon flavours. Visitors are welcome.

FARANDA WINES   SV
Wanneroo Road, Wanneroo, WA 6061

w *

Chasselas, Muscat and Grenache are made into small quantities of table wine here by the Faranda family and sold in flagons at the cellar door.

FERMOY ESTATE   MA
Metricup Road, Willyabrup, WA 6284

w, r *

The first releases from this new estate are expected soon. Red varieties grown are Cab Sauvignon and Pinot Noir; whites include Chardonnay and a Semillon/Sauv Blanc mix.

FOREST HILL VINEYARD   MB
Muir Highway, Mount Barker, WA 6324

w, r, ft **→

Formidable Betty Pearse runs this remote Mount Barker vineyard with her husband Tony. Originally started in 1965, half of their 50 acres (20 ha) are planted to Cab Sauvignon, with lesser amounts of Rh Riesling, Chardonnay, Traminer and Sauv Blanc. The remaining 10 acres (4 ha) is, as Betty puts it, a fruit salad of different varieties. As there is no winery here, Forest Hill's fine grapes have always been vinified by outsiders: **Sandalford** (pre-76), **Paul Conti** (76-83) and, since 1984, **Plantagenet**. This explains why some early bottles (made at Conti's Wanneroo winery) bore the name Conti Forest Hill, and for a while the property bore this same too. Forest Hill's excellent vineyard work and superior fruit stem partly from its close ties with WA's Dept. of Agriculture, which planted a 5-acre (2-ha) experimental vineyard here in 1965-66. The new wine-maker is Plantagenet's capable John Wade. His first 88 wines at Forest Hill are awaited with interest.

Forest Hill has acquired a reputation for its Rh Riesling wines; the 75, according to indefatigable Betty, has the distinction of being the most awarded wine in the West. The intense, rich lime juice of the 86 is classic Riesling at its Australian best, while the 85 Cabernet has more body, tannin, liquorice and fruit. Betty rates her Chardonnay highest, but the rich, smoky 80 was marred by an astringent finish. Port is made here too, including a pleasant Cab Sauvignon-based ruby. Visitors are welcome daily, 10am-4pm, except on national holidays.

♀   Star buy: Forest Hill Rh Riesling

FREYCINET ESTATE   MA
Lot 1, Gnararary Road, Margaret River, WA 6285

w=86 85, r=86   *→

Peter Gherardi of Freycinet is ideal wine-maker material: he has degrees in both Agriculture and Wine Science, and also works for the WA Dept. of Agriculture, keeping a close eye on Freycinet from his nearby office; his wife Jennifer also helps to run the estate. Freycinet was founded in 1978 but Peter, like many small part-time wine-makers, could only recently afford his own winery. Freycinet is now harvesting some mature fruit from its 20 acres (8 ha) of vines, which it turns into almost 3,000 cases of wine. Half of this acreage is planted to Cab Sauvignon, rounded off with Merlot and Cab Franc; the rest is divided between Semillon, Sauv Blanc, Chenin Blanc and Chardonnay. Chardonnay is the only unblended white; the Chenin Blanc and the Sauv Blanc are topped with Semillon. Best of the bunch are the fresh, appley 86 Chenin Blanc/Semillon and the herbaceous, sappy 86 Cab Sauvignon.

GALAFREY WINES   MB
145 Lower Stirling Terrace, Albany, WA 6330

w, r, sp   *

Founded in 1978 by Ian and Linda Tyrer, Galafrey is about to form a public company. This will enable it to increase the size of its vineyards and winery with a view to supplying the export market – especially the UK. Currently, it produces about 2,500 cases from 25 acres (10 ha) of local fruit. Ian vinifies all his wines in Albany at a huge converted wool warehouse. Rh Riesling and Cab Sauvignon account for two-thirds of production, Pinot Noir, Chardonnay and Muller-Thurgau for the rest. Recently Ian has been experimenting with sparkling varietal wines; so far he has produced a Rh Riesling Brut and a Cab Sauvignon Brut. Galafrey's wines are acceptable without being special. The best wine is the Rh Riesling, whose 84 vintage was a pleasant, racy, green, aromatic mouthful. The clean, raspberry-like 82 Pinot Noir and the fresh, grassy 83 Cabernet both demonstrate Galafrey's expertise.

GILLESPIE VINEYARDS   MA
Davis Road, Witchcliffe, WA 6286

w, r   *

Alastair Gillespie is wine-maker at this small family-owned estate. Surrounded by hills covered in gum forest, Gillespie is one of the most southerly vineyards in the region. There are 25 acres (10 ha) of Cab Sauvignon, Semillon, Sauv Blanc and Rh Riesling vines.

GLENALWYN WINES   SV
West Swan Road, West Swan, WA 6055

w, r, ft   *

The Pasalichs, like many other wine families in the region, came to the Swan from Yugoslavia. Dalmatian traditions live on at Glenalwyn with the emphasis on fortified wines. Table wines are also made from Chenin Blanc and Cab Sauvignon.

GOUNDREY WINES   MB
Langton, Muir Highway, Mount Barker, WA 6324

w, r, ft   *→

Michael and Alison Goundrey planted their first vines in 1970, "purely as a hobby". Michael was a sheep-shearing contractor, but the call of the vine proved irresistible. In spite of the Goundreys' hard work, it was not until 1983 that they turned professional, as they put it, and decided to live solely off the winery. In 1987, Goundrey Wines became a public company. Its operations are now centred on Denmark Cellars, the outgrown 1928 butter factory in Denmark, and the Langton property at Mount Barker where a new winery built from rammed earth topped with a shingled roof will be ready for the 1989 vintage.

Wine-maker Rodney Hooper divides Goundrey's 210 acres (85 ha) of vines, which include 115 acres (46 ha) of new plantings, into the premium Windy Hill range and the cheaper Denmark Cellars selection. The current split is roughly 70/30, but these proportions could change when expansion is over. However the new Denmark Cellars range, whose first vintage was 1988, will always be keenly priced. So far this has offered mostly blended varietal wines such as the Dry White and the sweet, fruity Autumn Red, but Late Harvest Riesling, Cabernet and port are also marketed. The Windy Hill selection consists of single varieties, including Rh Riesling, Chardonnay, Sauv Blanc, Cab Sauvignon and Shiraz. Half of Goundrey's acreage is occupied by Rh Riesling and Cab Sauvignon, the other half divided between Chardonnay, Sauv Blanc, Shiraz, Pinot Noir and Cab Franc.

Goundrey's recent investment in Langton with its new equipment, small French oak and a good wine-maker to control it all should mean finer wines. The Windy Hill Rh Riesling is its best wine and the full, fruity, peachy 84 vintage an agreeable representative of the Goundrey style. Windy Hill Cabernet is the best of the reds: the 84, aged in American oak, was richly if aggressively flavoured, but will need time to show at its best; the 85 is well thought of in Australia. Visitors are welcome at Denmark Cellars Mon–Sat, 10am–4pm; Sun, 12–4pm.

GRALYN CELLARS   MA
Caves Road, Willyabrup, WA 6284

w, r, ft, sp   *

Graham and Merilyn Hutton are joint owners/wine-makers of Gralyn – hence the winery's name. Their main concern is beef cattle but they also own 11 acres (4 ha) of Cab Sauvignon, Hermitage (Shiraz) and Rh Riesling planted in the early 1970s. Unlike other Margaret River estates, Gralyn makes table, fortified and sparkling wines. However, port is its chief preoccupation: six different versions are made, including Hermitage Port, Cabernet Port and, unusually, white port.

HAINAULT VINEYARD   DR
Walnut Road, Bickley, WA 6076

w, r   *→

Hainault is a cool-climate winery with high rainfall, situated half an hour east of Perth near the observatory. At 1,230 feet (375 m), it is one of WA's highest. The 11-acre (4-ha) vineyard, which is neither ploughed nor irrigated, is close-planted with seven varieties. Chardonnay leads the field, followed by Cab Sauvignon, Merlot, Semillon, Gewurztraminer, Pinot Noir and Cab Franc. With such young vines (some of them not yet producing) only just over 1,500 cases a year are made here. Peter Fimmel, Hainault's quality-minded owner/wine-maker, vinifies his grapes with French techniques firmly in mind. The Chardonnay, for instance, is barrel-fermented in oak, while the different components in his Bordeaux-style Cabernet/Merlot are vinified separately (with an extended maceration on skins for a fuller flavour) and blended just prior to bottling. This wine is a classic mix of 50% Cab Sauvignon, 45% Merlot and 5% Cab Franc. Fimmel hopes to release a non-vintage *méthode champenoise* Brut sparkler in late 1989. He rates the Chardonnay as his best wine, but the Cabernet/Merlot is his bestseller. With just six commercial vintages released, Hainault is still learning, but it is ahead of other Darling Ranges producers.

HAPP'S VINEYARD   MA
Commonage Road, Dunsborough, WA 6281

w=88 87, r=84 86 88, ft   *→***

Erland and Roslyn Happ have owned almost 15 acres (6 ha) of vines there since 1978. Happ's skilful viticultural techniques (including a split and separated vine canopy) have enabled him to harvest as much as 7 tonnes of grapes to the acre – more than any other wine producer in the region. His wines are more approachably priced than his neighbours' too. Happ specializes in ports, and making port is obviously a passion of his; even his red table wines have a port-like intensity to them. Still, anyone who can produce a Merlot of the quality of his amazing deep, purple-black 85 with its wonderful, luscious, plum liqueur scent and taste deserves nothing but congratulation. Like all of his straight Merlots this has 10% Cabernet blended in. The ports and the Merlots from this winery have picked up some impressive medals.

The grape varieties grown here include Cab Sauvignon, Shiraz, Merlot, Verdelho and Chardonnay for the table wines, with Muscat and the Portuguese varieties Touriga, Tinta Cao and Souzao for the fortifieds. A Cabernet/Merlot blend (two-thirds:one-third) accounts for most of Happ's output. In addition some 650 cases of Merlot are produced and about the same quantity of Shiraz, vintage port (a 50/50 Cabernet/Shiraz blend) and Fuchsia, an equal three-way blend of Cab Sauvignon, Merlot and Shiraz which is described by Happ as pink, slightly sweet and *spritzig*. The whites consist of smaller quantities of Verdelho, Chardonnay and Muscat (first introduced in 1988), with 50 cases of Solera, a wood-aged port style. All this adds up to just 5,000 cases a year. Visitors are welcome daily, 10am-5pm.
♀   Star buy: Happ's Merlot

HARTRIDGE   SW
Wanneroo Road, Wanneroo, WA 6065

w, r, ft   *

This small estate, run by the hard-working Sandows, makes table and fortified wine from Cab Sauvignon, Chenin Blanc, Chardonnay, Malbec and Pinot Noir grapes. Wines are sold at the cellar door.

HAY RIVER   MB
The Springs, Denmark Road, Mount Barker, WA 6324

r   *→→*

Goundrey makes the wines for this remote estate which lies close to the river that gives it its name. Founded in 1974, it is a one-grape, one-wine winery and its highly regarded Cab Sauvignon is, alas, sold only in WA.

HENLEY PARK WINES   SV
149 Swan Street, West Swan, WA 6055

w, r, ft   *

Owned by the Petersen family, Henley Park has a new wine-maker who is likely to continue producing a wide range of fortified and table wines. Small quantities of flagon and bottled wines are sold at the cellar door.

HIGHWAY WINES   SV
Great Northern Highway, Herne Hill, WA 6056

w, r, ft   *

Like many other wine-makers of Yugoslav descent in the Swan, Anthony Bakranich makes small amounts of table and fortified wines.

HOUGHTON   SV
Dale Road, Middle Swan, WA 6056

w=83 88 80, r=82 86 85, sw, ft, sp   *→→***

Houghton White Burgundy, sold abroad as Houghton Supreme Dry White, is WA's most famous wine and Australia's biggest-selling dry white alongside **Leo Buring's** (SA) Liebfrauwine. The West could not hope for a more appealing, fragrant, peachy ambassador – as demonstrated by the 1988 vintage, carefully vinified by chief wine-maker Peter Dawson. Its soft, peachy fruit, which is based on Chenin Blanc topped up with a little Muscadelle and dashes of Chardonnay, Verdelho and Semillon, has wide appeal.

Established in 1836, the estate was originally controlled by a three-member syndicate which included a certain Colonel Houghton who gave his name to the company. Houghton produced its first commercial vintage in 1859 and launched the White Burgundy in 1937. The business was acquired by **Thomas Hardy** (SA) in 1976 and Houghton appears to have blossomed under its ownership. Not only have its range and label design much improved (including its stylish logo of two golden swans), but – more importantly – so have the wines. The Dale Road site is an impressive place to visit. Recently the company bought and restored the homestead, built in 1863. Each year, 50,000 visitors come to taste the wines, visit the homestead and admire Houghton's new high-tech equipment. Opening times are Mon-Sat, 10am-5pm; Sun or public holidays, 11am-4pm.

Houghton produces around 270,000 cases a year, which makes it the largest WA producer by far, accounting for two-thirds of the state's crush. It runs three centres in the West and takes in 23 grape varieties from its own vineyards, besides buying in about 30% of its needs. Its largest plantings are of Rh Riesling, Chenin Blanc, Cab Sauvignon, Verdelho and Chardonnay grapes. The 125-acre (50-ha) estate here in the Swan Valley with its vast, well-equipped winery is Houghton's GHQ. In addition, it runs the 227-acre (92-ha) Moondah Brook Estate, an hour or so north of the Swan, and a 235-acre (95-ha) leased outpost in the Frankland River. Given that the labels of the estimated 21 table wines, two ports and two sparkling wines produced in these three centres feature the Houghton name prominently, all are dealt with here.

Houghton's table wine range, its cheapest and most commercial, contains wines such as the champion White Burgundy, as well as more modest offerings like the dusty, redcurranty 88 Cabernet Rosé, Chablis, Hermitage, Frankland River Rh Riesling and Cab Sauvignon. A diagonal colour stripe distinguishes this range. One notch up is the Wildflower Ridge range, whose watercolour labels bear the unmistakable Hardy look. The crisp, appley 87 Wildflower Chenin Blanc and the zesty-citric Semillon are ordinary, but appealing. The distinctive, full-flavoured Moondah Brook Estate wines are also on this level. These include the waxy, pineappley 88 Verdelho, the biscuity 87 Chardonnay and the spicy 85 Cab Sauvignon. The next step up is the Gold Reserve range, its oak-aged wines marked by a diagonal gold stripe. Try the glorious, waxy, gutsy 87 Gold Reserve Verdelho or the slightly less successful but pleasant, pineappley 86 Gold Reserve Chardonnay. Houghton's finest and priciest wines are the limited-quantity Show Reserves. These are mainly aged wines such as the delicious 83 Moondah Brook Show Reserve Verdelho whose greeny-gold colour and toasty, citric style is well worth seeking out. The Show Reserve White Burgundies or Supremes (the same wine with five years' ageing), such as the buttery, biscuity 81, prove again how good this wine is.
  ♀ Star buy: Houghton White Burgundy

HOWARD PARK   MB
Lot 11, Little River Road, Denmark, WA 6333

w, r *→›**

Originally in control of **Wynns'** large old winery at Coonawarra (SA) where he made some first-class wines, talented John Wade moved to the West with his wife several years ago, landing the job of wine-maker at **Plantagenet** in 1988. At the same time, he hung on to his own winery here, established in 1986. Wade makes just 500 cases of elegantly labelled wine a year and aims to maintain this manageable level for the time being. Production is divided between a Rh Riesling and a Cab Sauvignon. The first (86) and second (87) vintages were snapped up by enthusiastic WA wine drinkers. This is a winery to watch.

IOPPOLO'S WINES   SV
108 Pinjar Road, Wanneroo, WA 6065

w, r, ft *

The Ioppolo family makes minute quantities of traditional Swan table and fortified wines sold in flagons.

JADRAN WINES   SV
445 Reservoir Road, Orange Grove, WA 6109

w, r, ft, sp *

Jadran is south of Perth and therefore not strictly sited in the Swan, but the style of its wines puts it in this bracket. Besides the usual Swan mix of table and fortified wines, Jadran's wine-maker Stephen Radojkovich also makes sparkling wines.

JANE BROOK ESTATE WINES   SW
Toodyay Road, Middle Swan, WA 6056

w, r, ft *→

Named after the creek that flows through the estate Jane Brook was
originally known as Vignacourt. It was first established as a table grape
vineyard in 1911-12 and did not produce wine commercially until 1954.
David and Beverley Atkinson bought the winery in 1972 but waited
until 1984 to change the name. Today they own 25 acres (10 ha) in the
Swan, buying about 40% of their fruit from the Swan and the Margaret
River. Annual production is now 5,000 cases.

Sauv Blanc, Chardonnay, Shiraz, Cab Sauvignon and Merlot are
grown and made into wine here. In addition, Jane Brook makes a
macération carbonique Nouveau, a wood-aged Chenin Blanc (aged in
German oak) and a fortified range including Late Harvest Frontignan,
vintage and tawny ports, and Liqueur Tokay made from Muscat and
Verdelho grapes. The estate is gradually expanding to a planned 30
acres (12 ha), but home-grown grapes will always be supplemented by
bought-in fruit. Jane Brook's straight Chenin Blanc – for example the
racy, fruity, citrous 83 – is worth tasting; the odd sweaty, woody 84
wood-aged variety is not. The 83 Cab Sauvignon, with its ripe cassis
scent and taste, is worthwhile.

JINGALLA WINES   MB
Bolganup Dam Road, Porongurup, WA 6324

w, r *→→**

This estate, founded in 1979, is near the Porongurup National Park. Its
labels carry the Porongurup tag and depict the giant balancing rock that
is part of the local landscape. Jingalla is owned by partners Geoff and
Nita Clarke and Shelley and Barry Coad, who also have shares in
Goundrey. Wine-maker Rodney Hooper produces its range from 15
acres (6 ha) of Rh Riesling, Cab Sauvignon, Shiraz and Verdelho vines.
The best wine here is the Cab Sauvignon whose 86 won the top trophy
at the local show. Other Cabernet-based wines include the Cabernet
Rouge, made from 50/50 Cab Sauvignon/Shiraz, and Cab Sauvignon
Blend. Riesling comes in two versions – a straight Rh Riesling blend and
a sweet Select Late Harvest Riesling.

KARRELEA ESTATE   MB
Duck Road, Mount Barker, WA 6324

w, r **

Karrelea rocketed to fame by scooping up a Gold Medal at Perth for its
87 Rh Riesling. Amazingly, this was only Karrelea's second vintage, so a
bright future should be assured. **Plantagenet** makes its wines: a Sauv
Blanc completes the range of whites; reds include Cab Sauvignon, Pinot
Noir, Merlot and Cab Franc.

LAKEVILLE VINEYARDS   SV
1921 Albany Highway, Maddington, WA 6109

w, r, ft *

The usual mix of Swan fortifieds and red and white table wines are
made here, sold in flagons and larger sizes at the cellar door.

LAMONTS   SW
Bisdee Road, Millendon, WA 6056

w, r, ft *

Wine-maker Corin Lamont runs this estate with her family. Corin is the
daughter of Jack Mann, **Houghton's** much respected wine-maker until
1972, who is a consultant here. She follows his traditional methods,
avoiding cold fermentation and inoculated yeasts. Just 3,000 cases of
old-fashioned but intriguing wine are produced. Lamonts' 10 acres
(4 ha) of vines supply only half its fruit; the rest is bought in locally and
turned into fortifieds, Light Red Cabernet, Hermitage (Shiraz) and
Chardonnay. Home-produce includes a White Burgundy, a Cabernet,
a Cabernet Rosé, sweet white and Navera, a well-thought-of Liqueur
Muscat-style. The White Burgundy, a blend of 60% Verdelho, 20%
Semillon and 20% Muscadelle, usually accounts for half of production.
All wines are sold at the cellar door within a year of release.

LEEUWIN ESTATE   **MA**
Gnaraway Road, Margaret River, WA 6285
                    w=82 81 85 87, r=82 85 87 83, sp *→****
Tourists flock here to lap up Leeuwin's fine wines, eat in the superb
restaurant and admire its stunning setting among tall trees. Not all
will admire the drawbridge tower modelled, it appears, on a Greek
monastery cupola, nor the waterfall and showy rock garden. But tourist
glitz and showbiz is part of the Leeuwin style. Every year a sell-out
concert is held in the splendid grass amphitheatre near the winery,
featuring talents as diverse as the London Philharmonic and Ray
Charles. Visitors willing to make the three-hour trek south from Perth
are welcome daily (10am-4.30pm) at the winery, housed in a series of
unglamorous standard insulated sheds. Once inside, even the most
critical student of viticulture could not fail to be impressed by the
equipment. There is every kind of high-tech, high-cost wine gadget here
– rows of stainless steel fermenters, two giant Willmes presses, a
gleaming laboratory with the latest evaluation devices, acres of
temperature-controlled vinification and storage space, and piles of
pricy French oak barrels. The technology is awesome.

All this could be dismissed as a rich man's plaything – the rich man
in this case being Leeuwin's owner, Perth businessman Denis Horgan –
were it not for the fact that Leeuwin has made some of Australia's finest
wines since its first commercial vintage in 1979. Named after the Dutch
ship *Leeuwin* ("lioness") which first sighted this part of Australia, the
vineyard was founded in 1974. California's Robert Mondavi winery was
involved in the early days but, by 1980, wine-maker Bob Cartwright and
viticulturist John Brocksopp had learned all they could. Brocksopp's
techniques are highly regarded. He protects his crops from birds by
planting alternative sources of food: sunflowers for the parrots and
flowering trees for the silver-eyes. Of the Leeuwin Estate's 4,700 acres
(1,900 ha), some 220 acres (90 ha) surrounding the winery are planted
to grapes. Rh Riesling and Cab Sauvignon account for one-third each,
followed by Chardonnay, with smaller proportions of Pinot Noir,
Malbec, Gewurztraminer and Sauv Blanc. These are made into 30,000
cases a year – chiefly Rh Riesling and Cab Sauvignon; the Malbec is
normally blended in with the Cabernet. Leeuwin Estate's prices are the
steepest in the Margaret River, with $30 plus charged for the art series
Chardonnay and Pinot Noir. The labels, painted by leading artists such
as Sidney Nolan and John Olver, are some of the most attractive and
memorable in Australia.

The top Chardonnay here is the splendid buttery-herbaceous 85
with its full, cabbagey flavours, closely followed by the fresh, elegant,
pineappley, cinnamony 86. The sherbetty-buttery 84 with its austere,
steely palate and the tropical fruit and vanilla 80 are both a shade less
impressive. The Sauv Blanc is the next-best white, an excellent example
being the fresh, grassy, green bean-like 87. The flowery-grapey Rh
Rieslings develop with age as do the soft, spicy Gewurztraminers, but
neither wine rivals the Chardonnay or Sauvignon. Leeuwin has had
great success with its Pinot Noir, and deservedly so judging by the
sensational, voluptuous, plummy 83 or the toasty-liquorice 86 backed
up with some classic strawberry-like fruit on the palate. On the same
level as the 83 Pinot is the 82 Cabernet – intense, meaty, and green
pepper-like. Not far behind are the firm, blackcurranty-tobacco 84 and
the luscious, cassis-like 83. Australians are keen on the just-released
truffley, liqueur-like 79 Cab Sauvignon, but Europeans are likely to be
less keen. Leeuwin also makes a respectable, light, lemony *méthode
champenoise* 79 Blanc de Blancs of limited availability, which is served
in the restaurant here.

Leeuwin's self-proclaimed philosophy is the "pursuit of excellence".
Few would dispute that it has succeeded in its aim.

LENTON BRAE   **MA**
Caves Road, Willyabrup, WA 6284
                                                              w, r   *
This new estate has 27 acres (11 ha) of vineyards planted to Cab
Sauvignon, Merlot, Chardonnay, Sauv Blanc and Semillon. The first
vintage was expected in 1988.

LESCHENAULT WINES   SW
Minninup Road, Off Lakes Road, Gelorup, WA 6230

w, r, ft *

Leschenault, just south of Bunbury, is named after the French botanist who landed and surveyed the area in 1801. Barry and Betty Killerby founded the business in 1973. Although Barry is the official wine-maker, they have hired consultant Rob Bowen, formerly **Plantagenet's** wine-maker. No doubt their Roseworthy-trained daughter Anna, who works for **Rosemount** (NSW), also helps out. A wide variety of vines are grown in the 40-acre (16-ha) vineyard immediately in front of the winery, half planted to Cab Sauvignon and Shiraz, with the remainder split between Semillon, Chardonnay, Pinot Noir and Gewurztraminer; no fruit is bought in. Just 4,000 cases are produced and quality is variable. The Killerbys rate their Shiraz highest. Apart from the straight varietal wines, they produce April Red (a light, unwooded Shiraz and Cabernet-based red), Crystal Dessert Wine (a fortified late-picked Gewurztraminer/Chardonnay-based wine) and vintage ports (blends of Shiraz and Cabernet), sold under the Kempston and Bicentenary labels. Crystal Dessert Wine is their newest product.

LONG VALLEY WINES   SV
Haddrill Road, Baskerville, WA 6056

w, r *

This winery is named after its owners, the Vallalongas. Table wines are made here from half a dozen grapes, including Chardonnay and Shiraz.

LUISINI   SW
Wanneroo Road, Wanneroo, WA 6065

w, r, ft, sp *

The Mondello family makes a vast array of popular wines, including fortified, flavoured and sparkling wines.

MOONDAH BROOK ESTATE   See Houghton.

MOSS BROTHERS   MR
Caves Road, Willyabrup, WA 6282

w, r *

The 18 acres (7 ha) here produce 2,500 cases of premium white and red table wines. The first release was an 88 Semillon/Sauv Blanc.

MOSS WOOD   MA
Metricup Road, Willyabrup, WA 6284

w=84 85 87, r=75 77 80 83 85 87   *→***

The second couple to dive into the Margaret River after the **Vasse Felix** pioneers were Bill and Sandra Pannell who planted vines here in 1969. Roseworthy-trained wine-maker Keith Mugford arrived with his wife Clare in 1978, entered into a partnership with the Pannells and finally bought them out in 1985. Moss Wood – like Vasse Felix – had its early problems, chiefly in the form of bad weather which wiped out a few harvests. But Mugford achieved an early coup with the release of his 81 Pinot Noir, one of the first in the region to deliver the classic flavours of Burgundy. Moss Wood aims to be known as a high-quality winery and jettisons disappointing wines. The 21 acres (8 ha) of vines planted next to the winery consist of Cab Sauvignon, Semillon, Pinot Noir and Chardonnay. No grapes are bought in and just 3,000 bottles are produced. Mugford ferments his wines in small batches, hand-punching down the cap of his warm-fermented Cabernet four times a day. His Pinot Noir, also fermented warm in open tanks to extract maximum fruit flavour, receives the same attention. Chardonnay is fermented partly in cask and aged on its flavour-enhancing lees for nine months.

Except for the wooded and unwooded Semillons, all Moss Wood wines are priced at the upper end of the Margaret River scale (up to $24 a bottle). But anyone who tastes the glorious 82 Moss Wood Pinot Noir with its classic combination of smoke, liquorice and raspberry-like fruit is unlikely to grumble. The 86 displays the same refined combination of flavours but with more Pinot-like strawberry intensity on the palate, while the 87 is lighter but has the same classic plummy, liquorice-like palate. The Cabernet, judging from the rich, complex, cassis-herbaceous 86, is a winner; the 87 boasts a fine, green pepper-herbaceous style. These are some of the Margaret River's finest red wines. The whites are not in the same league, but the fragrant, spicy-buttery 86 Wood-Aged Semillon is a charming, balanced wine. The 86 Chardonnay, with its odd, oaky-grassy scent and taste is, alas, not. The Mugfords regard the Pinot Noir as their finest wine, but the Cab Sauvignon is their bestseller. In outstanding years such as 80 and 83 they produce a Special Reserve Cab Sauvignon which is given extra oak-ageing. Visitors are welcome here Mon-Sat, 10am-4pm.

MOUNT SHADFORTH WINES   MB
Mount Shadforth Drive, Denmark, WA 6330

w, r *

Mount Shadforth, founded by the Keeley family in 1981, is not far from Denmark, overlooking the Wilson Inlet and Southern Ocean. Vines planted here include Cab Sauvignon, Malbec and Rh Riesling. Wines are available locally in small quantities.

NARANG WINES   MB
Woodlands Road, Porongurup, WA 6324

w, r *→

Campbell and Annette McGready are farmers first and vignerons second like most of Mount Barker's wine folk; stud cattle are their main interest. As part of the farm's concerns they planted 10 acres (4 ha) of vines in 1979 on the north-western slopes of the Porongurup Range, dwarfed by the quirky-looking Gibraltar Rock depicted on Narang's label. The vineyard is sited at an altitude of 1,250 feet (380 m), making it one of the highest in WA, and it is frost-free. Half the vines are Rh Riesling, with a large plot of recently-planted Shiraz and a smidgen of Chardonnay. Narang is one of the smallest producers in WA. Just over 300 cases of well-thought-of Rh Riesling (made for them at **Plantagenet**) are released annually. The biggest crop was in 1988.

NARRIKUP WINES   MB
Off Albany Highway, Narrikup, WA 6326

w *

The Coxalls own this remote winery half-way between Mount Barker and Albany. Narrikup sells minute quantities of one wine, Rh Riesling, yet again made by **Plantagenet**.

NERONI WINES   SV
Great Northern Highway, Muchea, WA 6501

w, r, ft *

The Nescis make small amounts of table and fortified wines from Semillon, Pedro, Shiraz and Grenache grapes.

OLD MILL WINES   DR
Lot 8, Carolyn Place, Forrestfield, WA 6058

w, r, ft *

The Nesci family grows and vinifies Chenin Blanc, Shiraz, Cab Sauvignon and, more unusually, Zinfandel grapes. With just 10 acres (4 ha) of vines, limited quantities of dry, sweet and fortified wine are made here; these are sold mostly at the cellar door and in Perth.

OLIVE FARM WINES   SV
77 Great Eastern Highway, South Guildford, WA 6055

w, r, ft, sp *→

Claimed to be the oldest producing winery in Australia, Olive Farm is situated a few minutes' drive north of Perth Airport. The winery was founded in 1829 and cellar-door sales still take place in the original 19th-century cellars. Olive Farm Wines and its 35 acres (14 ha) of Swan vines are now controlled by the Yurisich family. There is an A-Z range of wine styles here, including table, fortified and sparkling wines. Some 6,500 cases are produced annually, mostly sold in Perth or at the cellar door. Olive Farm wines are locally regarded as among the best in the Swan. Visitors are welcome weekdays, 10.30am-5.30pm; Sat, 9am-3pm.

PATTERSON'S   MB
St Werburgh's Road, Mount Barker, WA 6324

                                                                  W   *
The Pattersons are schoolteachers and, no doubt, own this small
Chardonnay vineyard mainly as a hobby. Very little is produced.

PAUL CONTI   SW
529 Wanneroo Road, Wanneroo, WA 6065

                                                          w, r, ft   *→
This winery, situated close to the sea north of Perth, is occasionally
deemed to be part of the Swan scene. However, like other Wanneroo
estates, it is more appropriately covered here. Originally founded in
1948 as Contiville, Paul Conti's wines enjoy a good reputation and are
some of the best-produced in the area. They are now made solely from
Conti's own 42 acres (17 ha) of vines at Wanneroo, including Cab
Sauvignon, Grenache, Merlot, Shiraz (Hermitage) and Pinot Noir for
the reds, with Chardonnay, Chenin Blanc and Muscat (Frontignac) for
the whites; port is also produced. Most wines are sold locally.

PEEL ESTATE   SW
Fletcher Road, Baldivis, Mandurah, WA 6210

                                                          w, r, ft   *
Peel Estate is one of the first vineyards of the South-West Coastal Plain
that you come to driving south from Perth along the coastal corridor.
William Nairn, owner/wine-maker with several partners, has 37 acres
(15 ha) of vines here with a little of everything grown, including a 3-acre
(1-ha) clutch of Portuguese port grapes. Annual production is 5,000
bottles. Whites, consisting of Chenin Blanc, Chardonnay, Sauv Blanc,
Verdelho and Semillon, are given six months' maturation in oak; reds,
including Shiraz, Cab Sauvignon, Zinfandel, Merlot and Cab Franc, get
two years. Nairn's Cabernet is, he feels, his finest red, but his bestseller
is the Wood-Matured Chenin Blanc. Port is also made at Peel Estate.
Thriving cellar-door sales have ensured that few people outside WA
know of this winery.

PENWILL WINES   SV
Swan Street, West Swan, WA 6055

                                                                  ft   *
Little is known about this small winery in the Swan Valley, except that
it produces port.

PIERRO   MA
Caves Road, Willyabrup, WA 6284

                                            w=86 87, r=86 87   *→***
Pierro's owner, Michael Peterkin, is another member of the Margaret
River medical fraternity. He is married to the **Cullens'** daughter,
Shelley, who runs among other things her parents' excellent cellar-door
restaurant. His wines are highly thought of and also, it must be said,
highly priced. There is, however, so little available that the expense can
perhaps be justified on grounds of scarcity. Dr Peterkin trained at
Roseworthy and had his first vintage here in 1983. There are now 15
acres (6 ha) of vines, set on gently sloping land on the banks of the
Willyabrup Brook. About 40% is Chardonnay, with 20% each of Pinot
Noir and Sauv Blanc; the rest consists of the usual WA mix.

Just 3,000 cases are made each year, of which half go for cellar
sales. The remaining 500 cases each of Chardonnay, Pinot Noir and
Sauv Blanc are much sought after. Try the fresh, spicy, cinnamon scent
and rich vanilla palate of the delicious 87 Pierro Chardonnay; the 86
is a shade less successful. Pierro's 87 Pinot Noir, with its classic
strawberry-rose scent and sappy, sinewy palate, is also a good buy.
Founded in 1980, Pierro was one of the first of the new-generation
Margaret River vineyards. Its close spacing and its soil, water and
canopy management have made a major contribution to the finesse of
its wines. Peterkin practises medicine full-time. It says much for his
energy and discipline that he still finds time to run Pierro and act as
consultant to several other Margaret River and Mount Barker wineries.
Visitors are welcome every Wed, Sat and Sun, 10am-5pm.

PIESSE BROOK WINES   DR
731 Aldersyde Road, Bickley, WA 6076

w, r = 85 87 *

Not far from **Hainault**, Piesse Brook is another tiny Darling Ranges winery. It has produced wines under both the Woodhenge and Piesse Brook labels. The Piesse Brook, named after a late 19th-century explorer, runs through the estate. Founded in 1975, the winery has three partners, including wine-maker Brian Murphy. There are 6 producing acres (2.5 ha), mostly Cab Sauvignon with an acre each of Chardonnay and Shiraz (Hermitage). A few more acres of Chardonnay and Pinot Noir should come on stream in 1989. Just 250 cases a year of Cabernet/Shiraz (blended two-thirds:one-third) are made here at present. Most wine is sold in Australia but a little reaches Europe.

PINELLI WINES   SV
18 Bennett Street, Caversham, WA 6055

w, r, ft, sp *

This small family-run winery in the Swan Valley produces table, fortified and sparkling wines.

PLANTAGENET   MB
46 Albany Highway, Mount Barker, WA 6324

w, r, ft *→

Plantagenet's vineyard, planted in 1968, is not quite the oldest in the region; that distinction belongs to **Forest Hill**. But Plantagenet is nonetheless one of the founding fathers of the Mount Barker wine industry, with the earliest winery (an old apple-packing shed) in the region, dating from 1974. By 1975, Plantagenet had set up a contract system making wine for other local grape-growers. This has expanded into a large and profitable concern: about a third of Plantagenet's total crush is taken up by other wineries' grapes.

Plantagenet's original 5-acre (2-ha) plot of Cab Sauvignon and Shiraz has mushroomed to 70 acres (28 ha). In addition to these two varieties it now grows Rh Riesling, Chardonnay, Malbec and Pinot Noir here; about 30% of its grape needs are bought in. Of the 12,000 cases produced, about one-third is Rh Riesling and the remainder divided between the other wine varieties. A thousand cases each of bought-in, modestly-priced Chenin Blanc and Muscat (the bestselling wine) are also made. Plantagenet's portfolio includes Fleur, a light, Shiraz-based red blended by *macération carbonique*, a blended white and a port; the 87 Pinot Noir is on its way. Rob Bowen was wine-maker 1979-87 and it was he who produced the 81 Rh Riesling with its classic lime juice and kerosene-like taste, albeit let down by a soft middle palate. He was also responsible for the earthy, black pepper spice of the 83 Shiraz (Hermitage) and the light, restrained, raspberry-scented 83 Cab Sauvignon. Plantagenet regards Shiraz as its best wine, but the deep, purple-black 85 showed the same sort of rustic earthiness as the 83.

This important medal-winning winery has a high reputation in Australia. But it is under the expert aegis of its new wine-maker, John Wade, who started here with the 1988 vintage, that Plantagenet is likely to fulfil its true potential. One of its joint owners, Tony Smith, is the director of the new Omrah venture and some of Omrah's 240 acres (100 ha) of grapes (60% Chardonnay, 20% Cabernet, 15% Sauv Blanc and 5% Shiraz) will no doubt turn up in Plantagenet's wines soon.

POINT CREEK   MB
Porongurup Road, Porongurup, WA 6324

w *

Norman Hill and his wife produce small amounts of Rh Riesling, made for them at **Plantagenet**, and plan to release Chardonnay soon.

REDGATE   MA
Boodjidup Road, Margaret River, WA 6285

w = 83-87, r = 82-85, sw, ft *→**

Not far from **Leeuwin** in the southern section of the Margaret River, lies Redgate. The Ullingers, father and son, discovered this place set among all marri trees in 1977. Today 40 acres (16 ha) of Riesling, Semillon,

Sauv Blanc, Cab Sauvignon, Cab Franc and Pinot Noir are grown here. The Ullingers favour traditional wine-making methods – "nothing fancy or trendy", as they put it. Rieslings are made in both dry and *spätlese* styles, while the Semillon is oak-matured and the Sauvignon barrel-fermented. The Ullingers also make white port. Bill and Paul Ullinger consider the Cabernet their finest wine and the spicy-minty 84 with its elegant wood-influenced palate is undeniably good. Try too their fine 87 Semillon, with its fresh, grassy, herbaceous taste. The winery has recently changed its label from a bright red gate (what else?) to one of the anonymous modern variety.

REDMOND VINEYARD   MB
Redmond Road, Redmond, WA 6327

w, r   ∗→∗∗

Founded in 1975, Redmond now has 10 acres (4 ha) of vineyards. Vines grown include Rh Riesling, Cab Sauvignon, Gewurztraminer and Sauv Blanc. Both Rh Riesling and Cabernet have done well in local shows but for a few years **Alkoomi** bought all the grapes here. Redmond's future looks a little uncertain.

REVELRY WINES   SV
200 Argyle Street, Herne Hill, WA 6056

w, r   ∗

Stephen Illich of Revelry makes table wine and sells it, mostly in flagon containers, at the cellar door.

RIBBON VALE ESTATE   MA
Lot 5, Caves Road, Willyabrup, WA 6284

w, r   ∗

John James, Ribbon Vale's owner, mostly uses outside wine-making help in the shape of Jan and Michael Davies, a Roseworthy-trained husband and wife team, who also act as consultants to other Margaret River wineries including **Cape Clairault** and **Willespie**. James' training as an industrial chemist has enabled him to vinify several reds himself. He founded this 64-acre (26-ha) estate with its 17 acres (7 ha) of vines in 1977, but his first vintage was not until 1982. Just 2,000 cases are made of a Cabernet/Merlot blend, Semillon and a Semillon/Sauv Blanc mix; some Sauvignon is also produced. The most successful wines are the zesty, grassy 87 Sauv Blanc and the pleasant fresh, but a little dull Duet (a 50/50 Semillon/Sauvignon blend). As yet Ribbon Vale's toasty, hefty 86 Cabernet/Merlot (a 70/30 blend) is too earthy and robust to merit many compliments.

SANDALFORD   SV
West Swan Road, Caversham, WA 6055

w=88, r=84, sw, ft   ∗

John Septimus Roe came to WA with the first settlers in 1829, and founded Sandalford in 1840. The Inchcape Group owns most of it now but the Roe family retains a minority interest and is still involved in the wine-making. Christian Morlaes from **Chateau Remy** (VIC) is the new chief executive/wine-maker. In spite of this reshuffling, the scale of operations has not changed: some 50,000 cases are produced, making Sandalford the second-largest WA producer after **Houghton**. The estate does not buy in grapes, relying on its own 70 acres (28 ha) of vines in Caversham in the Swan Valley and 350 acres (140 ha) in the Margaret River near Willyabrup.

Fortified wines such as Tawny Port and Sandalera Liqueur are made at Caversham, as well as Cab Sauvignon, Zinfandel, rosé and the Chenin/Verdelho and Semillon/Chardonnay blended whites. Sandalford's Margaret River vines offer up finer fare in the shape of Riesling, Verdelho, Semillon, Cab Sauvignon, Shiraz, sweet wines such as Late Harvest Riesling and Auslese Rh Riesling, and vintage port. But the winery's range is above all commercial and its wine-making is not all that it might be. Sandalford rates the Margaret River Verdelho as its best wine but large quantities of Cab Sauvignon are also sold. Almost three-quarters of Sandalford's wines are sold in WA, the remaining quarter elsewhere in Australia.

SANDSTONE   MA
Carburnup River, WA 6280

w *

Roseworthy-trained Jan and Mike Davies, wine-makers and consultants to several Margaret River wineries, released their own wine in 1988. The 88 Sandstone Semillon is a pleasant, herbaceous, tropical fruit salad of a wine, with a shade too much spicy oak on the palate. Future releases are eagerly awaited.

SCARP VALLEY WINES   DR
6 Robertson Road, Gooseberry Hill, WA 6076

w, r *

An intriguing address for a vineyard, but little more is known about this Darling Ranges establishment.

SHEMARIN   MB
Harvey Road, Forest Hill, WA 6324

w, r *→

Ex-**Plantagenet** wine-maker Rob Bowen and his wife Denise have now moved to Perth, so whether their winery Shemarin will continue as before is uncertain. Small quantities of wine have been made since 1985 from the 5 acres (2 ha) of Sauv Blanc vines here and a little Chardonnay. Earlier vintages of mainly Zinfandel and Hermitage (Shiraz) have also been produced here from bought-in grapes. The 82 Zinfandel was a big, rich, gutsy mouthful.

SUSSEX VALE VINEYARD   MA
Harman's Mill Road, Willyabrup, WA 6284

w, r *

Cattle, sheep, goats and horses all have precedence over wine here. The Middleton family's 21-acre (8-ha) vineyard, planted in 1982, grows Sauv Blanc, Semillon, Chardonnay, Muscat, Cab Sauvignon, Pinot Noir and Shiraz. Stuart Pym is the wine-maker.

TALIJANCICH WINES   SV
121 Hyem Road, Millendon, WA 6056

w, r, ft *

At this winery, owned by the Talijancich family, table wines play second fiddle to the wide range of fortifieds which include Liqueur Muscat, Tokay and vintage port.

THOMAS WINES   SW
23-24 Crowd Road, Gelorup, WA 6230

r *→

Gil Thomas, a pharmacist by profession, caught the wine bug from Bill Pannell at **Moss Wood**. He has two small plots of vines: one, the local Briar Holme vineyard, grows Pinot Noir; the other, further inland, is planted with Cab Sauvignon. Very little is produced.

TINGLE-WOOD WINES   MB
Glenrowan Road, Denmark, WA 6333

w, r *

This tiny concern, started by "owner, manager, worker" Robert Wood with other members of his family in 1980, owes its intriguing name to the nearby forest of massive gum trees, known locally as tingle trees. With just 4 producing acres (1.5 ha), planted in 1976, and another 4 acres planted in 1984, Tingle-Wood has a long way to go before it progresses beyond cellar-door sales. **Goundrey** makes Tingle-Wood's 100 cases each of Riesling and Cab Sauvignon/Shiraz (a 60/40 blend). The new plantations here will soon produce a blend dominated by Gewurztraminer and rounded off with Sylvaner.

TWIN HILLS WINES   SV
Great Northern Highway, Baskerville, WA 6056

w, r, ft *

At Twin Hills, 25 acres (10 ha) of vines are turned into a wide range of table and fortified wines by the Kraljevich family.

VALLEY WINES SV
Lennard Street, Herne Hill, WA 6056

w, r, ft *

Antonio Zannino makes table, fortified and flavoured wines, supplying the local market, like many traditional Swan producers, with 25-litre containers of wine for home-bottling.

VASSE FELIX MA
Harman's South Road, Cowaramup, WA 6284

r=79 86, w=76 86 78, sp *→**

Founded as early as 1967, Vasse Felix was *the* wine pioneer of the Margaret River. It was Gladstone's 1965 report that persuaded Dr Tom Cullity, the first in a long line of medical vignerons here, of the region's viticultural potential. He was the first to plant a vineyard and the first to set up a winery. Early problems mostly revolved around the hungry silver-eye birds which decimated the grapes. Vasse Felix trained a falcon to protect its crop and thereafter adopted a flying falcon as its symbol. Englishman David Gregg joined Cullity as wine-maker and soon made good progress. Eventually David and his wife Anne leased the estate from Cullity and he became manager/wine-maker, as he is today. But it was not until 1987, when financier Robert Holmes à Court bought Vasse Felix, that its financial problems were over.

Vasse Felix's jewel of a 20-acre (8-ha) vineyard next door to the winery, planted mostly to Cab Sauvignon with a little Rh Riesling and less Hermitage, Malbec and Gewurztraminer, supplies only 30% of its fruit. The remainder comes from five vineyards half an hour to the south, which provide grapes for more Cab Sauvignon and the base wines for Vasse Felix's Classic Dry Red and White and its new *méthode champenoise* wine. The Greggs' exciting new sparkling wine project involves the completion of a building in which to vinify, age and sell the wine. Below the ageing rooms there will be an elegant tasting area where visitors to the winery (welcome here every day, 9.30am-4.30pm) will be encouraged to try a flute glass of the Vasse Felix fizz. *Gyropalettes* are used to riddle the wine and an early unfinished Brut non-vintage blend, based mostly on Pinot Noir with a touch of Chardonnay, Pinot Meunier and French Colombard, shows promise.

Over 8,000 cases a year are made here, 75% divided between sales of Cab Sauvignon and Classic Dry White (mostly Semillon with a little Sauvignon and Chenin Blanc). No one is going to get too excited by the latter whose fresh, leafy scent and taste is drinkable but a little ordinary. The 86 Cabernet is a different creature altogether – full, with a rich cassis scent and complex blackberry palate, albeit a touch jammy. Australians rave about Vasse Felix Cabernets, but they go down less well with Europeans. The light, juicy raspberry fruit of the Classic Red (made from lightly-extracted Cab Sauvignon, with some Pinot Noir and macerated Malbec) is again nothing to write home about; nor was the 86 Hermitage with its big, rich, farmyard style. Vasse Felix's Rieslings are made with a touch of *süss-reserve*. The fresh, lemony-lime scent and mango-like taste of the 88 Riesling was pleasant but the wine had a perplexingly bitter finish.

VINDARA SV
Great Northern Highway, Herne Hill, WA 6056

w, r, ft *

The Viskovich family has made table and fortified wines here since 1978 from about 12 acres (5 ha) of vines. All wines are sold at the cellar door, mostly in bulk for home-bottling.

WESTFIELD SV
Memorial Avenue, Baskerville, WA 6056

r=79 86, w=86, sw, ft *→

The Kosovichs, like many Yugoslav families, were lured to Australia by the prospect of gold. The present owners, John and Mary Kosovich, took over Westfield in 1957 from John's father, who had started the vineyard in 1922. What separates it from other Swan wineries run by families of Yugoslav descent is not its cool, dark, traditional cellar with hand-hewn timber beams but the quality of its wines, many of which have won WA medals. John admits that in 1957 Westfield was still making rough reds and fortifieds, like everyone else in the region. Gradually, throughout the 60s, he refined the wines until they reached their present quality. Today production is 80% table wine to 20% fortified; in the early 60s the opposite had been the case.

Not much more than 3,000 cases of wine are made each year from Westfield's 18 acres (7 ha) of vines. Fashionable Chardonnay takes the biggest share, followed by Cab Sauvignon, Verdelho, Chenin Blanc, Semillon and Shiraz, with a little Merlot, Muscat and Muscadelle. Australia absorbs all of these sensibly-priced wines. Kosovich views the Chardonnay as his best wine, but the somewhat oily, buttery 83 shows that the hot Swan is not ideal for this grape; the oily, perfumed richness of the 83 Semillon reveals the same problem. But the 84 Chenin Blanc with its lively, green, pear-drop style is a good example of Westfield's white wine expertise. Understandably given the heat, the reds are better. The 81 Cabernet/Shiraz enjoyed a big spicy nose and an equally big, spicy palate, though the straight 82 Cabernet was a touch jammy and burnt. Westfield also makes a lively Cabernet Blanc pink wine, redolent of blackcurrant leaf, and a sweet duo – Late-Picked Verdelho and Autumn Harvest, a Semillon/Verdelho blend. The fortifieds consist of a *flor* sherry and vintage port.

WIGNALLS KING RIVER MB
Chester Pass Road, Albany, WA 6330

w, r ∗→∗∗

William, Patricia and Robert Wignall's winery, founded in 1981 on the southern banks of the King River north of Albany, is WA's southernmost vineyard. Beneficial sea breezes whistling in off the King George Sound help to create a cool climate and a long growing season for its 21 acres (8 ha) of Pinot Noir, Chardonnay, Sauv Blanc, Cab Sauvignon, Cab Franc and Semillon. These are vinified by John Wade at **Plantagenet**. Current Wignalls output is under 2,000 cases, with a small amount of Frontignan bought in, vinified and sold at a low price. Great things are expected from Wignalls, not just because of the favourable micro-climate here but also because of the quality-minded vineyard work, with its organic approach. The Wignalls use a minimum of chemicals, relying on guinea-fowl to keep the insects down, and individually manicure the vines. This has brought them early medals: the Pinot Noir in particular has received considerable praise from the Australian wine world. Their chief problem is lack of supply, but the first Cabernet vintage has just been released and life should be easier when their new plantings come on stream in 1989-90.

WILLESPIE WINES MA
Harman's Mill Road, Willyabrup, WA 6284

w, r, sw, ft ∗

Schoolteachers Kevin and Marian Squance founded this firm in 1976 and now have 25 acres (10 ha) of vines; additional plantings will bring this up to 30 acres (12 ha). Grapes include Cab Sauvignon, Verdelho, Semillon, Rh Riesling, Sauv Blanc and Merlot. Like several other Margaret River estates Willespie Wines hires the roving Davies wine-making duo. Three separate varietal dry whites are made from their Verdelho, Rh Riesling and Semillon grapes, as well as a botrytis-affected Late Harvest Rh Riesling, Cab Sauvignon and vintage port based on Cab Sauvignon grapes. In time Willespie also expects to produce a Sauv Blanc wine.

WOODHENGE WINES See **Piesse Brook**.

WOODLANDS WINES MA
Lot 1, Corner Woodlands & Caves Roads, Willyabrup, WA 6284

w, r ∗

Founded in 1973, Woodlands is run by David and Heather Watson. Most of the 12-acre (5-ha) vineyard is planted to red varieties, although Chardonnay is also grown. Few wines have been released because the Watsons sell most of their grapes. Each vintage of the Cab Sauvignon, blended with a little Malbec, is named after a member of the family born in that year – hence the 81 "Andrew" Cabernet (which won a trophy at the national show in Canberra), the 83 "Elizabeth" vintage, and so on. A small amount of Pinot Noir was released recently and other reds are on their way. The first Chardonnay is expected in 1990.

WOODTHORPE ESTATE   DR
Richardson Road, Parkerville, WA 6553

                                                                    w, r, ft ★
Hugh Jackson is Woodthorpe's wine-maker/chief executive, but Balthasar van der Meer from **Darlington Vineyard** and others help out here. This small "weekend" winery makes a range of wines from Chenin Blanc, Colombard, Chardonnay, Shiraz and Cab Sauvignon grapes, sold under three labels: Woodvine for the whites, Woodthorpe for the reds and Woodvale for the Shiraz-based port.

WRIGHTS   MA
Harman's South Road, Cowaramup, WA 6284

                                                                    w, r, ft ★
Henry and Maureen Wright, who joined the wine world in 1973, have 30 acres (12 ha) of vines just across the road from **Vasse Felix**. Reds consist of Cab Sauvignon and Hermitage (Shiraz), whites of Rh Riesling, Semillon and Chardonnay. Their Hermitage has the greatest reputation and the Wrights feel it is their best wine. Sadly the last Hermitage I tasted, the 84, was suffering from wine faults. So was the 85 Cab Sauvignon, whose murky colour and farmyard scent showed it had spent too long on its lees. Wrights also produces a Semillon/Chardonnay/Sauv Blanc blend, as well as white and red ports based on Rh Riesling and Shiraz grapes respectively.

Northern Territory

Alice Springs, in the middle of the vast Australian outback, is just about the last place on earth one would expect to find a winery. The Northern Territory, with its bone-dry climate and infertile desert soil, is almost as poorly suited to viticulture as the Sahara. Nevertheless, against all expectations (and some would say good sense) there is a single stray winery situated 9 miles (15 km) south of Alice Springs in the Red Centre of Australia, which ekes out an existence and even produces drinkable wines that are a quality notch above souvenir status. As a result, Australia can justly claim to produce wine in every one of its states.

Northern Territory wineries

CHATEAU HORNSBY   §
Petrick Road, Alice Springs, NT 5750

                                                                 w, r, ft, sp ★
It takes courage and cussedness to establish an irrigated vineyard in a middle of nowhere as hot and inhospitable as Alice Springs. Clearly the plucky Hornsbys have plenty of both attributes. Suffice it to say that, so far, the viticultural merits of the red, arid, sun-baked semi-desert of Alice Springs have not proved sufficiently appetizing for others to set up in competition to their winery, Chateau Hornsby.

Denis and Miranda Hornsby founded their 7-acre (3-ha) vineyard in 1976. Today their wines include Cab Sauvignon and Shiraz for the reds, with Semillon and Rh Riesling for the whites. Surprisingly, given the tough climate in which grapes have to be picked before 9am every morning to avoid the blistering heat, the Hornsbys' efforts are approved of. Cellar-door sales and simple lunches are available daily; Sundays, with music and dancing, sound fun.

Queensland

❦

Queensland is better known for pineapples, orchids, crocodiles and the Great Barrier Reef than wines, yet this hot, humid state with its unloved monsoon belt is, surprisingly, not the viticultural white elephant one might suppose. This is principally because all its wineries, bar two, are situated way down on the New South Wales border in the Granite Belt region surrounding Stanthorpe. As elsewhere in Australia it was Italian families who fostered and, to some extent, founded the industry here. But Queensland's oldest winery, **Romavilla**, lies outside the Granite Belt and has no Italian connections. It was founded by an Englishman in 1863 and is still operating today.

Given the trying climate, Queensland's wine-producers did not bother to switch from unsuitable, inferior table grapes to decent *Vitis vinifera* wine grapes until the mid-1960s. This makes it one of the newest wine regions in the country. The switch was worth it, for while there has hardly been a stampede of grape-growers rushing to add to the state's 370 acres (150 ha) of vines, recent years have seen an encouraging revitalization of the industry. Who knows, perhaps one day Queensland's wines will be as famous as her pineapples.

Wine-producing regions

GRANITE BELT (GB)
The hilly Granite Belt, Australia's least-known wine region, lies roughly 140 miles (220 km) south-west of Brisbane, stretching from Wallangarra on the NSW border via the centres of Ballandean, Glen Aplin and Stanthorpe up to Dalveen in the north. Just 23 miles (60 km) long, and seldom more than 9 miles (16 km) wide, it is a compact belt. True to its name, the terrain consists of poor granite soil interspersed with large boulders. Early Italian settlers in the late 19th century grew table grapes with their other fruit. Today others have set up in the region alongside the Italian community. Protected on its western side from monsoon downpours by the Great Dividing Range, the Granite Belt still gets a good deal of damaging summer and vintage rainfall. It also suffers – odd though this may sound – from spring frosts and hail. But, at 2,360-3,280 feet (720-1,000 m), the Granite Belt has a relatively cool climate. The result is a longer growing season and finer fruit.

Distinctive regional wine-styles

BALANDEAN NOUVEAU
Spelt with one 'l' to distinguish it from the town, Balandean Nouveau is Queensland's only truly distinctive wine-style. This light, fresh, carbonic maceration wine, mostly Shiraz-based, is made by the cluster of producers in and around Ballandean and Stanthorpe. To maintain standards wines are submitted to an independent panel that judges which are worthy of the Balandean Nouveau name; not all go through. The region even has its own version of the French Beaujolais Nouveau race.

OTHER WINERIES (§)
There are two solitary Queensland wineries outside the Granite Belt region. **Romavilla**, situated some 280 miles (450 km) north-east of Brisbane at Roma, has been in operation for well over a hundred years. The much younger **Foster & Company**, which lies inland from Cairns in the remote Atherton Tablelands, has the distinction of being Australia's most northerly winery.

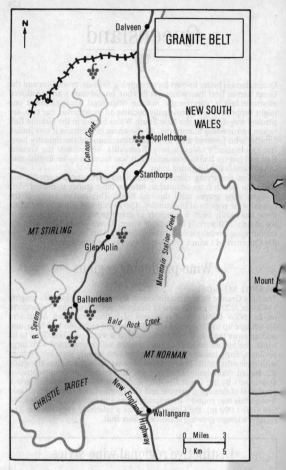

Queensland wineries

BALD MOUNTAIN
Old Wollongalla Road, Ballandean, QLD 4382

The Parsons are transforming their vineyard by planting new *Vitis vinifera* vines. Tiny quantities of Bald Mountain Shiraz, Sauvignon and Chardonnay have been released; their quality augurs well.

BALLANDEAN ESTATE   See Sundown Valley Vineyards.

BUNGAWARRA WINES
Bents Road, Ballandean, QLD 4382

Founded in 1975, Dr Philip and Lyn Christensen's estate has just 12 acres (5 ha) of vines. Philip makes 1,500 cases of inexpensive, straight varietal table wines and Liqueur Muscat. His Balandean Nouveau-style Cab Sauvignon and Chardonnay have gone down well in Australia.

QUEENSLAND

Wine Regions

1 GRANITE BELT

N

0   Miles   100
0   Km   200

GREAT DIVIDING RANGE

Cairns

Townsville

Hughenden

PACIFIC OCEAN

Winton

R Belyando

QUEENSLAND

Emerald

Rockhampton

R Burnet

Roma

Toowoomba

BRISBANE

R Balonne

1

Southport

Warwick

NEW SOUTH WALES

Stanthorpe

COSTANZO BROTHERS   **GB**
Sundown Road, Ballandean, QLD 4382

w, r ★
This traditional Italian estate, which has adopted new technology, sells
straightforward blended wines, made by Stan Costanzo, in bulk.

ELSINORE WINES   **GB**
Kerridges Road, Glen Aplin, QLD 4381

w, r, ft ★
Wine-maker Peter Love makes table and fortified wines from 45 acres
(18 ha) of Shiraz, Cab Sauvignon, Semillon and Chardonnay.

FELSBERG   GB
Townsends Road, Glen Aplin, QLD 4381

w, r   *

This winery was established by Otto, Peter and Anne Haag in 1983.
Otto makes table wine from 11 acres (4 ha) of various vines, which
benefit from their altitude of 2,800 feet (850 m).

FOSTER & COMPANY   §
Kalunga, Herberton, QLD 4872

w, r, sw   *

This remote winery, all alone in the far north of the state close to Cairns,
was founded in 1978. The climate here is not as blisteringly hot as might
be expected, owing to its position in the relatively high, cool Atherton
Tablelands. But it is nonetheless a warm region with high levels of
summer rainfall. Christopher and Diana Foster produce a range of
popular wines at cheap prices from 62 acres (25 ha) of vineyards still
partly planted with the foxy American vine *Vitis labrusca* which, along
with table grapes, was the original base for Queensland's wines.

J & N RICCA   GB
Sundown Road, Ballandean, QLD 4382

w, r   *

Joe Ricca is the wine-maker at this traditional Italian winery; his table
wine can be bought in bulk only.

KOMINOS WINES   GB
Accomodation Creek Road, Lyra, QLD 4352

w, r   *→

The Cominos (confusingly spelt with a C) are the owners here. Tony
Comino, the capable Riverina-trained wine-maker, produces a wide
range of table wines from 15 acres (6 ha) of grapes including Shiraz,
Pinot Noir and Cab Sauvignon for the reds, and Rh Riesling, Semillon,
Chenin Blanc and Chardonnay for the whites. Kominos was founded in
1976 but Tony's first commercial vintage was not until 1985. His wines
are deemed some of the best in Queensland.

MOUNT MAGNUS   GB
Donnelly's Castle Road, Pozieres, QLD 4352

w, r, ft   *

Mount Magnus, formerly Biltmore Cellars, is owned by John Matthews.
He produces table and fortified wine from 29 acres (12 ha) of Cab
Sauvignon, Shiraz, Chardonnay and Emerald Ruby grapes. The altitude
of around 3,300 feet (1,000 m) adds a quality edge to his popular-
sounding brands of "Mount Magnus", "Donnelly's" and "Sunstate".

OLD CAVES WINERY   GB
New England Highway, Stanthorpe, QLD 4380

w, r, ft, sp   *

David Zannatta, whose family set up Biltmore Cellars (now **Mount
Magnus**), makes table wines, fortifieds, sparkling wines, flavoured
wines and even mead at this winery, founded in 1980.

ROBINSONS FAMILY VINEYARDS   GB
Lyra Church Road, Lyra, QLD 4382

w, r, ft   *

Riverina-trained John Robinson runs this winery, established in 1969.
With two separate vineyards at Ballandean and Lyra, adding up to some
44 acres (18 ha), it is one of the largest Queensland estates. In addition
to table wines, the Robinsons produce ports and liqueurs.

ROMAVILLA   §
Northern Road, Roma, QLD 4455

w, r, sw, ft   *→

Remote Romavilla, founded in 1863 by Samuel Bassett, was once
known as Bassett's Romavilla. The present concern was established in
1975 and is owned by David Wall. Fortified wines have always been a
speciality here. Together with its table wines, these are made from

Romavilla's 49 acres (20 ha) of Durif, Mataro, Shiraz, Muscat, Syrian, Riesling, Chenin Blanc and Crouchen vines. The end result is some impressive Muscats, sherries and ports, alongside dry table wines and sweet white dessert wine-styles.

RUMBALARA GB
Fletcher Road, Fletcher, QLD 4381

w, r, sw, ft *

Retired Robert and Una Gray produce just over 3,000 cases of table and fortified wines a year, as well as vermouth and cider. Robert acquired his oenology degree from Riverina in 1981 and his son Chris recently followed in his footsteps. With only 15 acres (6 ha) of their own vines, they have to buy in half their grapes. These are turned into a range of single varietal wines, of which Semillon has won most praise from Australian critics. Blended wines include a Riesling/Sylvaner blend and a carbonic maceration Shiraz/Pinot Noir. The Grays founded their firm in 1974 and were the first in the region to produce fortified wine. Today fortifieds account for a quarter of total production, and range from Liqueur Muscat and Muscat-based dry and sweet vermouth to Shiraz-based vintage port.

STONE RIDGE VINEYARDS GB
Limberlost Road, Glen Aplin, QLD 4381

w, r *→

Jim Lawrie and Anne Kennedy have been joint owner/wine-makers here since 1981. They make about 700 cases a year of barrel-fermented, oak-aged Shiraz and Chardonnay from bought-in grapes. Their 5 acres (2 ha) of mixed vines are not yet bearing. Lawrie and Kennedy are clearly serious about their craft. In addition to a Bordeaux-inspired blended red, they hope that eventually their Rhône-inspired blended white – a combination of, Roussane, Viognier and Marsanne unusual for Australia – will prove as worthy as the French original.

SUNDOWN VALLEY VINEYARDS GB
Sundown Road, Ballandean, QLD 4382

w, r, sw, ft *→

This 37-acre (15-ha) quality-oriented winery is the largest producer in Queensland. Its annual production of 8,000 cases is divided between the Sundown Valley and finer Ballandean Estate labels. Almost all of its fruit comes from the firm's own vineyards, though a little is bought in locally. Started by Angelo and Mary Puglisi in 1970, Sundown was previously a table grape property which had been planted in 1930 by Angelo's grandfather. They made use of expert wine-making help from the Queensland Government's scientific team to turn their home-grown Shiraz, Cab Sauvignon, Cab Franc, Semillon, Chardonnay, Chenin Blanc, Sauv Blanc, Sylvaner and Riesling grapes into wine. Ballandean Estate's Light Red (a Shiraz/Cabernet blend) and Semillon are their two big sellers. The cheaper Sundown Valley collection offers popular wines such as Lambrusco and White Burgundy, as well as fortifieds such as Liqueur Muscat, Pioneer and Vintage ports. Plans include the release of a classier Ballandean Estate Print Label Series Chardonnay and Show Reserve Shiraz. Sundown is open daily, 9am-5pm.

WINEWOOD GB
Sundown Road, Ballandean, QLD 4382

w, r, sw *

Winewood, founded in 1985 and owned by Roseworthy-trained Ian Davis and his wife Jeanette, is one of the newest Ballandean-based wineries. They are determined that Winewood should remain a small, well-run, family-owned winery making "distinctive regional wines", rather than diluting the home product by buying in grapes. The 10 acres (4 ha) here of almost-mature Shiraz, Cab Sauvignon, Marsanne and Chardonnay vines produce around 500 cases a year. In addition to these tiny quantities of moderately-priced single varietal wines, Winewood also produces a botrytised Semillon as well as a Beaujolais carbonic maceration wine-style.

124

NEW ZEALAND WINES

Introduction

New Zealand has a much smaller wine-making industry than its huge
Antipodean neighbour, but the success of its best wines in recent years
has been no less phenomenal. The enthusiasm and self-sufficiency of its
wine-makers, combined with a cool-temperate climate well-suited to
white grape varieties, has crafted some superb world-class white wines.
In less than a decade, New Zealand wines have hurtled as if from
nowhere to the upper echelons of the wine world.

1819 on ...

The vine arrived in New Zealand just over three decades after its
establishment in Australia, when the Reverend Samuel Marsden, an
English missionary, planted out a small vineyard in 1819 at Kerikeri.
Marsden's vines, shipped across the Tasman Sea from New South
Wales, survived the difficult conditions of what is now Northland and
other plantings followed. But the first wines were not made until the
arrival of the itinerant wine pioneer James Busby, who encouraged
wine-making throughout the colony just as he had in Australia.

In the damper climate of New Zealand, without effective means to
combat mildew and rot, 19th-century wine-makers were fighting a
losing battle from the start. Worse setbacks were to come with the
growing strength of the prohibition movement towards the end of the
century. Fortunately the New Zealand Government, like its Australian
counterpart, encouraged the production of wine and in 1895 hired
Romeo Bragato, an Italian viticulturist from Australia, to tour the
country and assess its wine-making potential. His enthusiastic report
spawned a host of vineyards. It was Bragato too who revitalized the
Government Wine Research Station founded in 1897 at Te Kauwhata,
planting out experimental vines there – only to see his work ruined by
the arrival of phylloxera. However, hot on the heels of the aphid came a
wave of Dalmatian immigrants who were to shape the country's wine
industry from the turn of the century until the present day.

New Zealand's Dalmatian immigrants originally left their home-
land on the Yugoslavian coast to dig for kauri gum in the Northland
region. Many of them planted out vines around Auckland and began to
make wine. Their early wines, nicknamed "Dally
diesel", may have lacked quality but Dalmatian hard
work paid off. Today vineyards have spread throughout the North Island and are making progress in the
South Island; half of these are still owned and run by
their descendants.

Small is beautiful

With some 10,600 acres (4,290 ha) of vines and an
annual grape crush of 60,000 tonnes, New Zealand's
wine industry is tiny by comparison with that of its
neighbour Australia – roughly the same size, in fact,
as New South Wales' Hunter Valley region. This
small industry will shortly find itself under threat
from Australian wines, for in 1990 all trade barriers
between the two countries are due to be lifted. Large
Australian wine companies such as **Cape Mentelle**

Wine Regions

THE NORTH ISLAND

1 AUCKLAND
2 GISBORNE
3 HAWKE'S BAY
4 NORTHLAND
5 WAIKATO / BAY OF PLENTY
6 WAIRARAPA

THE SOUTH ISLAND

1 CANTERBURY
2 CENTRAL OTAGO
3 MARLBOROUGH
4 NELSON

NEW ZEALAND

0   Miles   300

0   Km   600

(WA), **Mildara** (VIC), **Wolf Blass** and **Yalumba** (SA) already have a firm foothold in New Zealand, while others such as **Thomas Hardy** (SA) buy grapes here to beef up their native Australian blends. Over the next five years New Zealand's wineries, especially the medium-sized concerns, are likely to be hard hit by a flood of cheaper, finer Australian wines. Most of the country's wine-makers are well aware of this. They realize too that in order to survive as a small wine-producing nation, when home consumption is static, if not falling, New Zealand should not try to compete in the cheap cask section of the market but continue to develop its overseas market for quality wines.

Maritime influence

New Zealand's climate can be described as cool-temperate with strong maritime influences. No point in either of the main islands is less than 70 miles (105 km) from the ocean and sea breezes, though they can cause damage to vines, have a beneficial effect overall on grape-growing conditions. The country's heavy rainfall, however, is detrimental to the vine's ripening programme; autumn downpours, frequent on the North Island, encourage high levels of humidity, which causes mildew, rot and other vine diseases.

The claim of New Zealand wine-makers to have completely "cool climate" vineyards is contested by Australian viticulturists, who point out that the climate here is more temperate than cool. Having said that, some parts of the country such as Central Otago are positively cold. If Australian wines suffer from too much sun then New Zealand wines suffer from too little. New Zealand does however avoid the extremes found in Australia and its vineyards, importantly, have a longer, slower growing season. This produces fruit with more flavour, finesse and extract, coupled with higher acidity and a lower alcohol content.

The dairy factor

Overseas visitors are particularly impressed, and surprised, by New Zealanders' wine technology. Even the smallest wineries bristle with stainless steel and modern wine gadgets, while the largest such as **Montana's** Marlborough operation look positively space-age when compared to European wineries. This technological know-how has largely been a by-product of New Zealand's dairy industry, where stainless steel and stringent hygiene controls are commonplace. What is remarkable about New Zealand's enthusiastic wine-makers, many of them Roseworthy-trained Australians, is their self-sufficiency. Unlike European wine-makers, who can phone up the manufacturer and order a spare part if anything should go wrong, New Zealanders of necessity have an intimate knowledge of their machines: if one breaks down it will be they who have to fix it. This accounts for a wealth of wine equipment in New Zealand sporting improvised attachments.

Grape varieties

New Zealand's boom-and-bust wine history has had a dramatic effect on its vineyards. During the mid-1960s and early 70s farmers were encouraged to turn spare land over to vines and treat them like any other cash crop. As a result, 80% of New Zealand's grapes today are grown not by the wine-makers themselves but by contract growers. Prices have escalated and quality has suffered. However, recent plantations of vines by wine-makers, especially in the South Island, are beginning to alleviate this problem.

The most widely-planted variety by far is Muller-Thurgau, which accounts for over a quarter of the country's vines. Muller-Thurgau spearheaded the transition from fortified to table wine production in the 60s and there are now over 3,000 acres (1,215 ha) of the variety in New Zealand. This is a direct result of German influence during the period, an influence which was further increased in 1979 when Dr

Helmut Becker from Geisenheim, the leading German wine institute, arrived here with a suitcase full of vine cuttings and the firm belief that New Zealand's climate closely resembled the grape-growing conditions in his native Germany.

German influence had important implications for viticulture in New Zealand because it swept away most low-quality hybrids such as the unpleasant-tasting Albany Surprise grape. However, with hindsight, it is clear that while parts of New Zealand do indeed mimic the climate of the Mosel and the Rhine others have greater similarities with the French regions of Bordeaux and Burgundy. Today New Zealand's finest wines are made from French, not German, varieties. And encouragingly, Chardonnay and Cabernet Sauvignon are now the country's second and third-largest plantings respectively.

Wine-styles

New Zealand's wines, like Australia's, tend to be a bit of a shock for first-time drinkers. The crisp, light, zingy, aromatic white wines made here have a depth of verdant flavour unmatched by Europe, California or Australia. Reds are not as successful, though Hawke's Bay Cabernet and South Island Pinot Noir have shown considerable promise.

Muller-Thurgau, grown mainly in the Gisborne, Hawke's Bay and Marlborough regions, is used in large quantities by **Montana** to make soft, slightly sweet, grapey, back-blended wines such as Blenheimer. Chardonnay, planted particularly in Marlborough, transforms into lighter, crisper wines than those of the North Island which are richer and often oak-aged. Although New Zealand produces six times as many white wines as reds, Cabernet Sauvignon grapes produced in Hawke's Bay's Bordeaux-like climate are blended with a little Merlot and Cabernet Franc to make some impressive rich, fruity wines. Marlborough has almost as many Cabernet Sauvignon vines but the style of its wines tends to be too light, grassy and herbaceous to compete with those of Hawke's Bay. The great Marlborough success story is Sauvignon Blanc, which has produced delicious, crisp, flowering currant wines that are truly world-class. Hawke's Bay Sauvignons tend to be richer and less vibrant. Some fine late harvest Rhine Rieslings have also been made by a handful of wineries, though straight versions lack finesse.

Other fine marriages between wine and region include Gisborne Gewurztraminer, which is a delightfully spicy, Alsace-like wine-style, and Canterbury's plummy, Burgundy-like Pinot Noirs. The country's climate also transforms Semillon into extraordinarily grassy, tart wines that can easily be confused with Sauvignon. Pinotage, the South African Pinot Noir-Cinsaut cross, is another New Zealand surprise that has yielded fine, full-flavoured, fleshy wines with berry-like fruit.

The North Island

Although three-quarters of New Zealand's vines are grown on the North Island, principally at Gisborne and Hawke's Bay, the climate here is far from ideal for viticulture, suffering as it does from rain, rot, viruses and vine diseases. The canny North Islanders, however, have found ways around these difficulties, moving out of the wettest regions, Northland and Auckland, and either acquiring vineyard land in the South Island or buying southern grapes in. This move to the south, above all to the Marlborough region, is set to continue: by 1991, it is estimated that as much as two-fifths of New Zealand's vines will be planted in the South Island. Nevertheless, some of the country's finest red wines have come from the North Island, especially from Hawke's Bay which has produced glorious Bordeaux-inspired wines.

Wine-producing regions

AUCKLAND (AU)

Auckland was one of the first regions in New Zealand to be planted, but in this wet, humid climate many vineyards still have virused vines which suffer from diseases such as leaf-roll. To combat these problems, most wineries now either own vineyards in Gisborne, Hawke's Bay and Marlborough or purchase grapes from these regions. Auckland's own vineyards used to provide a third of the country's grapes; now they provide less than 7%. However, its wineries remain well-placed for tourists. The region's 690 acres (280 ha) of vines are scattered around Auckland itself, mostly in the Kumeu-Huapai-Waimauku area and at Henderson. Principally a red wine region, the main variety grown is Cabernet Sauvignon, followed by Palomino used for sherry production.

GISBORNE (GI)

Since the mid-1960s, Gisborne's vines have expanded to cover some 3,200 acres (1,300 ha) of the area's fertile, high-yielding soil, making it the largest New Zealand wine region. Muller-Thurgau is the leading variety, followed by Dr Hogg Muscat, Chardonnay, Reichensteiner and Gewurztraminer. Gisborne's prime role is as a supplier of grapes for the cask wines of the major producers such as **Montana** and **Corbans**, and as such there are few wineries here. This is a pity because it does produce fine whites, especially spicy, Alsace-like Gewurztraminer and flavoursome Chardonnay and Sauvignon. Its reds are adversely affected by high rainfall particularly in the autumn, which causes late-ripening grapes such as Cabernet to swell, resulting in pale watery wines. Rot also causes problems, and phylloxera has devastated large tracts of vines. Grape-growers are tackling these problems by planting phylloxera-resistant vines and moving off the high-yielding plains to hillside sites.

HAWKE'S BAY (HW)

Currently the second-largest wine region in New Zealand with 3,200 acres (1,230 ha) under vine, Hawke's Bay is expected to overtake Gisborne by 1991. With more sunshine, less rainfall and lighter soils growing more balanced fruit, Hawke's Bay is much better suited to grape-growing and wine-making, and has many more wineries; it also suffers less from phylloxera. Like Gisborne, the region's largest planting by far is Muller-Thurgau – but, unlike Gisborne, red varieties grow happily here and Cabernet Sauvignon is the next-largest planting. Indeed, some of the country's finest reds come from Hawke's Bay. Several small boutique wineries have recently arrived in the region and this trend looks likely to continue.

Distinctive regional wine-styles

GISBORNE GEWURZTRAMINER
The dry, perfumed, spicy Gewurztraminers made in Gisborne (notably by **Matawhero**), with their classic, almost Alsatian palate reminiscent of lychees and roses, are as good as any in the world.

HAWKE'S BAY CHARDONNAY
Although other regions of New Zealand have larger plantings of this variety, Hawke's Bay is acknowledged as the leading producer of consistently big, rich, full-flavoured Chardonnays that take well to oak.

NORTH ISLAND MULLER-THURGAU
The only other variety in the North Island's tricky climate with a claim to world-class distinction is Muller-Thurgau. The soft, flowery-grapey, easy-drinking wines made here from this grape, usually back-blended with a touch of sweetness, are New Zealand's answer to Liebfraumilch.

NORTHLAND (NO)

Northland, New Zealand's most northerly region and the first to be planted with vines, is an hour north of Auckland. Traditionally, this has been a hybrid grape region producing ordinary table wines and fortifieds. There are now about 85 acres (35 ha) of vines, but wines are mostly sold in small quantities at the cellar door. Publicity generated by the **Antipodean** gave the region a valuable shot in the arm. Vines in this almost sub-tropical climate suffer from rain, rot and high humidity.

WAIKATO/BAY OF PLENTY (WK)

This region, situated some 45 miles (75 km) south of Auckland between Waikato and the Bay of Plenty, has long been associated with the vine. It was here that Romeo Bragato, New Zealand's first viticulturist, started an experimental vineyard at the end of the 19th century. His modern equivalent is the Australian Dr Richard Smart, based at the Government's Te Kauwhata Research Station, who is almost single-handedly raising viticultural awareness in New Zealand. Low yields and high rainfall have restricted vineyards here to just 290 acres (118 ha) – principally Muller-Thurgau, Sauvignon Blanc and Chenin Blanc.

WAIRARAPA (WR)

Wairarapa is New Zealand's most fashionable new wine region, though vines were grown here at the end of the 19th century before the arrival of prohibition. As with Australia's Margaret River region (WA), it was a scientist's report endorsing the region's soil and climate – in this case that of Dr Derek Milne, the co-founder of **Martinborough** – that encouraged the first modern plantings in 1979. Milne maintains that low rainfall during the growing season, free-draining soils and dry, sunny autumns add up to a Burgundian or Rheingau-type climate. Certainly, Wairarapa's climate is closer to Marlborough in the South Island than Hawke's Bay to the north. The main varieties grown are Pinot Noir, Chardonnay, Riesling, Sauvignon Blanc and Gewurztraminer. Recent success, particularly with Pinot Noir and Chardonnay, should attract more wine-makers into the region.

North Island wineries

ABEL & CO   **AU**
Pomona Road, Kumeu, Auckland

                                                                        w, r   *
Malcolm Abel founded this winery in 1970, releasing his first vintage in 1974. Since his untimely death, Dan Southee has taken over the 5,000-case production here. There is now a balanced range of reds made from Auckland fruit and whites made from Gisborne fruit, including Beaujolais Nouvelle Zelande, Cabernet and Chardonnay.

AKARANGI   **HW**
River Road, Havelock North

                                                                        w, r   *
The Osborne and Kiddle families, who jointly founded this 6-acre (2.5-ha) estate in 1988, release small quantities of table wines.

THE ANTIPODEAN   **NO**
PO Box 40088, Glenfield, Auckland

                                                                     r   *→**
Owned by barrister brothers James and Petar Vuletic, the Antipodean produced its first commercial vintage in 1985 and stepped into the European limelight in 1987 with a carefully crafted publicity campaign. Only one wine is produced here: a Bordeaux-inspired blend of Cab Sauvignon and Merlot (two-thirds:one-third) with a dash of Malbec, made from 5 acres (2 ha) of vines. The Vuletics vinify 350 cases of this wine in large wooden vats and give it two years' ageing in small oak *barriques*, racking every three months and fining with egg-whites in the French manner. The 85 had a fresh, green pepper scent backed up by a jammy, over-oaked palate, the finer 86 a strong, beefy, tarry scent and a tarry, sinewy palate. Both wines needed more fruit.

ASPEN RIDGE   WK
Waerenga Road, RD 1, Te Kauwhata, South Auckland

w, r, ft   *

This small winery just north of Lake Waikare, which produces a limited
range of wines, was founded by Alister McKissock who used to run the
Te Kauwhata Research Station.

ATA RANGI   WR
Puruatanga Road, PO Box 43, Martinborough, Wairarapa

w, r   *→

Clive Paton and his wife Phyllis, formerly at **Montana's** Blenheim
winery, founded Ata Rangi in 1980. They now have 10 acres (4 ha) of
vines, led by Cab Sauvignon and Pinot Noir, and a half-finished winery.
Low-cropping vines and hand-crafted wines aged in oak have ensured a
good reception for Ata Rangi's reds – among them Celebre, a Cabernet,
Syrah and Merlot blend. 1988 saw the release of the first barrel-
fermented Chardonnay.

BABICH   AU
Babich Road, Henderson, Auckland

w=86 87, r=85 87, ft   *→**

This Dalmatian establishment, founded in 1916 by Joe Babich, is one
of the oldest wineries in New Zealand that has remained under
continuous family ownership. Early wine-making days were tough and
Babich did most of the work himself – from growing grapes and
crushing them by foot to opening a shop in which to sell his wines.
Moving down to Henderson in 1919, he bought 60 acres (24 ha) of
wilderness where he farmed and planted Pinot Meunier vines.
Gradually wine-making got the upper hand here and Babich's sons,
Peter and Joe Jnr took over the business. Today they produce some
67,000 cases of wine a year, which makes their winery one of New
Zealand's largest concerns. Peter looks after the Babich vineyards and
administration, and Joe is the wine-maker. Their 70 acres (28 ha) of
Henderson vines and half-share in a Hawke's Bay vineyard together
provide 40% of the fruit needed for their wines.

Babich produces a full range of reds, whites, sherries and ports. Its
finest table wines, made from Hawke's Bay fruit, are bottled under
the Irongate label. The 87 Irongate Chardonnay with its rich, nutty
butterscotch scent and zingy, verdant, oaky palate is definitely their best
Chardonnay; the gold, almost amber 87 Henderson Chardonnay is still
fresh but its oaky, sappy palate masks the wine's fruit. Babich also
makes a successful aperitif-style Semillon/Chardonnay blend, whose 88
vintage offered a pleasant zesty, green mouthful. The flowering currant-
like 88 Sauvignon is a shade too tart and the charred, jammy, liquorice
and leaf-mould-like 86 Henderson Pinot Noir, though equally agreeable,
is not great. The next generation is now being groomed for the family
firm, with Peter's son David studying wine at Roseworthy in Australia.

BRAJKOVICH   See **Kumeu River**.

BROOKFIELDS   HW
RD 3, Napier

w, r   *

Peter Robertson, formerly with **McWilliam's**, makes 5,000 cases a year.
His 7 acres (3 ha) of Hawke's Bay Chardonnay and Sauvignon vines
supply only 20% of his fruit; the remainder is bought in locally. Wines
include a partially barrel-fermented Chardonnay and an oak-aged
Sauvignon. The 87 Sauvignon is a soft, pear-drop wine, while the big
chunky 87 Chardonnay needs time to fill out. Brookfields' best wine is a
Bordeaux-inspired Cabernet blend: the straight 86 Cabernet had a
delicate, smoky, cassis-like palate.

BRYLADD   NC
Main South Road, Pamapuria, RD 1, Kaitaia, Northland

w, r, ft   *

Owen Birss produces small quantities of traditional table and fortified
wines at this Northland winery.

CEDAR WINES   AU
Main Road, Kumeu, Auckland

w, ft   *

The Piskulich family makes sherry, port and a Moselle-style white wine
from 2 acres (1 ha) of Kumeu vines.

CHIFNEY   WR
Huangarua Road, Martinborough, Wairarapa

w, r   *→

Stan and Rosemary Chifney planted 10 acres (4 ha) of vines in 1980.
With the help of their daughter and son-in-law they produce, among
other wines, an award-winning Cab Sauvignon and Chardonnay.

C J PASK   HW
Korokipo Road, Hastings, Hawke's Bay

w, r   *→**

Chris Pask produces 6,000 high-quality cases of wine a year, selling
some of his 80 acres (32 ha) of fruit. Pask's Cab Sauvignon has pleased
both European and New Zealand palates. Other wines include the
white Estate Blend, Roys Hill White and Red, and well-regarded Pinot
Noir, Sauvignon and Chardonnay.

COLLARD BROTHERS   AU
303 Lincoln Road, Henderson, Auckland

w, r, sw   **→

Despite their English air, the Collards have been in New Zealand since
1910, when horticulturist John Collard founded the firm. The estate
initially only grew grapes, but John's son Lionel started to make wine.
Today Lionel's two sons Bruce, a senior wine judge, and Geoffrey, who
has studied wine in Germany and Bordeaux, are the wine-makers.
German influence is apparent in their fine Rh Riesling and sweet late
harvest Botrytised Riesling, but their French varieties are if anything
more impressive. The Collards have 50 acres (20 ha) of vines, divided
between a 40-acre (16 ha) plot at Rothesay in the Waikoukou Valley
and their 10-acre (4-ha) home vineyard. These supply half their fruit;
the rest is bought in, mainly from Marlborough and Te Kauwhata.
Whites such as Rothesay Chardonnay, Sauv Blanc and Rh Riesling
dominate the list. Try the fine, fresh, zesty, lemony-gooseberry 88
Rothesay Vineyard Sauv Blanc, the deliciously rich, buttery, nutty 87
Marlborough Chardonnay or the even finer elegant, refined, perfumed,
three-star 87 Rothesay Chardonnay. Do also try the highly successful
peachy 85 Dry Chenin Blanc. Reds consist of Private Bin Claret and a
Cabernet/Merlot blend, rounded off with Cab Franc.
 ☿   Star buy: Collard Brothers Rothesay Sauv Blanc & Chardonnay

CONTINENTAL   NO
PO Box 6041, Ruamanga, Whangarei

w, r, ft   *

Wine-maker Mario Vuletich and family run this traditional Dalmatian
estate, producing about 2,000 cases a year of table and fortified wines.

COOKS   WK
Paddy's Road, Te Kauwhata, South Auckland

w, r, sw, ft   *→**

Since its merger with **McWilliam's** in 1984 and the takeover by
Corbans in 1987, Cooks has become part of the second-biggest New
Zealand wine group. It now produces some 6 million bottles a year.
Cooks was started in 1969 by a group of Auckland businessmen who
decided to build a first-class winery that would vinify only superior
grape varieties. It was a fine plan, but price wars and heavy losses soon
forced the winery to cater for the cheaper end of the market. This led to
the release of Chasseur, an inexpensive, sweet blend of Muller-Thurgau,
Chenin Blanc and Chasselas in medium and dry versions, and the
Fernhill Muller-Thurgau and Chenin Blanc range.
    Cooks' Te Kauwhata and Napier wineries, formerly managed by
Corbans' chief wine-maker Kerry Hitchcock, now concentrate on two
ranges of wines: Chasseur, the cheaper range, and the Longridge of

Hawke's Bay selection. Cooks' Wine-makers Reserve wines are its finest. Export markets get the leafy, lemon peel-like Tolaga Bay Dry and Medium White, the soft, herbaceous Tolaga Bay Dry Red and the premium Cooks range. The latter includes the fragrant, zesty, flowering currant-like 88 Hawke's Bay Sauv Blanc, the light, appley 88 Chenin Blanc, the soft, oily Marlborough Sauv Blanc and the ripe vanilla and sandalwood-like 87 Marlborough Semillon, which has perhaps been over-oaked. Cooks' Cabernet has always offered pleasant, herbaceous, green pepper scents and tastes, but its best wine is the Chardonnay. The 88 Hawke's Bay has fine, fresh, oaky-pineappley flavours; the 80, also aged in American oak, was a glorious, full-bodied wine.

℩ Star buy: Cooks 88 Hawke's Bay Chardonnay

COOPERS CREEK   AU
Main Road, Huapai, Auckland

w=86, r   *→**

Coopers Creek was founded in 1980 by American Davis-trained wine-maker Randy Weaver and accountant Andrew Hendry, who met working for Penfolds (NZ). Roseworthy-trained Kim Crawford took over when Weaver went home in 1988. Coopers Creek produces about 17,000 cases a year, concentrating on dry, distinctive, full-flavoured wines. Popular wines include the spritzy, lemony, herbaceous 88 Coopers Dry Chenin Blanc/Semillon/Chardonnay and the tart, oaky, verdant 88 Fumé Blanc. The fine, oaky-toasty, hazelnut-like 87 Chardonnay from Hawke's Bay is higher-quality. Red wines include the 86 Cabernet/Merlot with its sturdy, burnt, herbaceous capsicum taste. At present, Coopers Creek buys in most of its grapes, its own 10 acres (4 ha) of Cab Sauvignon and Merlot at Huapai and 17 acres (7 ha) of Chardonnay and Pinot Noir at Hawke's Bay supplying only a quarter of its fruit. The unlovely-sounding, but delicious, barrel-fermented Swamp Road Chardonnay from Hawke's Bay is Coopers' best wine; the 86 vintage was clean, smoky and well made.

CORBANS   AU
PO Box 21-183, Henderson, Auckland

w, r, ft, sp   *→***

Having swallowed up **Cooks-McWilliam's** in 1987, Corbans is now the second-biggest wine firm in New Zealand after **Montana**. Its enormous range includes table, fortified, sparkling and flavoured wines, as well as wine coolers and fruit wines. Lebanese-born Assis Abrahim Corban, who founded Corbans in 1902 with less than 4 acres (1.5 ha) of vines, would not recognize the place. In spite of introducing new wine-styles throughout the 1940s, 50s, 60s and 70s, Corbans did not appear as innovative as its competitors. Norbert Seibel, a Geisenheim graduate, helped to improve its reputation in the early 80s, but the firm's finest hour came with the release in 1986 of its Stoneleigh Vineyard range, made from the fine fruit of a widely-acclaimed South Island vineyard.

Corbans produces some 9 million bottles of wine and 3 million wine casks a year, and owns wineries at Marlborough and Gisborne, as well as bottling facilities at Henderson. Excluding the Cooks-McWilliam's vineyards, Corbans has some 700 acres (280 ha) of vines – 200 acres (80 ha) at Marlborough and the rest at Hawke's Bay and Te Kauwhata. These supply only a third of its fruit; the rest is bought in. In 1988 the company also became involved in a \$2 million joint venture at Marlborough with South Australia's **Wolf Blass**. Kerry Hitchcock oversees production of the Liebestraum and Velluto Rosso ranges, the Robard & Butler range and sherries, ports and cask wines. Corbans' straight range includes the soft, spicy 83 Select Dry Gewurztraminer and the equally soft, fruity, supple 83 Cabernet/Merlot. The 83 Robard & Butler Dry Rh Riesling was a strong, peppery wine.

The Stoneleigh quartet is Corbans' finest range. The 88 Stoneleigh Sauvignon, with its wonderful fresh, green, nettley palate, is a three-star wine. The rich, ripe, chunky cassis-fruit 87 Stoneleigh Cab Sauvignon is almost as good and the soft, flowery, appley-citric 87 Rh Riesling is also attractive. The only real disappointment is the light, oaky 87 Stoneleigh Chardonnay, which has had too much oak treatment.

℩ Star buy: Corbans Stoneleigh Sauvignon & Cab Sauvignon

DELEGAT'S
Hepburn Road, Henderson, Auckland

AU

w, r, sw   *→★★★

Delegat's was founded in 1947 when Jim and Rose Delegat's father, who like their mother came from Yugoslavia, planted out vines at Henderson. The company has survived recent financial problems with the help of the Wilson Neill wine and spirit group which now part-owns it. In the late 1970s Delegat's hired wine-maker John Hancock, now at **Morton Estate**, who made some splendid, full, rich Chardonnay and freeze-concentrated *auslese* Muller-Thurgau wines. The present wine-maker is Brent Marris. Delegat's offers two different styles of wines: a straight varietal and regional range, and the finer Proprietors Reserve range. The three-star 87 Hawke's Bay Sauv Blanc, worth seeking out for its intense, zesty, herbaceous taste, is delicious; the zappy, flowering currant-like 88 is more delicate and restrained. Delegat's sources its Chardonnays from Gisborne. The soft, buttery 86 is pleasant and the 87 Chardonnay with its rich, butterscotch scent and buttery palate excellent. But both are eclipsed by the rich, oaky 86 Proprietors Reserve Chardonnay and the buttercup-gold, full, fat style of the 87.

♀ Star buy: Delegat's Proprietors Reserve Chardonnay

DE REDCLIFFE
RD 1, Pokeno, Auckland

AU

w, r   *

Founded in 1976, De Redcliffe is one of Auckland's small "boutique" wineries. Owner Chris Canning, who employs Riverina-trained Mark Compton as wine-maker, has 40 acres (16 ha) of vines supplying a third of his grapes. Hawke's Bay fruit is bought in to make an annual total of 19,000 cases, but both plantings and production are expanding fast. Chardonnay is the big seller, followed by the Semillon/Chardonnay blend: the 87 Chardonnay has a soft, ripe, appley-oaky, but somewhat dull mouthful. Visitors can stay at De Redcliffe's Hotel du Vin.

DRY RIVER
Puruatanga Road, Martinborough, Wairarapa

WR

w, r   *

Dry River, founded in 1979 by Dr Neil McCallum and his wife Dawn, produces 2,500 cases a year from 12 acres (5 ha) of vines, buying in a third of its fruit locally. Wines include a Sauv Blanc, Pinot Noir and, unusually, a well-regarded Pinot Gris.

ESK VALLEY
Main Road, Bayview, Napier

HW

w, r   *→

This sprawling establishment, formerly known as Glenvale, was bought in 1987 by **Villa Maria**. It now produces quality varietal table wines, such as Chardonnay and a Cab Sauvignon/Merlot blend (which did well in the Canberra show), exclusively from Hawke's Bay fruit. The straight 86 Private Bin Cabernet has a soft, light cassis taste.

ESKDALE
Main Road, Eskdale, Hawke's Bay

HW

w, r   *

Canadian Kim Salonius built this traditional winery with his own hands and now produces Chardonnay, Gewurztraminer and Cab Sauvignon.

FAIRHAVEN WINES
324 West Coast Road, Glen Eden, Auckland

AU

w, r, sw, ft   *

Founded in 1942, this winery sells small quantities of a wide variety of wines including sherries, dessert wines and table wines.

FINO VALLEY
283 Valley Road, Henderson, Auckland

AU

w, r, ft   *

Fino Valley makes a range of fortified and table wines which are mostly sold at the cellar door.

FULLERS   AU
Candia Road, Henderson, Auckland

                                                              w, r *
The Allens make table wines from 8 acres (3 ha) of vines, including
Palomino and Dr Hogg Muscat.

GOLDWATER ESTATE   AU
Putiki Bay, Waiheke Island

                                                              w, r *
Kim and Jeanette Goldwater, who are advised by the viticulturist Dr
Richard Smart, own 5 acres (2 ha) of two-tier trellised vines on Waiheke
Island, just across the isthmus from Auckland. They started here in
1978 and now make l,500 cases of Sauv Blanc, a Cabernet/Merlot/Cab
Franc blend and Rosé Cabernet, their newest wine.

HOLLY LODGE   WR
Upper Aramoho, Wanganui

                                                              w, r, ft *
Vance Crozier runs this touristic winery in Wairarapa, making a range
of table and fortified wines.

KARAMEA   WK
Tuhikara Road, RD 10, Frankton, Hamilton

                                                              w, r *
This small 4-acre (1.5-ha) outfit, founded by the Timbrells in 1980,
makes 700 cases of wines including Dry and Medium Breidecker and a
Pinot Noir; these are on sale at the winery.

KUMEU RIVER   AU
2 Highway 16, Kumeu, Auckland

                                           w=87 89, r=87 89, ft *→→*
The hard-working Brajkovichs, another family of Dalmatian descent,
founded this company in 1944, originally as San Marino Wines. Mate
Brajkovich, whose first job in New Zealand, aged 15, was to dig for
kauri gum with his father, is still head of the firm. He is assisted by his
sons, especially Roseworthy-trained Michael who has worked in
California and in Bordeaux for the Moueix family of Château Pétrus.
The Brajkovichs' 45 acres (18 ha) of Kumeu vines, some of which have
been trained by Michael to a u-shaped lyre system, supply 80% of their
fruit; the remainder is bought in locally. Annual production of 17,000
cases is divided between the Kumeu River, Brajkovich and San Marino
label wines. The Kumeu River trio of wines – Chardonnay, Sauvignon
and Merlot/Cabernet – are the Brajkovichs' finest offerings. Try the
delicious, full, biscuity-pineappley 87 Chardonnay, the robust, chunky,
earthy fruit of the 86 Merlot/Cabernet, or the dry, rich, creamy, apricot-
like botrytis-affected 87 Noble Dry Sauvignon. The Brajkovich range
includes Chardonnay, Cab Franc, Merlot and various blends; San
Marino is a more humble selection of cellar-door-style blended table
wines and fortifieds.
 ⚲ Star buy: Kumeu River 87 Chardonnay

KV WINES   AU
Riverhead Road, Kumeu, Auckland

                                                              w, r, ft *
The Vitasovich family, who founded this winery in 1973, produce a
variety of wines including a Seibel/Cabernet, a Palomino/Chenin Blanc
blend and fortifieds.

LIMEBURNERS BAY   AU
112 Hobsonville Road, Hobsonville, Auckland

                                                              w, r *→
This winery is situated at Limeburners Bay, just to the east of Kumeu
and Huapai. Alan and Jetta Laurenson planted their vineyard in 1977
and originally sold grapes to other wineries, starting to sell wine under
their own label in the early 80s. There are 27 acres (11 ha) of vines here,
planted to a range of mostly premium red grapes, and more are on their
way. About 4,000 cases of well-thought-of wines are made.

LINCOLN   AU
130 Lincoln Road, Henderson, Auckland

w, r, sw *→

With 60 acres (24 ha) of vines and a sizeable production, Lincoln is one of the larger New Zealand wineries. Its founder, Petar Fredatovich, worked as a stonemason before buying this property in 1937. Today his grandsons, Peter and John, run the firm with wine-making help from Nick Chan. Lincoln's vineyards are in Auckland, but grapes are also bought in from Hawke's Bay, Gisborne and Marlborough. Wines include the blended Brigham's Creek White and Red pair, varietals such as Gewurztraminer, Muller-Thurgau, Chardonnay and Cab Sauvignon, and Gamay Beaujolais, a light carbonic maceration red.

LOMBARDI   HW
PO Box 201, Havelock North

w, r, ft *

The Green family's 10 acres (4 ha) of vines supply about half the fruit needed to make 8,000 cases a year of Italian-influenced wines.

McWILLIAM'S (NZ)   HW
Church Road, Taradale, Hawke's Bay

w, r, ft, sp *

This Australian wine firm was operating in New Zealand as early as 1944 and grew larger in the 60s when it merged with Tom McDonald's winery. McDonald, a celebrated New Zealand wine-maker, remained in charge at McWilliam's until Bob Knappstein took over in 1976. McWilliam's took its New Zealand concern seriously, which no doubt accounts for the success of Cab Sauvignons such as the rich, deep, truffley 75. McWilliam's also made some fine Chardonnays: the 80 was a classy, smoky-toasty mouthful and the 81 had a glorious, buttery oak style. It is therefore a great pity that these wines are no more. Since its takeover by **Corbans** in 1987, the range has dwindled to wines such as the sparkling Marque Vue, Heritage Hock, Moselle, port and sherry.

MARKOVINA   AU
PO Box 86, Kumeu, Auckland

w, r, ft *

Ivan Markovina runs this small Auckland estate, where he produces limited quantities of various table and fortified wines.

MARTINBOROUGH VINEYARD   WR
Princess Street, Martinborough, Wairarapa

w, r *→

Wairarapa's reputation as a region has had much to do with the medal-winning performance of this winery, run as a partnership of the Schultz and Milne families. About 5,000 cases a year are produced from Martinborough's 25 acres (10 ha) of vines and local bought-in fruit. Roseworthy-trained wine-maker Larry McKenna, previously at **Delegat's**, hopes to double this. The site here was selected as being especially suited to Chardonnay and Pinot Noir, and these are its top varieties. Martinborough's Pinot Noir is regarded by many as the finest in New Zealand and its Chardonnay and Sauv Blanc have also been well received. Riesling and Gewurztraminer complete the range.

MATANGI VILLAGE VINEYARD   WK
PO Box 113, Matangi, Hamilton

w, r *

Rodger and Virginia Gallagher's 5 acres (2 ha) produce just 150 cases of wines such as Rh Riesling-based Waikato Gold and Cab Sauvignon.

MATAWHERO   GI
Riverpoint Road, RD 1, Gisborne

w=83 89 86, r=83 89 86 *→**

Denis Irwin, dubbed the "Matawhero Maniac" by the Antipodean press, is now back at Riverpoint Road after abandoning plans for a vineyard in Goulburn (VIC). The vineyard here was planted in 1968 by Denis' father Bill, whose early work with Gewurztraminer, Chardonnay,

Chenin Blanc and Pinot Noir vines gave Matawhero a quality lead over other New Zealand concerns. Denis built on his father's foundation, releasing the first commercial vintage in 1976. Matawhero now has 100 acres (40 ha) of vines. Annual production is 8,000 cases.

Matawhero's style is dry, distinctive and European-influenced: its exotic, dry, spicy Gewurztraminer, for example, tastes uncannily like an Alsace. Irwin puts this down to the traditional methods of Swiss wine-maker Hatsch Kalberer, who uses only the estate's own grapes and natural yeast for fermentation. The range consists of dry table wines. Gewurztraminer is the leading quality wine, followed by a flavoursome Chardonnay and, unusually for this region, a well-thought-of Cab Sauvignon/Merlot. The newest wine is a Sauvignon/Semillon blend. 1983 was an excellent year for this winery, so snaffle up all dry, spicy 83 Matawhero Gewurztraminers. The 82 Dry Reserve Gewurztraminer with its delicious, exotic Alsace-like spice is also a good buy.

♀ Star buy: Matawhero Gewurztraminer

MATUA VALLEY   **AU**
PO Box 100, Kumeu, Auckland

                                    w=87 88 86, r=87 86 88, sw, ft *→→*

Wine-maker Ross Spence, who trained at Fresno in California, and his brother Bill, who is in charge of sales and vineyards, have run Matua Valley since 1974. Their 50 acres (20 ha) of Hawke's Bay Cabernet and 110 acres (44 ha) of mixed Auckland varieties supply only a third of the fruit for their 67,000 cases a year; the rest is bought in from Hawke's Bay, Gisborne and Marlborough. Matua Valley's Sauvignon, for example the elegant, fresh, grassy, leafy 88, is one of its best wines; the Reserve version of the same vintage, although good, has been over-oaked. The Spence brothers' Chardonnay has always been worthwhile: the 87 Judd Estate Chardonnay, made from grapes grown in the Judd family's Gisborne's vineyards, offers pleasant, light, appley flavours, but the 87 Egan Estate Chardonnay with its fresh, ripe, biscuity-pineapple flavours is a finer wine. Look out for Matua Valley's fresh, grassy, raspberry-scented 86 Cab Sauvignon whose light, herbaceous fruit is definitely worth tasting; the deep, full, blackcurranty 85 was finer still.

MAYFAIR WINE CELLARS   **AU**
192 Sturges Road, Henderson, Auckland

                                                             w, r, ft *

The Ivicevich family, like many others, is now trying to change from sherries and other fortifieds to table wines at this 7-acre (3-ha) estate.

MAZURAN   **AU**
255 Lincoln Road, Henderson, Auckland

                                                             w, r, ft *→

The Mazurans once enjoyed a great reputation for their fine traditional sherries and ports. The family is no longer in charge here, though a son-in-law carries on old traditions.

THE MILLTON VINEYARD   **GI**
PO Box 66, Manutuke, Gisborne

                                                             w, r *→→*

Situated west of Matawhero and Gisborne, this purist, organically-minded winery is run by James and Annie Millton, who founded it in 1984. Their 50 acres (20 ha) of Poverty Bay vines supply all the fruit they need to produce 6,000 cases a year, mostly of a Sauvignon/Semillon blend, a barrel-fermented Chenin Blanc and a Chardonnay. Steinbery Muller-Thurgau and Cabernet Blush are their newest wines. They also make a highly-regarded botrytis Riesling. Their 87 Opou Vineyards Rh Riesling had delicate, peachy-flowery flavours.

MISSION   **HW**
PO Box 7043, Taradale, Hawke's Bay

                                                             w, r, ft *→

Mission, founded in 1851, is the oldest winery in New Zealand. As the name suggests, it was started by the Society of Mary, a French Catholic missionary order, which still owns the winery today, using its profits to run the seminary here at the foot of the Taradale Hills. Warwick Orchiston, who was formerly the wine-maker at **Vidal**, manages the winery. Wines are made by Paul Mooney, Mission's first lay wine-maker, and Brother Francis. Half of Mission's 100 acres (40 ha) of vines surround the winery, sheep farm and elegant Victorian seminary, visited by thousands every year. The other half are at Meeanee, the seminary's former location, which the missionaries were forced by floods to leave in 1910, transporting the building piece by piece to its present site.

With an annual production of 35,000 cases, Mission is one of the larger New Zealand wineries. Although it still produces sacramental wines and fortifieds, the majority of its output now consists of quality table wines. Its priciest offerings are its Cab Sauvignon, Cabernet/Merlot and Gewurztraminer. Mission rates its *barrique*-aged 88 Chanel Block Chardonnay Reserve as its finest wine. The 83 Chardonnay offered soft, ripe, pineappley flavours, and the 83 Cabernet/Merlot was a fruity, oaky wine. The 88 Sauvignon is light, zesty and spritzy. Visitors are welcome daily except Sun, 8am-5pm.

MORTON ESTATE   WK
RD 2, Katikati, Bay of Plenty

                                        w=86 83 85, r=86 83 85, sp   **→****
The discerning visitor may find Morton Estate's Cape Dutch façade somewhat bizarre in the idyllic surroundings of New Zealand's green and pleasant land; indeed, even the locals thought it was going to be a mosque or a crematorium when building work was underway. But Morton Brown felt that his remote site on the east coast would need a unique selling point to bring in customers. He need not have worried: his wines alone have taken care of that. After planting vines here in 1979, Brown hired brilliant Australian wine-maker John Hancock just in time to produce his first commercial vintage in 1983. **Mildara**, the large Victorian wine firm, bought Morton Estate in 1988. This injection of capital has meant more vineyards and plans for a processing plant at Hawke's Bay. There are now 260 acres (105 ha) of vines, mostly in Hawke's Bay, some of which are only just bearing; the home plot is planted entirely to Pinot Noir. About a third of Morton Estate's 42,000 cases are made from bought-in Hawke's Bay and Gisborne grapes.

John Hancock stands out from other New Zealand wine-makers because of his talent for producing a wide range of wines, from dry to sweet and from still to sparkling, all of which are first-class. Other estates may make a finer Sauvignon or a classier Cabernet but none can match his all-round wine-making ability. Anyone tasting the elegant, restrained flowering currant fruit of the 88 Hawke's Bay Sauv Blanc, the delicious, buttery-cinnamony 88 Chardonnay or the 86 Black Label Chardonnay Reserve with its deep, fruity, Burgundy-like oaky-toasty flavours can experience Hancock's wine expertise at first hand. Limited quantities are made of superior Black Label Chardonnay and Fumé Blanc. The latest 86 Cab Sauvignon, with its rich, liquorice taste, was a shade over-charred. Morton Estate also makes *méthode champenoise* wine, based on Pinot Noir and Chardonnay.
♈ Star buy: Black Label Chardonnay Reserve & Fumé Blanc

NAUTILUS See **Yalumba** (SA).

NGATARAWA   HW
Ngatarawa Road, Bridge Pa, Hastings

                                                        w, r, sw, ft   *
This winery is a partnership between Alwyn Corban, a scion of the **Corbans** wine dynasty who studied oenology at Davis, and Garry Glazebrook, whose family owns the land on which their 27-acre (11-ha) vineyard is planted. The winery is housed in the Glazebrook family's century-old stables, hence Ngatarawa's horse symbol. Apart from the Stables Classic White and Red blends, Corban also makes large quantities of Chardonnay and Sauv Blanc. "In exceptional years", Ngatarawa produces Glazebrook, a Bordeaux-inspired Cabernet blend, Botrytis Selection Riesling, and Alwyn, a premium hand-picked barrel-fermented Chardonnay. The 88 Sauv Blanc was an ordinary, musty wine and the 87 Stables Cab Sauvignon Red a dull, cassis-like offering.

NOBILO VINTNERS   **AU**
Station Road, Huapai, West Auckland
                                   w=76 85 86, r=70 76 78 83, sw   *→**
Inventive Nick Nobilo is chief wine-maker at this family-owned estate,
founded in 1943. Like most New Zealanders of Dalmatian descent, the
Nobilos came here to dig kauri gum early in the century. Nick Nobilo
Snr eventually saved enough to buy land at Huapai where he planted
vines in 1943. Nobilo has had a troubled financial history, but appears
to have weathered the storm and now produces 125,000 cases a year.
The firm's own 50 acres (20 ha) of Huapai vines, planted two-thirds to
Pinotage and one-third to Cab Sauvignon, provide just 10% of its fruit.
The bulk of its needs, mostly white varieties such as Muller-Thurgau,
Sauv Blanc and Chardonnay – Nobilo's three bestsellers – are bought in
from Gisborne, Hawke's Bay and Marlborough.
     An impressive 40,000 cases of Muller-Thurgau are sold under the
White Cloud label; this white wine is back-blended with *süss-reserve* to
provide an appealing light, sweet, grapey-flowery wine. Sauv Blanc,
with sales of 20,000 cases, is the next most popular bottling; the 88
Fumé Blanc wine had a zesty, tingly style overlaid with marzipan. The
Chardonnays include a fresh, light, pineappley 87 from Gisborne
and the fine, fresh, oaky-pineappley 87 Dixon Vineyard Chardonnay.
Nobilo rates this last wine as its finest, along with its red blend Concept
(two-thirds Pinotage:one-third Cabernet), which is made only in top
years. Try also the delicious light, soft 85 Gewurztraminer, tasting of
spicy lychees and roses. Nobilo's red wines have provided some of its
most memorable mouthfuls – especially its classic Pinot Noirs, such
as the delicious, savoury-gamey 78 Pinot Noir and the moreish, rich,
elegant 78 Pinotage. The latest vintages include the robust, earthy,
bloody 86 Pinotage and the gutsy, grassy, leaf-mould-like 84 Pinot Noir.
Nobilo's 76 Private Bin Claret had a lovely, rich, gamey-truffley taste.
Nobilo's finest red now is the 84 Cab Sauvignon with its well-made,
ripe, herbaceous, cassis-like scent and taste.
 ♀ Star buy: Nobilo 76 & 78 Pinot Noir & Pinotage

OLD RAILWAY WINERY   **AU**
PO Box 21-294, Henderson, Auckland
                                                                  w, r   *
Steve Pecar runs this small winery in the Auckland region, producing
red and white table wines.

OZICH   **AU**
219 Metcalf Road, Henderson, Auckland
                                                              w, r, sw, ft   *
This winery, founded in 1965, is run by Mate Ozich with his sons
Davorin and Miro. Their 20 acres (8 ha) of vines are made by Davorin
into a variety of table and fortified wines, including Chablis and St
Jerome Cabernet/Merlot, their best wine.

PACIFIC   **AU**
90 McLeod Road, Henderson, Auckland
                                                              w, r, sw, ft   *
This medium-sized winery, managed by Millie Erceg, produces mostly
coolers and wine casks. Steve Tubic, formerly at **Corbans**, is the wine-
maker. Pacific's Reserve wines are its finest, especially the Gewurztraminer. Sauvignon, Cab Sauvignon and fortifieds are also produced.

PAPA   **AU**
Station Road, Huapai, Auckland
                                                                  w, r   *
David Papa has produced some well-thought-of red wines at this small
Auckland winery.

PIERRE   **WI**
Elizabeth Street, Waikanae, Wairarapa
                                                                  w, r   *
Owner/wine-maker Peter Heginbotham founded Pierre in 1968. His
main wines are Cab Sauvignon and Pinot Noir.

PLEASANT VALLEY

AU

Henderson Valley Road, Newton, Auckland

w, r, ft   *

This traditional winery dates from 1902 when Stephan Yelas, another Dalmatian, planted vines here. The winery is still family-owned and the current Stephen, also called Stephen, is gradually bringing it up to date. Pleasant Valley is the premium range, Valley the cheaper selection.

REVINGTON VINEYARD

GI

110 Stout Street, Gisborne

w   *

Ross and Mary-Jane Revington bought a 10-acre (4-ha) vineyard at Ormond, about 11 miles (18 km) from Gisborne, in 1987. Just 200 cases of Chardonnay were released in 1988, Revington's first vintage.

RONGOPAI

WK

71 Waerenga Road, Te Kauwhata, South Auckland

w, r, sw   *→**

Tom van Dam and Geisenheim-trained Dr Rainer Eschenbruch, both previously at Te Kauwhata Research Station, founded Rongopai in 1982, releasing their first vintage in 1986. Rongopai produces about 3,000 cases a year from its own 10 acres (4 ha) of vines and bought-in grapes. Hawke's Bay Chardonnay is the major line but Rongopai also has a good reputation for its late harvest and auslese Rieslings.

SACRED HILL

HW

Pariawa, RD 6, Napier

w, r   *

Mark and David Mason's large vineyard produces a range of quality table wines, partly made from bought-in fruit.

ST GEORGE ESTATE

HW

St George's Road South, Hastings

w, r   *

Wine-maker Michael Bennett and Martin Elliot are joint owners of this 15-acre (6-ha) winery, founded in 1985. Half of the vines surround the winery; the remainder are in the Tukituki River valley. Most of their 3,000-case output is sold in their small restaurant, but a Cabernet/Merlot blend, Sauvignon and Chardonnay are available further afield.

ST NESBIT

AU

Hingaia Road, Papakura, Auckland

r   *→

Anthony Molloy, a full-time QC as well as St Nesbit's owner/wine-maker, began planting vines on the waterfront here in 1981 and today has almost 7 acres (3 ha) of vines. He hopes to increase this to 17 acres (7 ha) over the next five years and meanwhile keeps his customers satisfied with just 1,000 cases of a well-regarded Bordeaux-inspired Cab Sauvignon blend, rounded off with Merlot and Cab Franc.

SAPICH BROTHERS

AU

Forest Hill Road, Henderson, Auckland

w, r, ft   *

The Sapich family makes sherry and red and white table wines here from 45 acres (18 ha) of vines.

SEAVIEW

AU

Simpsons Road, Henderson, Auckland

ft   *

A variety of fortifieds are made at this small Auckland winery from just 3 acres (1 ha) of vines.

SEIBEL

AU

24 Kakariki Avenue, Mount Eden, Auckland

w   *

German-born and trained Norbert Seibel, formerly with **Corbans**, makes mainly Chardonnay, Sauvignon and Riesling from contract fruit.

SELAKS   AU
PO Box 34, Kumeu, Auckland

w=83, r=83, sw, ft *→

Selaks was founded in 1934 by the uncle of the present owner, Mate
Selak, who is now in the process of handing over the reins to his sons
Michael and Ivan. Michael is in charge of marketing and Ivan runs the
winery operation, aided by wine-maker Darryl Woolley. Like most
Dalmatian firms Selaks originally produced bulk wines, but unlike the
others it did not start producing premium bottled table wines until
1979. There are now 153 acres (62 ha) of mixed vines at Auckland,
Gisborne and Marlborough which supply three-quarters of Selaks' fruit.
The other quarter is bought in from these regions to make a total annual
production of 29,000 cases.

    Selaks' long list of wines includes popular offerings such as Pinot
Blush, a *méthode champenoise* Pinot Noir-based wine, Ice Wine,
Admiral's Port and Muscat Liqueur. Quality here has improved steadily
over the years. The 87 Semillon with its fresh, verdant, perfumed style is
unusually scented for a New Zealand wine, but good. The 87 Sauvignon/
Semillon, whose grassy style also has a highly perfumed quality, is
slightly less successful. Selaks' strong, coarse, grassy 88 Sauv Blanc is
not as good as previous Sauvignons like the 86 with its lovely, soft,
flowering currant-like character. The 87 Selaks Chardonnay was a
restrained, austere, pineappley wine. Two-thirds of the wine production
here is white and one-third red. Selaks has recently opened a restaurant
close to the winery.

SOLJANS   AU
263 Lincoln Road, Henderson, Auckland

w, r, sw, ft, sp *

Wine-maker Tony Soljan specializes in sherries and dessert wines,
mostly sold at the cellar door. A small selection of table wines are also
made, as well as a popular *spumante*-style sparkler.

STONECROFT   HW
RD 5, Mere Road, Hastings

w, r *

Owner/wine-maker Alan Limmer founded this 8-acre (3-ha) estate
in 1987. Stonecroft produces tiny quantities of table wines such as
Chardonnay and Cab Sauvignon, mostly sold at the cellar door.

STONELEIGH   See **Corbans**.

STONYRIDGE VINEYARD   AU
Onetangi Road, Ostend, Waiheke Island

r *

Waiheke Island's second winery was founded in 1982 by Stephen and
Jane White. Like **Goldwater Estate** they have just 5 acres (2 ha) of
vines, and produce tiny quantities of Stonyridge Larose, a Cabernet
blend, and a straight second label Airfield Cabernet, using "classic
Bordeaux techniques".

TE HANA   NO
PO Box 23, Wellsford, Northland

w, r, ft *

Ron Becroft has 35 acres (14 ha) of vines, from which he makes a
limited selection of table and fortified wines.

TE KAIRANGA   WR
Martins Road, Martinborough, Wairarapa

w, r *

Te Kairanga was founded in 1983 and had its first vintage in 1986. Tom
and Robin Draper, the major shareholders here, hire Stan Chifney of
Chifney to produce their 8,000 cases of wines. There are over 100 acres
(40 ha) of vines, but half have only just been planted: when they come
on stream production will quadruple. Chardonnay is the leading wine
and the Drapers aim to produce large quantities of a Bordeaux-inspired
blend and a Pinot Noir.

TE MATA   HW
PO Box 335, Havelock North

w, r *→****
John Buck's whimsical architect-designed house with its sprawling structure and skinny chimneys overlooks Coleraine, one of the finest red vineyards in New Zealand. These 62 acres (25 ha) of vines, owned as a partnership between John and Wendy Buck and Michael and June Morris since 1978, provide all the fruit for Te Mata's annual 20,000-case production. It took Buck and Morris eight hard years of searching to find this quality hillside site with its Bordeaux-like micro-climate, reasonably low yields and long-growing season. Today half the acreage is planted to the celebrated Coleraine Red mix of Cab Sauvignon, Merlot and Cab Franc, the remainder to Chardonnay and Sauv Blanc.

Te Mata's Coleraine Cabernet/Merlot, made by wine-maker Peter Cowley, is widely regarded as one of the top New Zealand reds; ample evidence of this is provided by the ripe, exuberant fruit displayed in wines such as the rich, elegant, perfumed 83 or the intensely rich, complex, cassis, mint and eucalyptus-like 85. Castle Hill Sauv Blanc, which includes the easy-drinking, ripe gooseberry 86, is Te Mata's second-biggest line after Coleraine. Chardonnay, sold under the Elston label, is in another league as demonstrated by the smashing, big, rich, pineappley palate of the 86. Te Mata also produces a second Sauvignon under the Cape Crest label and an Estate Reserve Rosé.
  ♀ Star buy: Te Mata Coleraine Cabernet/Merlot

TOTARA   WK
RD 1, Thames

w, r, sw *
Gilbert Chan, whose ancestors were Cantonese distillers, runs this Chinese-inspired winery. Speciality wines include Fu Gai, a sweet Muscat-based blend, and kiwi fruit liqueur.

VIDAL   HW
913 St Aubyns Street East, Hastings

w, r, ft, sp *→***
Anthony Joseph Vidal came to New Zealand from Spain in 1888 to work for his uncle Joseph Soler, Wanganui's pioneering wine-maker. Since he founded the company in 1905, it has expanded considerably and is now part of the **Villa Maria** group. Visitors to St Aubyns Street can still see the original brick winery which has been turned into a handsome tourist centre/wine bar. Roseworthy-trained Kate Marris produces two ranges of varietal table wines, both sourced entirely from Hawke's Bay fruit: the superior Reserve and the straight Private Bin selections. A well-thought-of *méthode champenoise* sparkler (two-thirds Chardonnay:one-third Pinot Noir) is also made. The winery's most popular offering is a barrel-fermented Chardonnay, but Vidal regards the wonderful, fragrant 87 Reserve Cabernet/Merlot as its finest wine. The 86 Chardonnay Reserve is a gutsy, intense, buttery-oaky mouthful, though the straight 88 Fumé Blanc is not very exciting. Also worth seeking out are the superb *barrique*-fermented 87 Gisborne Chardonnay, whose rich, buttery-oaky butterscotch taste was almost Burgundian in style, and Vidal's Cab Sauvignon Reserves; the best of these was the fine, ripe, cassis-fruit 87.
  ♀ Star buy: Vidal Cab Sauvignon Reserve

VILAGRAD   WK
Rukuhia Road, Ngahinepouri, Hamilton

w, r, ft *
The Nooyen family, which has owned this winery since 1922, makes small amounts of fortified and table wines.

VILLA MARIA   AU
5 Kirkbridge Road, Mangere, Auckland

w, r, sw *→***
George Fistonich, the determined businessman of Dalmatian descent who runs Villa Maria and **Vidal** in Hawke's Bay, has weathered a number of storms in his career. From a tricky start when he took over

his father's small, ill-equipped vineyard in 1961, Fistonich built up Villa Maria into the country's third-largest wine producer, only to see it go under. Now, with production much reduced, the firm is part-owned by an investment company and aims to survive by producing superior varietal bottled wines, leaving the cheaper wines to others.

Villa Maria's grapes, most of which are now bought from contract growers in Gisborne, Hawke's Bay, Wairarapa and Auckland, are vinified by Roseworthy-trained wine-maker Kym Milne. The black label Reserve wines are this winery's finest. They include a Cab Sauvignon/ Merlot blend, *barrique*-fermented Chardonnay, Gewurztraminer, Sauv Blanc and straight Cab Sauvignon. Beneath the Reserves is the Private Bin range, which offers the same varietal selection but with a Muller-Thurgau instead of the Sauvignon. Quality here is high. The top wine is undoubtedly the glorious three-star 87 Barrique-Fermented Chardonnay with its big, ripe, utterly delicious buttery-oaky style. The pleasant, fresh, pineappley-appley style of the straight 88 Private Bin Chardonnay is good too. Sauvignon is another Villa Maria success story: the 87 Private Bin is a very fresh, zesty, tropical fruit wine. The 87 Reserve Gewurztraminer has pleasant, spicy, lychee-like flavours.
℣ Star buy: Villa Maria 87 Barrique-Fermented Chardonnay

WEST BROOK   AU
34 Awaroa Road, Henderson, Auckland

w, r, ft   ★

Anthony Ivicevich has 7 acres (3 ha) of Cabernet and Merlot vines at Henderson which supply 10% of his fruit. The grapes for sherry and white wine production are bought in from Auckland, Gisborne and Hawke's Bay. About 8,000 cases of wine are made annually. Cheap wines, sherries and ports are sold under the Panorama label.

WINDY HILL   AU
Simpsons Road, Henderson, Auckland

w, r, ft   ★

Windy Hill's founder, Milan Erceg, built a reputation for his sherries and red wines. His son Paul now carries on these traditions, making wines from his 8-acre (3-ha) vineyard.

The South Island

New Zealand's once-insignificant South Island has turned out to be the saviour of the country's wine industry. Although vines were planted in Nelson and Central Otago during the late 19th century, most had fallen into disrepair prior to the arrival of **Montana** in 1973. Montana's pioneering plantings at Blenheim persuaded wine-makers that this sunny, relatively rain-free island could make good wine, and since then there has been a rush to plant vineyards in the south. It is not only New Zealand companies that have seen the potential of the South Island's soil and climate: A number of Australian wineries have invested in joint ventures at Marlborough and others has joined the rush to buy grapes here. Top of their shopping list is Marlborough Sauvignon Blanc, whose effortless varietal intensity is rarely if ever achieved in Australia.

Wine-producing regions

CANTERBURY (CB)

Canterbury's 250 acres (100 ha) of vines are mainly planted close to Christchurch or at Waipara to the north, most vineyards lying on silt loams and stony silts. Given Canterbury's cool climate and low rainfall, it is not surprising that Rhine Riesling is the biggest planting, followed by Chardonnay, Pinot Noir and Muller-Thurgau. Warm, dry summers and autumns encourage a long growing season which gives grapes extra flavour and finesse, though in some years the cold climate prevents full ripening; spring and autumn frosts can cause trouble too. So far Pinot Noir and Rhine Riesling have been Canterbury's most impressive wines, but only time will reveal the styles best suited to this fledgling wine-producing region and its recently-established wineries.

CENTRAL OTAGO (CO)
Situated way down on the south-east coast far beyond Canterbury, this region grew vines in the late 19th century and was pronounced suitable for wine-making by Romeo Bragato. Not many can have taken his advice for today there are just 37 acres (15 ha) of vines here and only a handful of wineries. With a climate cooler than Germany, Central Otago could well prove too cold for larger-scale grape-growing. But determined growers have pressed ahead, planting vines in protected sun-traps, and a further 25 acres (10 ha) are being planted.

MARLBOROUGH (ML)
With more than 2,770 acres (1,120 ha) under vine, Marlborough is New Zealand's third-largest wine region after Gisborne and Hawke's Bay. By 1991 it could well be the largest. Its long, dry summers, variable stony-gravelly soils and relatively rain-free autumns are well suited to grape-growing; Blenheim, for example, is usually the sunniest spot in New Zealand and the vines here need to be irrigated. **Montana**, which first spotted Marlborough's potential, planted extensive vineyards here on the flat, fertile Wairau plains in the mid-1970s, building a huge modern winery at Blenheim. Now **Corbans** and other wineries also source their grapes here. White varieties, especially Sauvignon Blanc, benefit most from Marlborough's slow-ripening climate. Rhine Riesling has also produced some crisp, flowery, flavoursome wines. Muller-Thurgau is the largest planting, followed by Sauvignon Blanc, Chardonnay, Rhine Riesling and Cabernet Sauvignon. Red wines here have strong herbaceous overtones that indicate a lack of sun.

Distinctive regional wine-styles

MARLBOROUGH SAUVIGNON BLANC
New Zealand's reputation as a producer of fine wine has had more to do with the success of this wine-style than with any other since **Cloudy Bay's** Sauvignon Blanc captured the attention of the wine world. Hawke's Bay and Gisborne both have sizeable plantings of this grape, but only in Marlborough does it transform into an intense, zesty, nettly, flowering currant-like mouthful – a match for any wine that Sancerre can offer. Occasionally wine-makers here produce overpowering, verdant capsicum Sauvignons. There is no need for such aggressively-styled wines: Marlborough's Sauvignon Blanc grapes have stacks of finesse and flavour; wine-makers don't need to go looking for it.

SOUTH ISLAND PINOT NOIR
Pinot Noir is a grape variety as difficult to vinify as it is to grow, but New Zealand's South Island may yet crack it. The recent clutch of delicate, plummy Pinot Noirs, especially from **St Helena** in Canterbury, are likely to prove more than a flash in the pan.

NELSON (NL)
Like Central Otago, this beautiful hilly region grew vines in the late 19th century. Today, with just 84 acres (34 ha) under vine, Nelson's wines are rarely sold outside the region and there are no plans as yet for new vineyards or wineries. This is a pity because its wines deserve to be better known. Nelson admittedly has some viticultural drawbacks more in common with the North Island than the South, chiefly in the form of damaging autumn rain, and it is difficult to reach by road. Chardonnay and Rhine Riesling are the two major plantings.

South Island wineries

AMBERLEY ESTATE   CB
Reserve Road, Amberley, North Canterbury

w *

Jeremy and Lee Prater, who founded Amberley in 1979, own 10 acres (4 ha) of vines surrounding their cellar. Rh Riesling and Chardonnay are their two biggest lines, but they also produce a back-blended medium dry Muller-Thurgau, Gewurztraminer, and a "Swiss-style" Dry Riesling Sylvaner. Current annual production here is 1,000 cases.

CELLIER LE BRUN   ML
28 Gee Street, Renwick, Blenheim

w, sp *

Frenchman Daniel Le Brun's family has made wine in Champagne for centuries. Daniel himself wanted to do something different so he emigrated to New Zealand, bought land here in 1980 and, armed with a vast French Coq champagne press, he started to make *méthode champenoise* fizz. Le Brun's vineyards are planted to Chardonnay, Pinot Noir and a little Pinot Meunier, from which he produces vintage, non-vintage, pink and Chardonnay-based sparklers as well as a still white wine. Quality here shows promise.

CLOUDY BAY   ML
Jacksons Road, Blenheim

w=85 87 86, r   *→*****

Cloudy Bay-mania swept the Antipodes and Britain the moment this winery's first Sauvignon was released. In 1989, this wine had to be rationed to British customers in the manner of a top *cru classé* Claret. If ever there was proof of New Zealand's world-class wine-making status this is it. Cloudy Bay Sauvignon, enriched with Semillon, has an extra dash of mouth-filling fruit and flavour that eclipses even the finest French offerings such as Sancerre and Pouilly Fumé. This winery is the New Zealand arm of **Cape Mentelle**, David Hohnen's award-winning WA winery. Hohnen was tempted across the Tasman Sea by the clear superiority of New Zealand Sauvignon and founded Cloudy Bay in 1985, making the first vintage from **Corbans'** fruit. Luck was on his side for 85, 86 and 87 were all great vintages, and so a cult wine was born. 1988 was not such a good vintage but Cloudy Bay-mania has shown little sign of abating and America hasn't even tasted the stuff yet.

Cloudy Bay's 100 acres (40 ha) of vines, grown in the stony, free-draining soil surrounding the Jacksons Road winery, provide Rose-worthy-trained wine-maker Kevin Judd, formerly at **Selaks**, with half of his fruit for the annual 22,000-case production; the rest is bought in locally, frequently from the Corbans Stoneleigh vineyard. The first 85 Sauvignon with its strong, verdant, asparagus and celery flavours is still showing well, as is the delicious, nettley, flowering currant-like 87. The 88, though good, has a more delicate, flowery quality. In spite of the Sauvignon's success, Hohnen believes that Cloudy Bay's Chardonnay is the better wine. The 86 with its rich, pineappley fruit and cinnamon-like oak is certainly fine and the elegant, cinnamony 87 is not far behind. Cloudy Bay's latest offering is a powerful, herbaceous, green pepper-like 87 Cabernet/Merlot blend.
℥ Star buy: Cloudy Bay Sauvignon

GIESEN   CB
Burnham, Christchurch

w, r, sw, sp   *→

German-born brothers Marcel, Alex and Theo Giesen come from a Rhine Valley wine-making family. Smitten by the New Zealand way of life on a visit from Germany, they decided to move here permanently and founded Giesen in 1984. Baden-trained Marcel is the chief wine-maker, Alex the viticulturist and Theo the marketing man. Their 1,000 cases of well-thought-of wines, made from 53 acres (21 ha) of vines, include dry and medium Riesling, Muller-Thurgau and a Blanc de Blancs *méthode champenoise* fizz.

GLENMARK   CB
Waipara, RD 3, Amberley, Canterbury

w, r, sw *

John McCaskey, Glenmark's owner, and wine-maker Bill Rebich have
11 acres (4 ha) of vines at Waipara. This acreage supplies almost all the
fruit they need to produce 2,500 cases of wines a year, including Dry
and Medium Rh Riesling, Pinot Noir, and the Waipara Red and White
blends (which are Cab Sauvignon-based and Gewurztraminer-based
respectively). A further 5 acres (2 ha) of Cab Sauvignon and Sauv Blanc
vineyards are planned.

GROVE MILL   ML
1 Dodson Street, Blenheim

w, r *

Food technologist and trained wine-maker David Pearce founded this
new "boutique" winery in 1987. His 6,000 cases of wines, made from
contract grapes, include Sauv Blanc, medium-dry Rh Riesling and a
Bordeaux-inspired blend.

HUNTER'S   ML
Rapaura Road, RD 3, Blenheim

w, r *→→*

Since Ernie Hunter died in a car crash, his viticulturist wife Jane has
carried on courageously here without him. Founded in 1982, Hunter's
has 40 acres (16 ha) of Marlborough vines, which provide a mere fifth of
its needs; the rest is bought in locally. Wine-maker John Belsham, with
help from Dr Tony Jordan, makes 20,000 cases a year. Muller-Thurgau
and Chardonnay are the two big sellers. The Chardonnay is barrel-
fermented, and the oak-aged Sauvignon and reds fermented at warm
temperatures. With the imminent launch of a carbonic maceration
Pinot Noir and a Cab Sauvignon, Hunter's first reds, production is
likely to increase to 25,000 cases. A blended Spring Creek Estate Dry
Red and White have also been introduced "to preserve the integrity of
the first label". Hunter's delicious, flowery 88 Rh Riesling is a splendid
example of this winery's expertise, as is its restrained, leafy, delicate 88
Sauv Blanc. The 88 Chardonnay had a similarly restrained pineappley,
flowery, green appley style. Hunter's 87 Pinot Noir is somewhat soft
and jammy, but has definite plummy fruit.
⟁ Star buy: Hunter's 88 Rh Riesling

KOREPO   NL
Korepo Road, RD 1, Upper Moutere, Nelson

w, r, sw, sp *

Directly overlooking Ruby Bay and the Tasman Sea, Craig and Jane
Gass' vineyard lies in one of New Zealand's most idyllic locations.
Korepo was founded in the mid-1970s and now has about 10 acres (4
ha) of mixed vines, including Chardonnay, Cabernet and Sauv Blanc, as
well as an on-site restaurant. Among its wines is a popular sparkling
wine called Olly's Folly.

LARCOMB   CB
Larcombs Road, RD 5, Christchurch

w, r *

The Thoms run this small new Canterbury vineyard and winery, selling
wines such as Breidecker, Rh Riesling, Pinot Noir and Gewurztraminer
mostly at the cellar door.

MERLEN WINES   ML
PO Box 8, Renwick, Blenheim

w, r *→

Geisenhein-trained wine-maker Almuth Lorenz, best known for her
early acclaimed vintages at **Hunter's**, decided to go it alone in 1987
when she founded Merlen. Almuth now has 10 acres (4 ha) of vines
here, planted principally to Chardonnay (which is barrel-fermented),
Semillon and Gewurztraminer; Muller-Thurgau, Rh Riesling and Sauv
Blanc grapes are bought in. Merlen's 4,000 cases of wine are sold by
mail order and at the cellar door.

MONTANA ML
PO Box 18293, Glen Innes, Auckland

w, r, sw, sp ∗→∗∗∗∗

Montana is New Zealand's largest wine company by far. With 2,000 acres (800 ha) of vines providing just a third of its annual 28,000-tonne crush, the company processes almost half of the country's total grape harvest. As well as its bottling hall and sizeable winery in Auckland, Montana has other wineries in Gisborne, Marlborough and Hawke's Bay supervised by four wine-makers. Although its head office is in Auckland, 60% of Montana's vines are planted in Marlborough and it is this region which most clearly epitomizes the Montana style. The company was founded near Auckland by Dalmatian-born Ivan Yukich, who began selling his wine in the mid-1940s using the brand name Montana, but it did not seriously launch itself onto the market until 1968. The brilliant decision in 1973 to plant vines at Marlborough, dismissed as "sheep country" by other wineries, proved the making of Montana. It survived the departure of the Yukich family in the mid-70s and a depression in the industry, buying Penfolds (NZ) in 1986.

Montana's comprehensive range of wines is now controlled by Peter Hubscher. The brands that take up most of the tank space in the company's Marlborough and Gisborne wineries are the popular Wohnsiedler and the medium-dry Blenheimer, a sort of New Zealand Liebfraumilch made from Muller-Thurgau; Rhiur Riesling is another medium-sweet white. Montana also makes large quantities of commercial dry wines under the Chablise and Beauer Station Dry White labels, of which the red equivalent is Fairhall Claret. Besides its comprehensive range of sparklers, from sweet, grapey Bernardino Spumante through to classy *méthode champenoise* fizz, sold under the Hyland and Lindauer labels, Montana has also joined forces with Deutz to produce a joint-venture fizz. Hubscher is already rating this as his finest wine, but until it is released the consistently good Marlborough single varietal wines will remain the most impressive. The finest of these is undoubtedly the Sauvignon Blanc, whose 88 is a wonderful, intense, nettley-herbaceous mouthful. The fresh, pineappley 88 Chardonnay is also good, but lacks depth when compared to North Island offerings. Other Marlborough whites, such as the citric, grapey 87 Rh Riesling and the 87 Gewurz-traminer with its rose scent and lychee-like spice, are worthwhile.

Montana's Marlborough range reds are still not in the same league as its whites, though the 86 Cab Sauvignon/Pinotage with its grassy, liquorice-like scent and herbaceous, leaf-mould-like palate is worth-while. The 86 Cab Sauvignon with its warm, truffley, herbaceous palate is the best Cabernet yet from this winery. Montana's acquisition of Penfolds (NZ) has ensured the continuation of a limited range of ordinary varietal wines, cask wines and sherries.
  ♀ Star buy: Montana Marlborough Sauv Blanc

NEUDORF VINEYARDS NL
Neudorf Road, RD 2, Upper Moutere, Nelson

w, r ∗

Neudorf's 9 acres (3.5 ha) of vines, planted in 1978 in an extraordinarily beautiful setting, are owned by Tim and Judy Finn. Tim makes 3,000 cases, mainly of Chardonnay, Cabernet, Pinot Noir and Semillon.

PENFOLDS (NZ)   See Montana.

RANZAU NL
Patons Road, Hope, Nelson

w, r ∗

Trevor Lewis and family planted Ranzau's 4 acres (1.5 ha) of vines in 1983 and make just 400 cases of wine a year in their spare time.

RIPPON VINEYARD CO
Mount Aspiring Road, PO Box 175, Wanaka, Central Otago

w, r ∗

Rolfe and Lois Mills' 10-acre (4-ha) vineyard overlooking Lake Wanaka is the largest in Central Otago. They make a range of wines including Muller-Thurgau, Riesling and Gewurztraminer.

ST HELENA   CB
Coutts Island, Belfast, Christchurch

                                                                  w, r   *→**

Founded in 1981 by the Mundy family and others, St Helena put
Canterbury on the world wine map with a remarkable 82 Pinot Noir,
whose deep, spicy, plummy fruit was truly Burgundian in style, and
a less impressive but rich, oaky 83. Both wines were made here by
wine enthusiast Danny Schuster, now replaced as wine-maker by
Geisenheim-trained Mark Rattray. The 63 acres (25 ha) of vines are half
planted to Pinot Noir, with the other half a mixture of white varieties
such as Chardonnay and Rh Riesling. St Helena's Pinot Blanc and
Chardonnay have also pleased New Zealand judges.

TARAMEA   CO
Speagrass Flat Road, RD 1, Queenstown

                                                                    w, r   *

Anne Pinckney makes small quantities of red and white table wines at
this Central Otago winery.

TE WHARE RA   ML
Anglesea Street, Renwick, Blenheim

                                                                 w, r, sw   *→

Te Whare Ra, meaning "house in the sun", is owned by Allen and Joyce
Hogan. The estate has 10 acres (4 ha) of vines including Chardonnay,
Cab Sauvignon and Rh Riesling; these provide almost all the winery's
fruit. Allen Hogan's sweet botrytised wines, made using techniques
learned from Rainer Eschenbruch at **Rongopai**, established Te Whare
Ra's reputation. He now produces *beerenauslese* and *trockenbeerenauslese* styles under the Botrytis Berry and Botrytis Bunch labels.

TORLESSE   CB
Jowers Road, West Melton, Canterbury

                                                                    w, r   *

Torlesse is the brand name of the Main West Winery, a new Canterbury
concern founded in 1986 by 18 shareholders, half of whom supply
grapes for the venture. The range of wines here has not yet been
decided, though wine-makers Thomas Reckert and Danny Schuster,
the latter of whom was formerly at **St Helena**, have produced Rh
Riesling, Gewurztraminer and Pinot Noir.

VAVASOUR   ML
PO Box 27, Seddon, Blenheim

                                                                    w, r   *

Peter Vavasour, this winery's owner, and viticulturist Richard Bowling
are the latest newcomers to the Marlborough region. Vavasour intends
to concentrate on red varieties, producing a Bordeaux-inspired Cabernet
blend and a Pinot Noir.

VICTORY GRAPE WINES   NL
Main Road South, Stoke, Nelson

                                                                    w, r   *

Managed by Rod Neil, Victory Grape Wines produces tiny quantities of
wines such as Muller-Thurgau and Pinot Noir.

WEINGUT SEIFRIED   NL
PO Box 18, Upper Moutere, Nelson

                                                                w, r, sw   *→*

Weingut Seifried, founded by Hermann and Agnes Seifried in 1973, has
60 acres (24 ha) of vines, making it the biggest Nelson vineyard by far.
German-born Hermann makes the wines and his New Zealand wife
Agnes looks after administration. Rh Riesling, made in a variety of
styles, takes up a third of their annual output, followed by Pinot Noir,
Chardonnay, Sauv Blanc and a little Gewurztraminer. A second 40-acre
(16-ha) Chardonnay and Sauv Blanc vineyard is being planted in stoney
sand near Rabbit Island in Ruby Bay. Weingut Seifried's elegant, ripe,
flowery Redwood Valley Estate 87 Sauv Blanc and its equally fresh,
verdant, appley 87 Chardonnay were both good wines.

Index

Page numbers in bold type refer to each winery's principal entry.